THE INSIDE STORY

Self-Evaluations Reflecting Basic Rorschach Types

Molly Harrower
Dawn Bowers
University of Florida

 LAWRENCE ERLBAUM ASSOCIATES, PUBLISHERS
1987   Hillsdale, New Jersey   Hove and London

Lawrence Erlbaum Associates, Inc., Publishers
365 Broadway
Hillsdale, New Jersey 07642

Library of Congress Cataloging-in-Publication Data

Harrower, Molly, 1906–
  The inside story.

  Bibliography: p.
  Includes indexes.
  1. Rorschach test. 2. Self-evaluation. I. Bowers,
Dawn, 1950–   . II. Title. [DNLM: 1. Rorschach Test.
WM 145 H323i]
BF698.8.R5H37   1987   155.2′842   87-6892
ISBN 0-89859-990-3

Printed in the United States of America
10 9 8 7 6 5 4 3 2 1

Contents

7
The High *FM,* *114*

8
The Ambi-Equal Classification, *134*

9
The Rare Extrovert, *181*

Acknowledgments

Our contributors need more than the usual acknowledgment, since without them there would be no Inside Story. Their names follow: Dawn Bowers, Deanna Brooks, Peggy Brooks, Bill Bruck, Candide DeLeon, Devorah Depper, Sharon Ellis, Joe Fritsch, Lisl Goodman, Judy Gorrell, Nancy McGinnis Haynes, Jan Hembree, Nili Hillman, Sherry Hulfish, Thomas King, Judy Kizer, Leo Litsky, Sheldon Magaliff, Lynne Magner, Rupert McPherson, Fred Ripin, Eugene Sass, Jackie Schecter, Ronnie Smith, Judy Steinberg, Craig Updegrove, and "Z."

There were a few contributors whom, despite every effort, we were unable to trace so that they could be notified of the inclusion of their work. We hope that finding themselves as part-authors will be a pleasant experience.

Thanks also go to Eileen Fennell for her help in the early stages of this work, and to two indispensable, indefatigable secretaries, Margaret Deale of Greenport and Gopher C. Dragon of Gainesville.

Introduction

During the last 11 years, I have had the opportunity to teach Projective Techniques, particularly the Rorschach, in a way consistent with my diagnostic and therapeutic beliefs.

From 1964 to 1967, I gave the Rorschach course at the New School for Social Research in New York City; from 1968 to 1975, my classes were part of the clinical graduate program at the University of Florida.

At the New School I faced a change in the curriculum whereby a year's course was cut to one of 6 months' duration; at the University of Florida, a shift from semesters to quarters left only 10 weeks to provide the training period prior to a student's utilizing the Rorschach technique in clinical situations.

Clearly, systematic and *extensive* basic training was not possible; equally clearly, a drastic change in the concept of what training could achieve was called for.

The time seemed ripe, therefore, to give an *intensive,* rather than extensive experience; to train the student to look inward and understand the duality of himself and his instrument.

Some 300 students were exposed to this method of teaching over the 11 years. Classes averaged 25 participants. The format of the course, the syllabus, together with some of the charts and handouts used, are presented in chapter 1.

This book contains illustrative self-evaluations, since the major assignment of the class—the event toward which others were oriented—was the study of the Rorschach-Self. For the final assignment, each participant had to turn in his or her own personal Rorschach record, scored, tabulated, and interpreted; the interpretation being related to an understanding of the Rorschach findings in reference to other forms of self-knowledge.

As these self-evaluations accumulated over the years, it became clear that they represented a cross section of possible Rorschach personalities. Rorschach look-alikes began to emerge. Students began to ask what does it "feel like" to be a person with such and such a psychogram. The "in" language bore increasing evidence that scores and ratios were becoming meaningful. "My W to M ratio is such that I just can't get the assignment in on time," was a joking excuse! Or, "I just don't have enough 'small d' to look up the references." "My CFs got the better of me last night when I was so annoyed."

The beginning chapters of this volume give examples from across the years of some of the basic Rorschach patterns: the very high R, the low R, the high F% as contrasted with the low F%; the high M, the introvert, the high FM, and the ambi-equal record.

We have also included examples of how self-evaluations work in special cases. For example, how do established therapists look back after 20 years? Can a career be chosen or changed with reference to, or in the light of, Rorschach self-knowledge: Medicine? Administration? Can insight be derived into family relationships by understanding the Rorschach types of the members?

I spoke of being able to teach in accordance with my beliefs and values; for many years I have hammered away at the idea that one must be aware in any given projective method where one's own blind spots lie and what one's own productive, idiosyncratic sensitivities can be, before one can use this instrument to its best advantage. I have expressed this in several places, but perhaps this quote best illustrates my meaning (Harrower, 1965b).

> The student should know his own performance in the projectives, so that he will not unconsciously ally himself with patients with similar psycho-diagnostic patterns or, conversely, react with undue severity to the producers of test protocols diametrically opposite to his own. The point is rarely emphasized, but this author considers it of prime importance. The psychodiagnostician badly needs to understand his own productions on all the test instruments that he uses. Moreover, he should have the opportunity to go over and discuss a report written on his test production by an experienced and wise psychodiagnostic practitioner. Unless this is done, he will find himself automatically assuming that somehow or other his own productions constitute a base line of normality. He will too readily read pathology into test profiles that are dissimilar to his own and, conversely, will find condoning circumstances where striking similarities pertain.

Kurt Koffka has a statement in his first chapter of the *Principles of Gestalt Psychology* (1935), which is a challenge to every author:

> Writing a book is a social act. Is one justified in demanding cooperation of

society for such an enterprise? What good can society, or a small fraction of it, at best derive from it?" (Koffka, 1935)

So, I may ask, who should take time to read these self-evaluations? I suggest that any instructor in the Rorschach method will get an exciting experience in the use of this method. It will be found that much of the seemingly routine facets of scoring will take on a new look for the class as students turn to their own responses to find the various determinants. A class rapport develops in which the instructor plays a vital role. The class is alive.

Any student about to learn the Rorschach method has an eagerness about his own record; this is built in and useable to great advantage — seeing the "inside selves" of others will, we feel, prove of interest to psychology students in training.

REFERENCES

1. Harrower, Molly. (1965). Clinical psychologists at work. In B. Wolman (Ed.), *Handbook of clinical psychology*. New York: McGraw-Hill.
2. Koffka, Kurt. (1935). *Principles of gestalt psychology*. New York: Harcourt, Brace and Company.

THE
INSIDE
STORY

1

The Instruction–Insight Method

The outline of the Instruction–Insight course is roughly as follows: The first of the 20 three-hour sessions is devoted to the *experience* of taking a full battery of the projectives in a never-again-to-be-achieved naive state. This is a modified group procedure, since each of the students has his own set of Rorschach cards and his own projective notebook in which to write his responses. This booklet, printed in the 1950s for research purposes, contains, in addition to the 20 pages for recording Rorschach responses and marking their locations on small diagrams, the Szondi faces, modified TAT cards, a shortened version of the Holsopple Miale Sentence Completion Test, and pages for figure drawings and the Most Unpleasant Concept. During the three-hour session, students proceed at their own pace, finishing the test at home if necessary.

In the second session, a discussion takes place about the experiences of taking the Rorschach; students count their own responses, and the range of the total Rs within the group comes to light. This wide spectrum of each individual's total number of responses is put up on the blackboard. Usually, there is a spread of as much as 50 or 60 points, with total responses as low as 10 and as many as 80. This is the first indication to each student of the large individual variations he or she may expect to find in his or her own subsequent testing experiences.

Surprise, some anxiety, and delight are expressed. When these have been ventilated, the collecting of the group record, or class record, begins. Going around the class, each student contributes one of his or her own responses, starting with Card I, to which 4 or 5 responses are collected, until approximately 60 or 70 responses have been recorded for the 10 blots. Each student therefore contributes three or four times, depending on the size of the class.

Collecting these responses is a crucial part of this method of teaching. It allows individuals to expose some of their personal perceptive experiences, but in a way that does not impinge on their privacy. Each student is being represented, but the total class record becomes that of another person, who acquires an entity and, when finally scored and assessed, can be spoken of freely, criticized or applauded in various ways. Over the years, various names have become attached to these "class persons"—"HH" or "Herman" being one with whom we all became very familiar.

A few students, as we shall see later, used these hypothetical entities in developing their own Inside Stories, contrasting and comparing their own productions with the "person" behind the class record.

When responses have been collected from the class, the instructor may add a few additional percepts if some needed illustrative material is missing. For example, a bizarre response might be inserted for one of the cards so that the "flavor" of such a perceptual distortion can be experienced; or an *F* minus response might be added, to demonstrate the kind of response so scored.

Although students write down each of the offered responses, we have found that their recordings in the stress of the moment are not always accurate; some responses may have been missed or scantily recorded. Therefore, we have always found it is helpful if the instructor or a student assistant types up the class record and has a xerox copy available for each student at the next session. Those are usually put on legal-sized paper, the responses well to the left-hand side, with ample space left to the right for the scoring categories.

We list here responses offered to Cards I and X by each of the three different classes, 1969, 1970, and 1971.

1969	1970	1971
An ornamental axe-head.	A female, standing naked	A bat
A twirling ballerina.	Two figures on either side, cross between bat and bear	Three acrobats. They're excessively clothed. Two on the sides are supporting the one in the middle.
A cross-eyed fox.	A jack-o-lantern.	Two king's helpers dragging central figure to the king.
A pelvic girdle.	Two ballerinas, on one toe swinging her leg up.	Boxing gloves.

Responses to Card X during the same years, 1969, 1970, and 1971:

1969	*1970*	*1971*
The two pink figures I saw as humming birds.	Two insects, balancing something.	A rabbit with green fog emerging from his eyes giving a green-like quality.
Fluffy white dog in the center (the yellow-eyed dog).	Two yellow rosebuds.	A crab crawling.
A parade towards the Eiffel Tower.	Two green lizards.	Artistic/autistic orgasm.
A great tree trunk with bushes (gray top).	Funny-faced man, yellow eyes, green mustache, gray nose, pink hair, fireworks exploding around him.	A flower garden in the early spring.
Two sea horses.	An aquarium scene, tropical fish, plants, gaily colored.	Two iguanas arguing, holding a bridge.
Rabbit's face.		An underwater scene with many different creatures.

The subsequent sessions are concerned with assigning the correct scoring to the class record, with discussions as to the meaning of locations, determinants, the variety of content, popular and original responses. To these standard methods of describing a response, I have added columns which allow a discussion of sequence analysis, symbolism, and the richness or sparsity of a response, where appropriate, as shown in Table 1–1.

TABLE 1-1

Responses	Scoring						
	Location	Determinant	Content	Original-Popular	Sequence Analysis	Symbolism	Rich-Sparse
	Where?	Why?	What?	Often?	When?	Meaning?	How?
Bat	W	Its shape F	Animal	25 times out of 30 in class	First, a safe "how-do you-do"	—	Sparse
Acrobats clothed, supporting, stretching, etc.	W	Moving, supporting, stretching, clothed M	Humans	Seen once	Tells a lot at once	Possible symbols	Rich
Two king's helpers dragging central figure to the king.	W	Moving, dragging M	Humans	Seen once		Symbols?	Rich
Boxing gloves Leathery feel	d	F, Fc Shape, and texture	Objects	Seen six times	Retreat to small area and object.	Some kind of aggres-sion?	

Note: From "The Rorschach and Self-Understanding: The Instruction–Insight Method" by M. Harrower, 1977, *Journal of Personality Assessment, 41,* p. 453. Copyright 1977 by the Society for Personality Assessment. Reprinted by permission.

Table 1-1 shows how the four responses to Card I collected from the class record of 1971, have been recorded under the seven ways of describing them.

The first response—a bat—was seen in the blot as a whole (*Location*). The "determining factor" for this being seen as a bat was its shape (*Determinant*). An animal was the subject matter classification (*Content*). How often was such a percept—bat—experienced? In this instance, it was given by 25 out of the 30 class participants; therefore it was *Popular,* or experienced often. The importance of a place of the response within the total number of responses is significant. Thus, we ask, *When* was a response given (*Sequence Analysis*). Its place as the *first* experience suggests that an appropriate way to embark on a new task has been chosen. Was there any symbolism contained in the answer *bat*? Possible, but unlikely. But in terms of the richness or restrictedness of a single word, *bat* would be considered sparse on a rich/sparse scale.

The explanation and discussion of the determinants is always left to the last of these scoring sessions. I have found over the years that students have more difficulty with these, both in understanding and utilizing them appropriately. But having coped successfully with the other six categories, and having become somewhat more at home in dealing with the inkblots, the flurry of anxiety with unfamiliar material has subsided and the 13 determinants can be handled without difficulty.

We return now to the further development of the Instruction-Insight method. During the fifth or sixth session (classes vary slightly in the time needed to feel at home with the basic scoring), a psychogram is made for the class protocol, and the basic ratios are recorded. The psychogram for the class record of 1972 is shown here. With scoring, the basic ratios, and a psychogram to work with, *interpretation* of the "class person" can begin. It is possible to be quite candid in the discussion of his or her assets and possible difficulties. Each student has some investment in the record but is not entirely responsible for it.

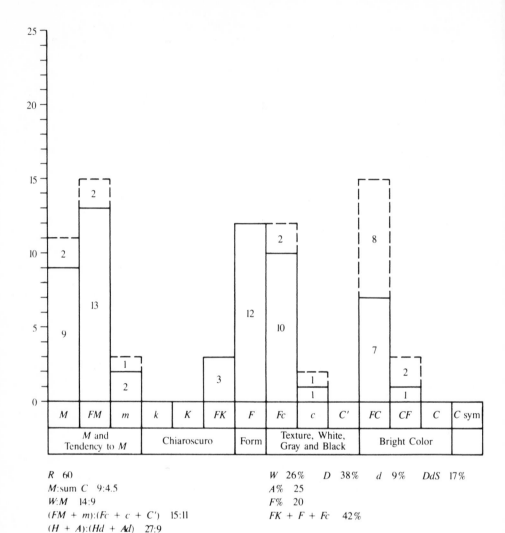

M	FM	m	k	K	FK	F	Fc	c	C'	FC	CF	C	C sym
9	13	2		3		12	10	1	1	7	2	1	

| M and Tendency to M | | Chiaroscuro | | | | Form | Texture, White, Gray and Black | | | Bright Color | | | |

R   60

M:sum C   9:4.5

W:M   14:9

(FM + m):(Fc + c + C')   15:11

(H + A):(Hd + Ad)   27:9

W   26%   D   38%   d   9%   DdS   17%

A%   25

F%   20

FK + F + Fc   42%

FIG. 1-1.   A psychogram for the class record of 1972

The principles of interpretation take up the next three class periods. In the tenth session, students begin to develop their own style of interpretation and assume the responsibility of writing up the "class person."

During the initial 10 sessions, as each new facet of scoring, tabulating, and interpretation is dealt with in class, the students work alone without help or discussion of their own personal record, which they took during their first encounter with the inkblots. The second half of the Instruction–Insight course—that is, during the next 10 three-hour sessions—attention is turned to a record that each student must administer, score, and then present to the class. An extra session, in which students administer the test to each other, has preceded this administration of the blots to some selected "subject."

Thus, using our scored and interpreted class record for comparison, each student-administered record is presented and discussed. The student who is presenting must make copies of the record available for every member of the class. Full scoring and the psychogram must also be presented as part of the handout. The interpretation of such student-presented records, however, is done by the class as a whole. These presentations are handled, at the suggestion of the instructor, in many different ways. To start with, the class as a whole comments on what they consider to be the outstanding qualities of the record under consideration, or, as an alternative, the students may spend 15 minutes drafting a couple of paragraphs of interpretation, which will then be read to the class for comparison and discussion. On yet another occasion, the outstanding characteristics of the record that is being presented may be listed on the board while the class as a whole states what should be considered the interpretive meaning of each.

The frame of reference of our interpretations may change. We might relate at one time to a hypothetical request from a referring physician, or we might orient the reports that were to be written on two of the presented cases in such a way as to reply to a hypothetical marriage counselor asking questions about a couple with problems.

On their own time, outside the class, the students work on their own personal Rorschach records. Each student scores his or her record, finds the ratios, and makes the psychogram. They are urged to start thinking about their "Rorschach self" and to imagine building or accumulating a "library" of records as a result of the individual presentation to the class.

In the long take-home exam, for the first time, the students share with the instructor their own record and its analysis, drawing upon their self-knowledge, the assessment of friends, and material from their group or individual therapy, to substantiate their projective findings.

Examples of these self-evaluations form the basis of *The Inside Story.*

2

The High *R* Experience
Self-Evaluation of Records
with 166 and 120 Responses

Rorschach records with over 100 responses are rare indeed. Most authorities consider somewhere in the mid-thirties to be the most usual number given. Rorschach, himself, felt that any number between 15 and 30 could be considered average; though he adds that there are rarely less than 15 but quite frequently more than 30 (Rorschach, 1942). Klopfer (1954) mentioned between 20 and 40 as an average number; Alcock's (1963) figures are from 25 to 40. Group administration of the Rorschach has yielded similar figures (Harrower & Steiner, 1951).

Can one be too productive? Too creative? Too original? Or, asked in another way, what price does one pay for a wealth of associative material, epitomized in a Rorschach record with 166 responses, 44 of which are *M*, the majority being scored as original?

In this chapter we consider the inner experiences of two psychologists in training with 166 and 120 total responses, total *R,* respectively. In the presentation of this material, we first give the Rorschach record in its entirety (Table 2-1), the psychogram of Student 1, (Figure 2-1), and this student's overall statement on her record. Although a detailed sequence analysis was written on each of the 10 cards, we have selected her comments on Cards I and IX as representative.

TABLE 2-1
Rorschach Responses of Student 1

Card I			
1. Man's profile—head silouhetted	*de*	F	*Hd*
2. Profile of Richard Nixon . . . cartoon caricature	*de*	F	*Hd*

TABLE 2-1
(Continued)

Card I

3. Chesspiece . . . a knight	S	F	obj
4. Airplane and aerial view from above	W	FK	obj
5. Two claw pincers	d	F	Ad
6. Blue cheese . . . dark is blue mold part and white is creamy lighter part	W	c	food
7. Boy scout eagle emblem	D	F	sign
8. Two breasts	d	F	sex
9. Woman lying on side of hill	d	M	H
10. Two dogs with floppy ears, or a dog by a pool and his reflection in water	D	FM	A
11. Food particle enclosed by an amoeba	ds	m	obj/A
12. Smoke	W	K, C'	smoke
13. Coiled snake	di	FM	A
14. Child on sled sledding	di	M	H
15. Puppet	S	F	Hobj
16. 18th century woman leading singing in sunday school	D	M	H
17. Baby on beach playing with ball	d	M	H
18. A turkish lady dancing	di	M	H

Card II

1. Rose petals	di	FC	pla
2. Clitoris and female genitalia	D	FC	sex
3. Abraised rocks	W	Fc	ntr
4. Sun setting	d	CF, FK	ntr
5. Epiglottis in throat	ds	F	H anat
6. Man with broken nose sticking out tongue	de	F, m	Hd
7. Eastern temple spire	d	F	arch
8. Surfer lying on surf board riding waves	di	M	H
9. Albino sting ray in ocean	S	FM, C' FK	A
10. Ruby red fat lips	D	FC	Hd
11. Engraved woman in stone	di	F, Fc	H
12. Two persons dancing with shriner hats	W	M, FC	H
13. Mushroom	S	F, C'	pla
14. Bromine gas	di	C, K	ntr
15. Two persons scaling wall or indian wrestling	W	M	H

Card III

1. Two playboy bunnies serving drinks	W	M	H
2. Shirred crepe	W	Fc	cloth
3. Guy with guitar OD'd	D	M	H
4. Half of a sharp denotation	DS	F−	music

TABLE 2–1
(Continued)

Card III

5. Two men pointing in straight up direction at birds in sky	D	M, FM	H, A
6. Strait of Gibraltar	D	FK	map
7. Fine cloth ripping	DS	m, Fc	cloth
8. Red bowtie	D	FC	cloth
9. Fetal pig	D	FC	A
10. Guy with beard, glasses . . . a jockey mounted on a horse	D	M, Fv	H
11. Cold ice crystals hanging	d	Fc	ntr
12. Nagg and Nell popping out of cans	D	M	H
13. Diver tucking to do flips into water	D	M	H
14. Gypsy woman conferring with another . . . ominous feeling. . . . long dangling earrings	d	F, m	Hd
15. Plant just sprouting from ground	dd	F, m	pla
16. Person's bottom	D	F	Hd
17. Man with bowtie and sunglasses	WS	F	Hd

Card IV

1. Giraffe with broken neck	D	FM	A
2. Either a woman touching hands to knees exercising or a diver doing jacknife	ds	M	H
3. Underground tunnel	di	FK, C'	ntr
4. Spinal vertebrae	d	F	Hanat
5. Clown with big feet	W	M	H
6. Poised alligator	di	FM	A
7. Nun swathed in black	di	M, C'	H
8. Granite	W	Fc	pla
9. Prickly pear cactus	de	Fc	pla
10. Head of bull or water buffalo	D	F	Ad
11. Person about to be levitated	d	M, m	H
12. Gray clouds under smothering clouds	W	K, C'	clouds
13. Chipped arrowhead	d	Fc	obj
14. Person pulling bubble gum that's stuck to his nose	DS	M	H
15. Tulip unfolding	d	F, m	pla

Card V

1. A stapler	d	F	obj
2. Seam that is bulky	di	k	obj
3. Woman lying on hill with folded arms	d	M	H
4. A bat or butterfly pondering terrain below	W	FM	A
5. Fairy with tiny wings . . . tinkerbell	d	M	H

TABLE 2-1
(Continued)

Card V

6. Two old mountain men with long goatees . . . heads resting against the same rock	W	F, Fc	Hd
7. Mexican ruin	d	F	arch
8. Sleeping alligator	d	FM	A
9. Person pointing with outstretched hand	d	F	Hd
10. Pregnant woman lying on back, asleep	d	M	H
11. Fault in land	di	k	geog
12. Woman sitting with legs apart reading	D	M	H
13. Person stepping out of closet into light	dd	M, C'	Hd
14. Chicken drumstick	d	F	food

Card VI

1. Salt crystal	W	Fc	ntr obj
2. Nurse with funny hat . . . Cherry Ames type	d	M	H
3. Chromosomes . . . chromatids during crossing and migration	di	m	
4. Aztec emblem	D	F	sign
5. Grandmother with bun waving hankie	d	M	H
6. Chick pea split open	di	F	obj
7. Butter churn	W	F	obj
8. Type of eye I usually draw when doodling	ds	F	
9. Two sophists in debate	d	M	H
10. Baby birds with heads popping out of nest	di	FM	A
11. Separation of light into spectrum of colors	ds	F, F/C	col proj
12. Leg jammed into wall	d	F, m	Hd
13. Man or paper doll split open and folded apart . . . like the paper doll chains	W	F	H
14. Totem pole	D	F	obj
15. Hot dog bun split open . . . person's fingers holding it and hot dog protruding from one end	W	F, m	food
16. Guitar	D	F	mus
17. Sliding board (figure) on ground	W	FK	obj
18. Foot with protruding big toe	d	F	Hd
19. Frog . . . eyes, legs hunched underneath	d	FM	A

TABLE 2–1
(Continued)

Card VI

---

20. Penis . . . perfect shape	*Di*	*F*	sex
21. Woman lying in bubble bath with foot dangling out, sudsing self	*d*	*M*	*H*
22. Hermit crab	*d*	*F*	*A*

Card VII

---

1. Vagina and pubic area . . . naked woman sitting on see-through plexiglass chair with legs outstretched	*W*	*FK, M*	sex, *H*
2. Two persons throwing kisses	*W*	*M*	*H*
3. Two persons on hands and knees playing horse	*D*	*M*	*H*
4. Muscle with fat superimposed	*di*	*Fc*	*H* anat
5. Rounded arrowhead or spear head	*S*	*Fc*	obj
6. Furrow in garden	*ds*	*k*	earth
7. Gorilla head	*di*	*F*	*Ad*
8. Camel sitting on haunches	*D*	*FM*	*A*
9. Topview of man flexing muscles . . . Popeye and Brutus type that pop out serially on top of each other	*W*	*Fv*	*Hd*
10. Pebbled stairs with moss over them	*de*	*Fc*	obj
11. Amorphous cancer eating insides of person	*WS*	*m, Fv*	
12. Person strangling dog		Could Not Find	
13. A waist cincher cinching	*ds*	*m*	obj
14. Man with syphilitic nose	*D*	*F, m*	*Hd*

Card VIII

---

1. Different cell stains	*W*	*CF*	color
2. Spinal vertebrae	*ds*	*F*	*H* anat
3. Pink weasels climbing cliffs	*D*	*FM*	*A*
4. Spinal disc	*D*	*F*	*H* anat
5. Dinosaurs in water . . . heads jutting out	*d*	*FM, FC*	*A*
6. Priest with arms out blessing people	*D*	*M*	*H*
7. Pansy	*D*	*CF*	pla
8. Mercury lobbing into puddle	*D*	*CF, m*	obj
9. Cotton candy	*D*	*CF*	food
10. Holes and tears in bread dough . . . elastic and sticky . . . being kneaded	*W*	*Fc, m*	obj
11. Booted feet hanging off bed	*d*	*F*	*Hd*
12. Man whose tongue just bitten off and half tongue falling out of mouth	*DS*	*F, m*	*Hd*

TABLE 2-1
(Continued)

Card VIII

13. Sailboat with sails	D	F	obj
14. Person hanging onto rope from helicopter	ds	M	H
15. Bruises	W	CF	Hd
16. Kangeroo with kids in pouch hopping along	D	FM	A
17. Atomic mushroom	W	CF, K	explosion

Card IX

1. Merlins playing violins	D	M	H
2. Pelvic bone	D	F	H anat
3. Cannons firing	d	FC, C	fire
4. Goat head	W	F	Ad
5. Animal, horse breathing fire out nostrils	W	FM, C	A, fire
6. Woman chasing girl . . . or girl being followed by shadow enlarged behind her	D	M, C'	H
7. Fungi	W	CF	pla
8. Water, lake, beach, trees against horizon	DS	FC, FK	ntr
9. Two skinny parents holding skinny kid . . . from American Gothic	di	M	H
10. Molten lava	di	CF	fire
11. Back of porcupine	de	Fc	Ad
12. Don Quixote on horse and Pancho feeding it	ds	M, FM	H, A
13. Person on large pogo stick pogoing	D	M	H
14. Person dragging another by hair—Tarzan-Jane type	D	M	H
15. Walruses snoozing in sun	D	FM	A
16. Hunter with hat eating apple	d	M	H
17. Radiation of light from tungsten coil filament	ds	FC	light
18. Bleeding madras plaid material	W	CF	cloth
19. Birth . . . symbolic emergence	W	Csym	sym
20. Mamillary bodies	di	FC	anat

Card X

1. Face of person with component parts . . . yellow amoeba for eyes, caterpillars for side of face, and long sideburns, orange bird for mouth, green bats for eyebrows, and brown crabs for ears	W (D)	F	Hd
2. Green bunnies on pogo sticks	D	FM	A
3. Two grey mice peering through periscope in submarine	D	FM, C'	A

TABLE 2-1
(Continued)

Card X

4. Golgi I type neuron	D	F	ana
5. Siamese twins attached by stomach	D	M	H
6. Two fingers of dentist prying open someone's mouth	ds	F, m	Hd
7. Woman in blue lifting dead husband . . . in mourning	D	M, FC	H
8. Horse falling off cloud	D	FM, K	A, cloud
9. The highwayman with light in hand on horse	D	M, FM, CF	H, A, light
10. Crushed ant	D	F	A
11. Demonic figure pushing trunk over cliff	d	M	H
12. Blood spot in yolk of egg	D	FC	Embryo
13. Parasites . . . all parasites	W	CF	A
14. Earth, sky, sun, abstract painting	W	C sym	sym
15. Two demonic guys splitting apart harmony with resistance from two trying to hold it together	W	M	H, sym

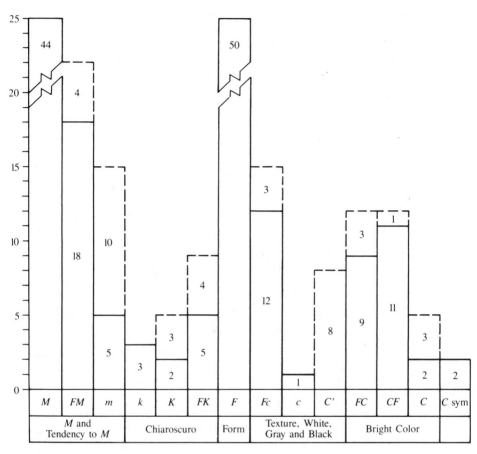

M	FM	m	k	K	FK	F	Fc	c	C'	FC	CF	C	C sym
44	4					50					1		
	18	10		3	4		3			3			
			3	3	5	12		8	9	11	3		
	5			2			1					2	2

| | M and Tendency to M | | Chiaroscuro | | | Form | Texture, White, Gray and Black | | | Bright Color | | | |

R   166

M:sum C   44:18.5

W:M   36:44

(FM + m):(Fc + c + C')   23:13

(H + A):(Hd + Ad)   63:30

W   22%   D   27%   d   19%   DdS   31%

A%   17

F%   30

FK + F + Fc   41%

FIG. 2-1.   A psychogram of Student 1

Self-Evaluation of Student 1

The difficulty I've had in compiling and analyzing my Rorschach protocol is most dramatically reflected in several aspects of my psychogram . . . the high number of responses (R = 166), the low W:M ratio (38:44), the low D% (27%) and high DdS percent (31%).

For the problem lies in sculpting some coherent order out of a kaleidoscope of images that fuse and flow together. While it has always been difficult for me to organize papers and ideas, this has become most pronounced in attempting to piece together aspects of my personality. Trying to get in touch with those Pandora parts of myself has triggered a great deal of anxiety, for there are large chunks in my emotional phenomenology that I've been unable to understand, especially in my attempts to do so now. There are a few basic givens that I intellectually acknowledge about myself.

I know that control . . . of my feelings . . . is a dominant and recurrent leitmotif in my life: I tend to encapsulate and sit on my emotions and don't know how to integrate them into the mainstream of my life. I know that I'm highly guarded and self-critical. I have some ambivalence about sexuality, which seems to be related to my emotional need–fear of dependency dilemma . . . and accented somewhat by feminist sentiments. I also know that I feel ambivalent about my mother, her relationship with my sister, and her relationship with me.

In retrospect, I'm not sure that I'm happy trying to evaluate me these past weeks . . . I feel that I've touched on some important life themes, but the emotional undercurrents that are presented in my phenomenal foreground remain amorphous and threatening and I'm lacking the *W* to understand. Do attempts at self-analysis always have such impact on people?

On the other hand, I was surprised at how relaxing and fun taking the Rorschach was . . . it was a flowing stream of images. My hypothesis is that had the Rorschach been administered by an 'official examiner,' my total number of responses would have dropped and my *F%,* increased. To a large extent, I'm very much the introvert the *M:C* ratio connotes. On other personality tests (MMPI and Cattell 16 PF), I fall off the scales on introversion. While I can be very sociable and party-going-ish, this happens only sporadically. Although I don't see myself as being a very dependent person, it is important for me to be around other people. Times when I've lived alone and relatively isolated for long periods, I tend to get bogged down in my *DdS* approach to the world. I need significant other folks around to help me define and validate reality at times. Related to my copious number of Rorschach responses is my most "horrible concept" . . . being bored. Being afraid that I won't be able to interest myself in life probably compels me to generate lots of gobbledygook. When I went through my initial identity crisis, it struck me that the world wasn't intrinsically interesting and that I had to make it so. And the stricture I placed on myself was avoiding the mundane, the obvious.

I wonder if this relates to my dominant *DdS* manner of viewing the Rorschach.

CARD I

In trying to discern a pattern ... a perceptual sequencing pattern ... I am first struck that I telescope in and out, vacillating between smaller and larger perceptual units in no apparent order. Is this confusion, or flexibility, or my defenses in optimal working order?

Before perceiving the blot as a whole, however, I first deal with rather miniscule edge details (man's profile, profile of Richard Nixon). Do these two small head responses reflect my apprehension about the "testing" situation? I know that when I'm anxious, I tend to tune into minutia details. In new places, whether academic or social, especially where I'm not sure what's expected of me, I find it difficult to feel at ease enough to globally appraise what is happening. Rather, I can analytically dissect bits and pieces, something I'm quite good at. As soon as I feel "secure" and comfortable, the picture does emerge, as do the *W* and *M* responses to this card. Tardily, but they do arrive. Even in the next response (airplane ... aerial view from above) where I venture to take a "global" view, I've distanced myself, and in doing so have given myself enough rope to remove myself quickly by tightening in the subsequent response, "two claw pincers."

One of the more interesting sequences of responses on this card— the *m* response followed by the *K* —clues me in to a conflict between feeling freely versus feeling afraid of what's to happen when I'm not in control. This emerges nicely in the response "food particle being engulfed by an amoeba." Even now, just in commenting about it, I feel "queasy" and it makes perfectly good sense that I am that particle being engulfed. This feeling of being overpowered indeed invokes anxiety, and this is reflected in the next response, smoke. Following the smoke response, this uneasiness is epitomized in the sexually symbolic snake—a dangerous and lethal penis poised to strike??? Sexuality is threatening to me, and I think it's related to a more global fear of letting go with my feelings. It is much easier and "safer" for me to deal with people on an intellectual, rather than emotional/sexual level. In the next response (child on sled sledding), I escape from the snake by retreating behind the playful innocence of a child.

Although *M* responses are not immediately accessible and take some time before they emerge, they are alive, albeit small *d* perceptions of people—mostly women and children, dancing, singing, playing. Initially, I am somewhat struck that my entire record is replete with lonely women (who are they?) and then I glance around my apartment and see that all my paintings and prints and wall hangings are also women . . . alone, sultry, cold. To a large extent, they seem to be a personal symbol of how I see myself as being alone, and distanced and offset. At the same time, I really don't feel lonely. Perhaps most interesting was my initial obliviousness to the biggest *M* on this card—a woman leading singing in Sunday school. Whereas the alone-type women on this card and throughout the remaining cards are me, this woman certainly is not. And it comes to mind that this might be my mother, a devoutly religious person.

Altogether, this card nicely gleans how I tighten as a coping maneuver for maintaining control, how the creepy anxious feelings arise when I feel overpowered, and how I distance myself.

CARD IX

I'm having tremendous difficulty analyzing my color cards. And, this probably bespeaks as much the difficulty I have in accepting, understanding, and expressing my feelings as the responses themselves indicate.

I was initially drawn to the top detail of the card with the mythical merlins playing their violins. I seemed to have recovered somewhat from the emotional shock of the last card and attempt to more constructively channel my color responses. There are more *FC* and *M* responses and fewer *CF* responses here than on the previous color card. After the "merlins," I "tighten" my perception via a sexualized anxiety response which explodes into cannons firing. Furthermore, I seem to vacillate between the "fire" type responses and the constricted goat head and pelvic bones. I think that I might be fluctuating back and forth because I don't want to confront for any length of time the strong, yet misunderstood emotionally reactive part of myself.

Perhaps most interesting on this card is the ambivalence that emerges in the response where I couldn't decide who was chasing whom—"either a woman chasing a small girl, or the small girl being chased by her shadow." Essentially, it doesn't matter, because it relays the same message: I'm being chased by an internalized parent, and I do have many ambivalent feelings toward my mother, which I haven't yet sorted through.

The next response (fungi) where all the colors run together in blobby puddle probably represents the dissatisfaction I've experienced in our relationship. I then distance myself from the puddle in a subsequent vista response of the terrain. And, this is my favorite of all my responses on the Rorschach, because the form and the colors are a perfect match, giving rise to the perception. Significant to my ambivalence about parenting are the two adults from American Gothic holding their child between them so sterilely, and this sterile coldness emerges in the next response of "porcupine bristles." (Harrower, 1977, pp. 453, 456, 458, 459)

It would be a mistake to assume that an unusually rich flow of associative material in and of itself tells the whole story with respect to the "inside" worlds of these two highly Rorschach-productive individuals. As every Rorschach worker knows, no one component of the record is of significance in itself. In this and subsequent chapters we group together records according to one outstanding characteristic, and while this is justified in some ways, it is quite arbitrary in others.

RORSCHACH RESPONSES, PSYCHOGRAM, AND SELF-EVALUATION OF STUDENT 2

A glimpse into the inner world of another highly productive student with 120 Rorschach responses is presented in Table 2-2. Her Rorschach record, psychogram (Figure 2-2), and some of her interpretations follow.

TABLE 2-2
Rorschach Responses of Student 2

Card I				
1. Bat	W	F	A	P
2. Women with hands in air, yelling; shadows moving on either side	W	M, mF, K	H	
3. Wolves flying up and off	D + D	FM	A	
4. Woman looks beheaded	D	M	H	
5. Woman's face looks evil and black	d	F, m, FC'	Hd	

Card II				
1. Two people squatting, facing each other, with hands together, knees touching, toes bent back	W	M	H	
2. Two people talking vigorously, clashes in argument, anger	W	M, m	H	
3. Blood dripping or splattering	D	C, m	blood	
4. Wind blowing from center—bodies look as though something blowing them (don't see wind, only effect)	D	mF, FC	H, wind	
5. Church steeple	S	F	arch	
6. Penis head	d	F	sex	

TABLE 2-2
(Continued)

Card II

5. Church steeple	S	F	arch
6. Penis head	d	F	sex
7. Mountain scene, red clouds	D	CF, FK	N
v 1. Fat beetle with antennae, crawling	D	FM	A
v 9. Rocket firing (include red)	SD	Fm, CF	obj, fire, smoke
10. Vaginal tract	d	FC	sex
11. Seed about to sprout, a stem (seems moving up)	d	Fm	pl
12. Praying hands	d	F	Hd, hands
13. Butterfly	D	F	A
14. Heart-shape	D	FC	At

Card III

1. Indians dancing around cooking pot, holding hands (tribal aborigine people). Are women because have busts, long chins, long necks, belt around waist, collar around neck	W`	M, F, F,	H, apparel, obj
2. Stomach and esophagus	D	FC	At
3. Dripping blood into a puddle	D	mF, CF	blood
4. Kidneys	D	FC	At
5. Butterfly	D	F	A
6. Penises	d	F	sex
7. Two doggies trying to get away, running around but women holding them	W`	M, FM	A, H
v 8. Male heads of tribesmen with arms flung up, spinning around in small circle, beards, pudgy faces	D	F, m	Hd
v 9. Bow tie	D	F	clothes
v 10. Elongated fish	D	F	A
v 11. X-ray or skeleton of chest and ribs	D	k	X-ray, At
v 12. Figures swirling around while two Indian chiefs watch them (the Indian chiefs are the red D's) as in a ritual or ceremony	W	M, F, m	H
v 13. Blood dripping into puddle	D	CF, mF	blood

Card IV

1. Bear skin rug with protruding feet, whiskers	W	Fc	A, obj
2. Maps	D	F	maps
3. Intercourse	W	M	H, Hd, sex

TABLE 2-2
(Continued)

Card IV

4. Goofy, speaking, talking, or laughing (head only)	*D*	*F, m*	*(A)*
5. Alligator's head, growling	*d*	*F, m*	Ad
6. Rocket going through space	*D*	*Fm*	obj
7. Profile, long nose	*de*	*F*	*Hd*
8. Profile	*de*	*F*	*Hd*
9. Man's face, snobby expression, slanted eyes	*S*	*F, m*	*Hd*
10. Something dripping or falling	*D*	*m*	obj
11. Rug, looks furry and cuddly	*W*	*Fc*	obj
12. Bear walking, giant bear or monster, so large can see soles on feet as is walking	*W*	*FM*	*A*
> 13. Forest and trees, clouds—all reflecting in lake	*W*	*FK*	*N*
> 14. Cloud takes ambiguous shape of barking dog	*D*	*F*	cloud, Ad
> 15. Alligator with mouth open	*D*	*F*	Ad

Card V

1. Flying bat with feet and antennae	*W*	*FM*	*A*
2. Alligator or crocodile	*D*	*F*	Ad
3. Tweezers	*D*	*F*	obj
4. Bat looks as though has cape over him with hood on	*W*	*F*	clo
5. Profile with puckering lips	*de*	*F, m*	*Hd*
6. Profile (partly)	*de*	*F*	*Hd*
7. Two busts	*d*	*F*	obj
8. Two penises	*d*	*F*	sex
9. Two men joined at rear	*d*	*F*	*H*
10. Shading looks like a caricature of a happy face, say Mickey Mouse	*di*	*F, m*	*(A)*
v 11. Snakes rising from basket at sound of flute (India) are Cobras	*d*	*FM*	*A*
v 12. Profile (see booklet)	*de*	*F*	*Hd*
v 13. Penis entering vagina	*S, dd*	*Fm*	sex
v 14. Seed growing through dirt	*S, dd*	*Fm, C'*	pl, dirt

Card VI

1. Bear skin rug, furry, upside down	*W*	*Fc*	A, obj
2. Penis	*D*	*F*	sex
3. Goofy	*d*	*F*	*(A)*
4. Wooden twisting instrument used for cooking, twirling around	*D*	*Fm*	obj
5. Looks like looking in a microscope	*d*	*FK*	

TABLE 2–2
(Continued)

Card VI

v 6.	Gorilla with outstretched hand,	*W`*	*FM*	*A*
> 7.	Top half looks like cloudy day at the beach with surf hitting shore	*D*	*FK, m*	*N*, cloud

Card VII

1.	Two little young Indian girls facing each other with hands pointed other way, feet touching, with dirty noses and chins	*W*	*M, C'*	*H*, dirt
2.	Caricatures with fierce angry expressions with horn	*D*	*F, m*	*Hd*
3.	Blades of knives	*D*	*F*	obj
4.	Another shaft or canal	*d*	*F*	shaft, canal
5.	Turnover pies	*D*	*Fc*	food
6.	Profile of warrior (Greek) inside knives	*di*	*F*	*Hd*
> 7.	Bowl or pot with pig legs	*S*	*F*	obj

Card VIII

1.	Bears climbing up mat	*W*	*FM*	*A*
2.	Top of skeleton head from dorsal view (of animal) plus a little of backbone	*D*	*k*	*AAt*
3.	Hands praying	*d*	*F*	hands
4.	Lion heads looking inward and upward	*D*	*F–*	*A*, obj
5.	Dress with three main stripes	*D*	*FC*	clo
6.	Hands reaching out to panthers paws	*d*	*Fm*	*Hd*, hands
> 7.	Panther walking over rocks near stream, reflection in water	*W*	*FM*	*A*
v 8.	Ghost with mean eyes, dripping hands	*D*	*M, F, m*	*(H)* hands
v 9.	Rocket firing	*d*	*mF, FC*	obj, fire
v 10.	Frog jumping	*D*	*FM*	*A*
11.	Scarred eyes	*dd*	*F, m*	*Hd*
> 12.	Teeth of tiger with mouth open	*d*	*F*	*AAt*

Card IX

1.	Painting with a Venus or lovely girl rising from center as symbol of youth and beauty, with hands touching from people on side, gods.	*D*	*F, Csym*	Art, myth, abst.
2.	Hip bones	*D*	*F*	*HAt*

TABLE 2-2
(Continued)

Card IX

3. Spaces between man's arm and his body	dr	F	Hd
4. Cotton candy puffs	D	CF, Fc	food
5. Green fingers	d	F	Hd
6. Shrinking man, ephemeral man shrinking to size	D	M, K	(H)
7. Dragons fighting, breathing fire	D	FM, CF	(A), fire
> 8. Big black cloud hanging over lake with orange and pink being less dense clouds, at sunset, reflections in water	W	CF	N, cloud
v 9. Pigs faces, facing outward, with mouths open	D	F	A
v 10. Penis spraying (pink)	D	Fm, CF	sex
v 11. Rocket—more so when right side up, taking off	D	Fm, CF	obj, fire

---

Card X

1. Spring-time picture	W	Csym	N	
with colors, yellow birds	D	FM, FC	A	
blue flowers	D	FC	pl	
blue spiders	D	FM, FC	A	P
green worms	D	FM, FC	A	P
spacious (white)	S	C'		
brown tree limbs	D	FC	pl	
2. Praying hands	d	F	hands	
3. Statues facing each other as if growing from ground	d	Fm	obj	
4. Dripping blood	D	CF, m	blood	
5. Pink puffy clouds	D	CF, Fc	clouds	
6. Boy Jesus or angel with hands in air with head or curly blond hair, perhaps wreath around	S	M, Cproj	myth	
7. Birds with scrapes, so that skin is broken with blood (assuming skin, not feathers)	D	FM, CF, Fc	A, blood	
8. Looks as though all figures looking toward or reaching for the gray pole at top center, only thing with straight sides (geometrical)	W	FM	A	
9. Young girls holding hands, looking up, floating in air (ephemeral figures)	D	M	H	

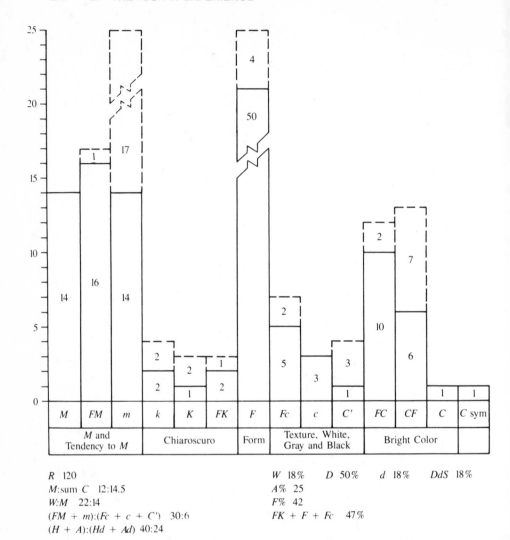

M	*FM*	*m*	*k*	*K*	*FK*	*F*	*Fc*	*c*	*C'*	*FC*	*CF*	*C*	*C* sym

| *M* and Tendency to *M* | | | Chiaroscuro | | | Form | Texture, White, Gray and Black | | | Bright Color | | | |

R 120
M:sum *C*   12:14.5
W:*M*   22:14
(*FM* + *m*):(*Fc* + *c* + *C'*)   30:6
(*H* + *A*):(*Hd* + *Ad*) 40:24

W 18%   *D* 50%   *d* 18%   *DdS* 18%
A% 25
F% 42
FK + *F* + *Fc*   47%

FIG. 2-2.   A psychogram of Student 2

Some of Student 2's problems and insights are given here. Speaking of herself in the third person, the code name E.N. is used.

Self-Evaluation of Student 2

The high number of *m* is the most detrimental feature of this protocol, that is, E.N. is experiencing being over-whelmed by uncontrollable

forces. The quality of the m responses is strong and volatile
(4 dripping blood, 4 rockets firing, 2 penis movements), the content
of which would seem to indicate strong emotional reactions to sex,
perhaps traumatic experiences. Thus, the m could reflect the conflict
between sexual impulses and a strict super-ego. Nine blatant sex
responses show that there is some concern about sex. Also on two
occasions, the sex responses were immediately followed by the
response "a seed growing."

Religious ideas are found in the symbolic "praying hands," and the
mythological and abstract response that includes "gods," and the "boy
Jesus" (Card X, 6). This picture is supported when taking into account
that E.N. was a literal Catholic until age 20 when her conflicts about
sex and guilt resulted in a clean break from the Church and a painful
growth process toward sexual fulfillment, and deeper personal
intimacy. Yet it appears that the residue of Catholicism still remains
and is still causing some intrapsychic conflict.

There appears to be a definite conflict in what the childhood
experience was like for this person and how she now sees herself—a
conflict between a more basic core and how she has evolved. Family
life for this person consisted of an ambitious, strong, and sensitive
father who believed in responsibility, commitment to an ideal, the
need to stay and stick with it, to fight for what one wanted. Much
attention was paid to argument, to cute and acute hostility. The mother
was sensitive, guilt-ridden and somtimes cool. Siblings were
competitive, emotionally reactive and ambitious. Thus, the learned
and taught values, especially aggression, were experiences against the
real nature of E.N. This is presently experienced in the feeling of
discomfort in accepting the aggressive and assertive part of herself.

How is this person handling this conflict? Content analysis shows
hostility and anger in 10 responses, indicative perhaps of conflict
reflected in the m, as a means of handling anxiety.

Overall, the psychogram looks to be one of a person functioning
at a more than average level. Though E.N. is functioning adequately
in terms of adjustment, she is not in terms of comfort. It has been
confirmed by her therapist that this person definitely has difficulty
accepting resources that appear to be available to her. Her
insecurity and self-doubt inhibit her from making full use of her
creativity, warmth, and intellectual abilities.

Students 1 and 2 differ in some important ways, despite their unusual
common denominator of a wealth of images. Take, for example, their
respective $W:M$ ratios. Student 2, with 22:14, came closer to the 2:1 ratio

considered to be that which makes for easier functioning—"easier" in the sense that the executive arm, as one might call it, the organizing *W* capacity, is not overloaded, and can keep pace with the creative suggestions carried by the *M* capacity. For Student 1, as she so beautifully put it, a major problem is "sculpting some coherent order from the kaleidoscope of images and ideas that fuse and flow together." For Student 2, this was not the problem; her concerns lie elsewhere.

A second difference lies in the *M:*sum *C* ratio. Student 1, despite the fact that her color scores are high (18.5), still would be rated as an introvert, the 44 *M*'s clearly dominating. In her choice of inner or outer directed activities, the inner world has the greater pull. Student 2, on the other hand, has virtually identical "pulls" from inside and outside (*M* = 14; sum *C* = 12.5). Notice also the difference in their *FM* scores, when compared to the *M* column.

From the inner experiences of two high productivity persons, we will consider next the individual with one response per card. How do their worlds differ?

3

The Low R Experience
Self-Evaluation of Records with Under 22 Responses

The inner world of Student 3 was in sharp contrast to those of Students 1 and 2 in the previous chapter. We are now looking at the type of record where only one response was given per card, and where that response is a Whole. We are confronted by dramatic differences in perceptual experiences.

But within this low R, somewhat simplified record, there is the same scoring procedure to be handled, the same ratios to be understood and interpreted, and personal data and behavioral reactions to be linked with their Rorschach equivalents.

In the self-evaluation, speaking of himself as the "Subject," we find that Student 3 was dealing successfully with his W compulsion, describing well his "adamant refusal" to see details. We find his acceptance of his introversial leanings, and the realization of his minimal emotional involvement. In dealing with his emotional responses, however, he underestimated the personal pressures reflected in his "atomic explosion" scoring this response incorrectly (K) without reference to the emotional coloring.

He was also concerned with his, then, lower than average, $F\%$. However, at the time his record was taken (early 1960s), the generally accepted percentage for F responses was, as he states, between 45% and 55%. It was not until some years later that the $F\%$ derived from several student groups, dropped into the 25% range. This unusual phenomenon seems to have been clearly related to cultural changes during the "do-your-own-thing" era, resulting in increasing disregard for authority and the established order.

Student 3's Rorschach responses (Table 3-1), his psychogram (Figure 3-2) and part of his self-evaluation now follow:

TABLE 3-1
Self-Evaluation of Student 3

1. face of wolf	W	F	A
2. two dancing clowns	W	M, FC	H
3. two men lifting heavy object	W'	M	H
4. head of wild bear	W	F	A
5. bat in flight	W	FM	A
6. insect under microscope	W	F	A
7. two ladies chatting	W	M	H
8. two climbing animals	W	FM	A
9. atomic explosion	W	K	Clouds
10. underwater scene	W	FM, FC	A

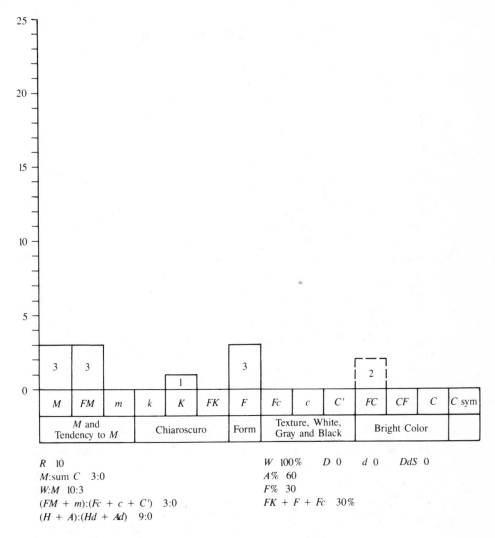

FIG. 3-1. A psychogram of Student 3

sees the forest and not the trees. He is more likely to be a generalist than a specialist. When he was unable to associate Card IX with anything with which he was familiar, he inverted the card to see a *W,* rather than try to describe a component of it.

He adamantly refuses to see not only *Dd*s, but *d*s and *D*s as well. Thus, we have evidence that his unitary approach could border on a compulsion to generalize. In actual life, the subject *does* approach the world as a whole.

In this subject's record there is total exclusion of the color group. Predominance of *M*s shows creative ability, inner life, more introversion than extraversion, and more intensive rather than extensive rapport with people. A high degree of *M,* as with this subject, shows difficulty in approaching the outside world. High *M*s with few *C*s could depict a danger of slipping off into fantasy. More *C*s are needed for such a person to counter balance the *M*s and thus allow the subject greater emotional expression.

In real life this subject has a problem in giving vent to his emotions. The presence of *FM*s in this subject's record is a healthy sign and tends to lessen the hold that fantasy has on him.

Rorschach distinguishes between flexion and extension *M*s. Subjects who predominantly see *M*s in extension as figures stretching or rising are different from those who predominantly see figures flexing. Flexion expresses passivity. Our subject showed all extensions *M*s.

F responses show intellectual control. Our subject has *F* 30% which is below the optimum level, perhaps his ability to make full use of his intellectual capacity is impaired by his degree of fantasy; for such a person, a decrease in fantasy might increase the use of his intellectual resources.

In summarizing the portrayal of our subject in this test, one can say he is introversive, aware of his instinctual drives, and inhibited emotionally. His intellectuality is in conflict with his fantasy, and with his drives. More emotional expression is needed to offset his introversion. This person is likely to have few, but strong friendship ties. Our subject approaches life as a whole. He is an active, striving introvert, rather than a passive one.

He is overwhelmingly a generalist with a minimum of analytic ability. The Rorschach is relevant and very accurate in describing the subject's behavior, thinking, and emotionality in real life situations.

THE LOW *R*
RORSCHACH RESPONSES, PSYCHOGRAM,
AND SELF-EVALUATION OF STUDENT 4

Student 4's 21 Rorschach responses, though twice that of Student 3, is still below the expected average and is still in marked contrast to the productions of Students 1 and 2. His responses also share with Student 3 an emphasis on *W* responses, marked introversion, and lack of responsiveness to the colored cards. When the responses are examined individually, Student 4's Rorschach record shows some explicitly accepted sexual responses, the presence of white space responses, and more differentiated percepts requiring additional determinants to describe them. It is also selected because of amplification given to each answer, something that does not occur in the record of Student 3.

Student 4 utilized a format in relating the Rorschach findings to the information which he gave about himself. We will see that he immediately commented, by way of parentheses, on the use he made of some of his scoring observations. By this he proved that he based his statements on Rorschach's interpretive principles. The instructor suggested this format at various stages in the learning of the interpretive process, believing it to be an important aspect of the insight-instruction method and a reminder that, ultimately, reports on patients should include evidence that diagnostic comments or judgments are based on legitimate interpretive principles. Some students stuck to this method; others abandoned it for more personalized styles.

Student 4 (or Tom as he speaks of himself) made good use of content, thus becoming more personal, and to that extent, more insightful. One might say from this self-evaluation (presented in Table 3-1) that it was not necessary to have a wealth of original material in a record for the inside evaluator to reveal some material that is close to the core of the self.

TABLE 3-1
Rorschach Record of Student 4

Card I			
1. Two dogs holding on to a pole	*W*	*FM, F*	*A*, obj
2. A mask	*W*	*F*	mask
3. Face of a monster, with horns	*W, S*	*F*	*(Ad)*

Card II			
1. Two Siamese men in a test of strength	*W*	*M*	*H*
2. "Mt. Rushmore" type stone face	*d*	*F*	Art
3. A jet plane flying	*S*	*Fm*	obj

TABLE 3–1
(Continued)

Card III				
1. Two African women bouncing a bow-shaped object back and forth with their breasts. They each have a low-slung penis and are preparing to urinate into pitchers.	W	M, FC, F	H, Sex, obj	P

Card IV				
1. A fox terrier with 2 human feet, flattened out, or falling	W	FM	(A)	
2. A monster whose penis or tail is the head of a fox terrier	W	M	(H), sex	
3. Two cocker spaniels with faces at rear of terrier, smelling	W, S	FM	A, sex	

Card V				
1. A bat flying	W	FM	A	P
2. Alligator heads	d	F	Ad	

Card VI				
1. Ghost-like English judge in chair at bar. He has long white hair and some kind of bird on his head.	W	M, FM Fc, F	(H), A, obj	O

Card VII				
1. Two elephants rearing up, back to back	W	FM	A	
2. Clown faces	D	F	Hd	

Card VIII				
1. Two rats being pulled up by an octopus-like monster	D, S	FM	A	P
2. Goat heads, embryonic stage	D	FC	Ad	

Card IX				
1. Two witches giving each other the "whammy" (the evil-eye, a la "L'il Abner" comic strip)	D	M	(H)	

TABLE 3-1
(Continued)

Card IX				
2. Two "B'rer Rabbits," smiling, face, neck, bow tie (human-like comic strip character)	W, S	M	(Hd)	

Card X				
1. Two flying men fighting each other with crabs	D, S	M, FM	H, A	P
2. Two worms, eye to eye	D	FM	A	

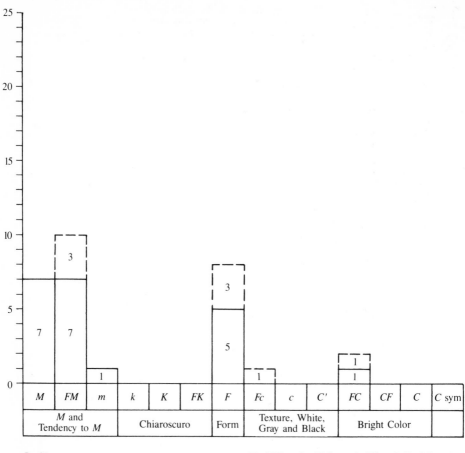

FIG. 3-2.   A psychogram of Student 4

R   21   W   57%   D   29%   d   9%   DdS   5%
M:sum C   7:.5   A%   48
W:M   12:7   F%   24
(FM + m):(Fc + c + C')   8:0   FK + F + Fc   24%
(H + A):(Hd + Ad)   14:4

Self-Evaluation of Student 4

"Tom" is able to organize material, relate details, and be concerned with the abstract and theoretical. There is sufficient creative ability for intellectual achievement. (Good *W:M* ratio. This is in line with IQ of 144 as measured by the WAIS in 1963.) However, his thoughts tend to be commonplace and narrow in range. (*A*% content. This is generally true. I am not really ambitious intellectually.) He seems to be stubborn and negativistic. (One *S* and five additional. Correct. I can become quite rigid in the face of suggestions from others, especially authority figures. I like to do things in my own way, without supervision.)

He accepts impulses readily and they do not interfere with the picture he has of himself as a mature individual. (*M:FM.* I believe this to be a fair statement, but I find myself resisting the acceptance of the hostility and aggressive feelings in my Rorschach.) He relies upon his inner life more than upon his environment for comfort or for stimulation. He has a rich fantasy life and is sufficiently in control of his impulses to give stability. (*M; M:C.* I do have some wonderful daydreams in which sexual, educational, and occupational goals are realized.)

There appears to be a denial or repression of the need for affection, which may constitute a major handicap in general adjustment. Socialized responses tend to be superficial, and responsiveness to environmental stimuli is limited. He is not able to identify closely with people. (Absence of *FK Fc;* low *FC;* a number of "human-like" responses.) (This is most probably accurate. I felt rejected by my parents, am generally a "loner," and have some difficulty relating to others.)

Tom has hostile and aggressive feelings, which he attempts to control. The Siamese men and their strength contest, the witches engaging in nonphysical combat, the two men using crabs to do the fighting for them. (I consider these feelings to be under adequate control. The Rorschach does not show that "barbed" humor is often used as an escape hatch.)

There may be a problem in sexual identification. (The phallic women on Card III. Intelligent, aggressive females do make me feel uneasy (castration fear), so this may be a valid judgment.) He has guilt feelings about sexual practices. (The response of a "ghost-like" judge on the "Sex" card (Card VI) beautifully illustrates my guilt reaction to masturbation during my Catholic youth.) It may be that he equates sex with animal rather than human function. (Responses to Cards IV and VI.)

THE LOW *R*
RORSCHACH RESPONSES, PSYCHOGRAM,
AND SELF–EVALUATION OF STUDENT 5

Excerpts from Student 5's insightful and courageous report show that even with relative poverty of Rorschach responses (low *R*), very keen insight can be derived from their study. This student made the most of his somewhat restricted psychological world, and was able to focus on his key problems.

In Student 5's self-evaluation, he spoke of three areas—his *W*%, his *FM*s, and his *A* score—as reflecting problems that he was dealing with in his therapeutic sessions. On the face of it, these scores (*W*% = 44%, *FM* = 3, and *A*% = 31%) are not unusual, but for Student 5, they triggered associations that related very clearly to his current self-evaluation.

The *W*% took him back to a time when his organizing ability was outstanding and had the flavor of satisfaction and success—then this fell apart, but he needed to show that he was once highly competent in this area.

His *FM* score is certainly not noted for its excess or inadequacy numerically. But the content and descriptive accounts have understandably a disturbing flavor for him: "Two bears climbing on the partially decomposed carcass of a large sea animal" or again, "Two crabs attacking two men and tearing them to pieces." His basic drives at this stage were beyond his control.

The *A*% which he also sparked to—though again not in itself unusual—allowed an insight to surface and it is this insight which he then deals with in his self-evaluation (see Table 3–3).

TABLE 3–3
Rorschach Responses of Student 5

Card *I*				
1. two elephants drinking	*W*	*FM*	*A*	
out of a large bottle	*D*	*F*	obj	
Card *II*				
1. two men in costume playing				
patty-cake	*W*	*M*	*H*	*P*
Card *III*				
1. two Negro savages beating				
tom-toms	*D*	*M*	*H*	*P*
2. a butterfly between the savages	*D*	*F*	*A*	*P*
3. two bloody things are hanging				
above the heads of the savages	*D*	*CF*	Blood	

TABLE 3-3
(Continued)

Card IV				
1. a great animal rug of some sort. It looks as if it came from a bear.	W	Fc	A-obj	P
Card V				
1. a bat	W	F	A	P
Card VI				
1. indian totem perched on top of an animal skin	W	Fc	A-obj	P
Card VII				
1. two imps facing each other and perched on clouds	W	M, K	H	
Card VIII				
1. two bears climbing on the partially decomposed carcass of a large sea animal	D D	FM c	A A-obj	P
Card IX				
1. two witches, appearing out of a great fire	W	M, CF	H	
2. a jet spouts between the witches	D	CF, m		
Card X				
1. two crabs attacking two men and tearing them to pieces	D	FM	A, H	P
2. a straight object at top made of iron or steel	dd	F	obj	

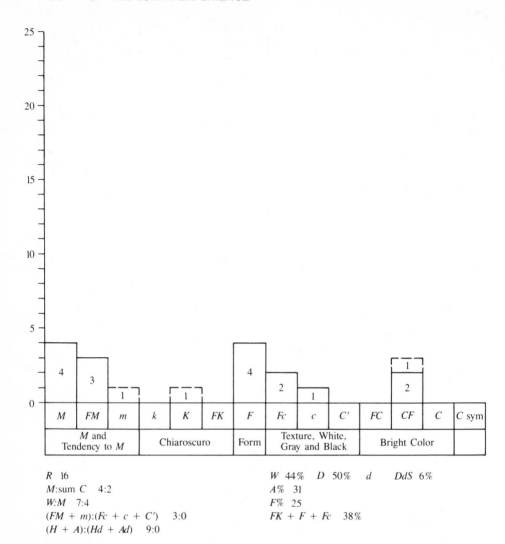

FIG. 3-3. A psychogram of Student 5

Self-Evaluation of Student 5

For the past five years, I have been undergoing intensive (four sessions a week) psychoanalysis. It is truly amazing how this Rorschach record exposes most of my problems—even succeeds in crystallizing them to a painful degree. It contains three key indicators: high percentage of *W, FM,* and Animal responses.

In discussing the *W,* I should report that when in high school and later at the university, I was often president of my class or chairman of an important committee. I possessed *organizational interest and ability.* I was usually able to size up the situation and pull things together.

However, some time around my second year out of college things began to afflict me. I wasn't making friends, felt sexually frustrated most of the time, and couldn't hold a job, and was generally agitated and anxious. It was then that I entered analysis.

After three years of treatment, I began to discover why I was having all this difficulty. The Rorschach *FM* predominance explains a good deal of this. I was unable to handle my *drive* impulses. I'd feel the need to succeed with a girl, a job, or a social situation—and overlook the fact that one has to withstand something before he gets what he wants. I was beginning to see the extent of my *infantility.* It was making life a continual series of dead end frustrations. Of all tenacious handicaps—emotional ones are among the most resistant to alleviation. In analysis, I am still learning that maturity takes place only through the withstanding of unpleasantness and postponed goal achievement.

Animal responses are verified in my ownership of a Rhodesian Ridgeback dog and Siamese cat for five years. Since I wasn't able to grow enough to endure friendship's trials and tribulations—I had to have something. The dog and the cat were my way of *protecting myself from reality.* Having walked and fed them respectively, I felt that my obligations to living were fulfilled.

Another conflict—that involving *high popular and popular* vs. *FM, F,* and *M* weightedness on the *psychogram fulcrum* —exists in actuality. Because of my *confusion, repression,* and *unreality* —I never know when I'm myself. Therefore, I may act as the environment expects me to do rather than in a way more intimately and really related to my inner self. However, I am happy to report that slowly but surely (and expensively) I am learning that it's better to be *really pained* in the world than euphorically neurotic.

STUDENT WITH BRAIN TUMOR

In order that these records with low *R* be seen in proper perspective, they should be contrasted with the minimum production of a brain tumor case. This student with an IQ of 146 was suddenly found to be doing very poor work in his studies. He was initially suspected of being a disciplinary problem. However, during a medical checkup both the EEG and the Rorschach suggested a tumor, which was verified at operation. His record appears in Table 3-4.

TABLE 3-4
Student with Brain Tumor

---

 1. the skull of a horse
 2. . . .
 3. . . .
 4. . . .
 5. like a bat
 6. a piece of sky
 7. . . .
 8. . . .
 9. . . .
10. a piece of lobster

Our students' low *R* records have none of the pathological features seen in this case. Note the failure to respond in any way to several of the cards, and the poor form of three of the four answers. The student's Psychogram appears in Figure 3-4.

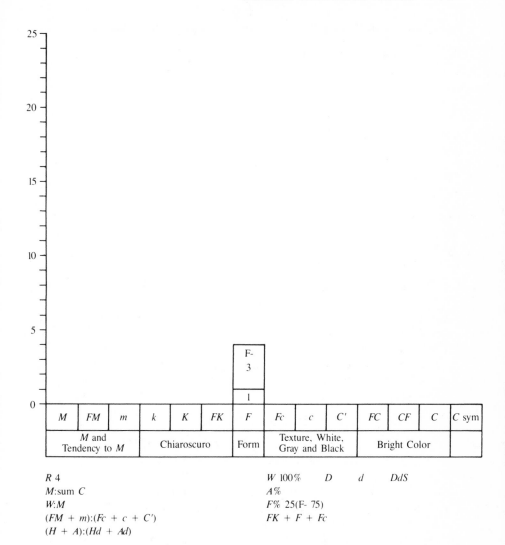

FIG. 3–4. A psychogram of brain tumor case

4

The High *F* Experience

In chapter 1 we spoke of determinants dominating a psychogram. This is graphically illustrated in the charted responses of Students 6 and 7, which show the *F* columns clearly in command with percents of 63 and 55, respectively. For these two students, logical thinking and the acceptance of, or need for, formal control plays a major role in their psychological makeups.

RORSCHACH RESPONSES, PSYCHOGRAM, AND SELF–EVALUATION OF STUDENT 6

Student 6 tackled his main inadequacy head on. He was fully aware of his lack of emotional freedom and also aware that he viewed other people as apt to be critical of him or "frowning" at him.

He was able to accept his somewhat restricted range of psychic reactivity, and to cash in on his assets. These assets were a careful and logical approach to his work. At one time Student 6 considered going into medicine, feeling that somewhat safer than dealing face to face with the psychological problems of patients. However, his final decision was to concentrate on psychological research, and he received a reward for having made the best contribution in the research field in his last year of graduate school. The Rorschach record of Student 6 is shown in Table 4-1 and his psychogram, in Figure 4-1.

TABLE 4-1
Rorschach Record of Student 6

Card I				
1. A leering face, diabolical, fiendish	WS	F, m	Hd	
2. Some kind of horned animal that is enraged or growling	WS	F, m	Ad	
Card II				
1. Two hooded figures (people) in heavy robes sitting facing each other with palms touching	W	M	H	P
2. Two bear-like creatures with front paws and rear legs touching	D	F	A	P
Card III				
1. Two exotic dancers facing each other with their hands laid on some object, like a crown, between them	W	M	H	P
Card IV				
1. A dragon's head emerging from a cave in the side of a mountain	W	FM	Ad, Ntr	
Card V				
1. A bat flying toward the top of the card	W	FM	A	P
2. A butterfly flying toward the bottom of the card	W	FM	A	P
3. A man in a kind of flying apparatus with wings attached to his arms; he is standing on the ground with the wings drooping at his sides	W	M	H, obj	
Card VI				
1. A bearskin rug	W	Fc	A obj	P
2. View of a man's crotch from underneath; his penis is erect	W	F	sex	
Card VII				
1. Two fists with "thumbs up"	D	F	Hd	
2. Two arms with hands in position for thumbing a ride	D	F	Hd	
3. Two Indian heads facing each other with feathers sticking up in back	D	F	Hd	
4. Vagina	di	F	sex	

TABLE 4–1
(Continued)

Card VIII				
1. Two lizard-like creatures	D	F	A	P
2. A butterfly	D	F	A	
3. An airplane pilot's face; he has his helmet, goggles, and oxygen mask on	WS	F	Hd, obj	
4. An insect's head	WS	F	Ad	

Card IX			
1. The bottom part of the picture reminds me of the kind of dress which has sleeves puffed up at the shoulder	D	F	obj
2. The bottom part could also be the upper torso of a very muscular man	D	(FC)	Hd
3. The upper part of the picture could be a grotesque head or mask	D	Fv	obj

Card X			
1. A frowning man with rather long hair and a moustache	WS	F, m	Hd
2. Flowers and colored leaves (on both sides of the picture)	D	FC	Ntr

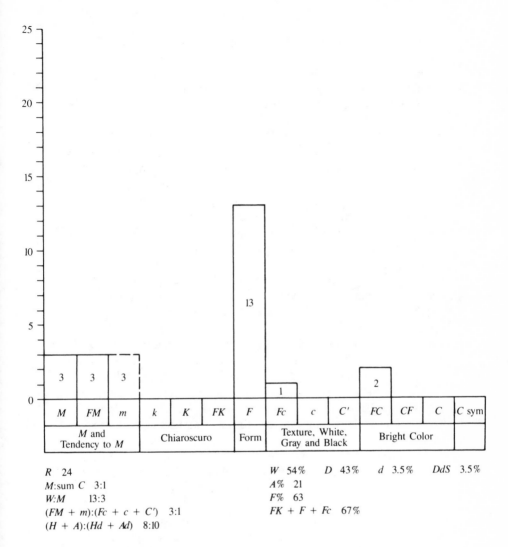

	M	FM	m	k	K	FK	F	Fc	c	C'	FC	CF	C	C sym
	3	3	3				13	1				2		
	M and Tendency to *M*			Chiaroscuro			Form	Texture, White, Gray and Black			Bright Color			

R 24
M:sum *C* 3:1
W:M   13:3
(*FM* + *m*):(*Fc* + *c* + *C'*) 3:1
(*H* + *A*):(*Hd* + *Ad*) 8:10

W 54%   *D* 43%   *d* 3.5%   *DdS* 3.5%
A% 21
F% 63
FK + *F* + *Fc* 67%

FIG. 4-1. A psychogram of Student 6

Self-Evaluation of Student 6

A prominent feature of my record is the high logical control column, 63%. The interpretation usually given a high *F*% is that it indicates a tendency toward rigidity and constriction, and I feel that this interpretation is accurate in my case. In much of my interaction with other people I feel that I behave in a somewhat guarded manner, being unwilling to "let go" and to respond according to the demands of the moment.

Nevertheless, my $F\%$ is not exceedingly high, indicating the possibility of some degree of spontaneity. In situations where I feel comfortable (e.g., with close friends) I can act more spontaneously.

Responses in other determinant categories are necessarily few as a consequence of the relatively high $F\%$. *A minimum of three M* responses is expected from the well-adjusted intelligent adult. The fact that I gave this minimum may be interpreted as indicating that my inner life is developed to some extent but is certainly not a rich one. The ratio of my inner needs to my extroverted activities is 3:1, certainly in agreement with my experience of withdrawing from the social milieu to seek stimulation from within. I have always thought of my inner world as comforting and a nice place to be. I guess it could be said with some accuracy that my inner world serves as a retreat for me, and that it is a comfortable retreat, not so much because it is richly developed but because it allows escape from the world which can prove threatening at times (note response 1 to Card I and response 1 to Card X).

The psychogram shows three *FM* responses. A total of two *FM*s would probably be more accurate since the two *FM* responses to Card V are very similar. Two *FM*s in relation to three *M*s and the moderately high F% is an indication of impulse control. I do not deny the existence of impulses within me but I do feel that I keep my impulses (especially impulses toward anger and sexual impulses) in close check.

A striking feature of my psychogram is the lack of responses at the color end. Two *FC* responses are recorded but it should be noted that one of these is bracketed. My *FC* response to Card XIII is bracketed because I did not feel it was a full-blooded *FC,* being determined more by form than color. Even the few color responses I did make, then, had a form component. This lack of development at the color end of the psychogram, in conjunction with the high $F\%$, is an indication of excessive control of emotions. I have always thought of myself as lacking in spontaneity and being reserved in my emotional expression. Some recent experiences have led me to see that the degree of control I exert is greater than I had previously thought. The psychogram tends to support my conclusions based on these experiences.

My total number of responses to the cards is 24. The total number of separate responses may be closer to 20, however, since in Cards I, V, VIII, and IX 2 "different" responses were given to the same portion of the blot. Eliminating one of the duplicate responses on each of these cards would result in a total of 20 responses. Adequate productivity is said to have been achieved if between 21 and 40 responses are made. My 20 responses (or even 24) place me at the lower end of the adequate range. I am not sure that I can account for this finding. I suppose that this rather low number of responses may be interpreted as indicating a lack of creativity. Some support for this interpretation is provided by the $W{:}M$ ratio, which is slightly higher than 4:1. A $W{:}M$ ratio higher than 2:1 is often interpreted as indicating intellectual ambitions that are too high for the person's creative potential. I do not know my own IQ but I have often felt that my academic success has been the result not so much of my inherent intellectual capacity as it has been the result of hard work. I should add that even after eliminating one of the duplicated responses on each of Cards I, V, VIII, and IX, the W responses constitute 50% of the total. This indicates that I have some ability to organize, to relate details, and to think abstractly.

Three additional m responses are found in my record. One interpretation of m responses is that they are an indicator of tension. This could certainly be true in my case in light of my high degree of control. Another interpretation of m responses is that they represent outer forces that the person cannot control. If the concept of outer forces can be extended to include other persons then I think this interpretation is most apt in my case. I think the ms in my record represent threatening others, others who may ridicule me or disapprove of me (note the "leering face" of Card I and the "frowning man" of Card X).

Despite the somewhat negative features of the psychogram, I do not feel I am a hopeless case. In support of this contention I cite my growing awareness of my rather high degree of control and low emotional expressiveness and my desire to do something about altering these features of my personality. Although my capacity for expressing emotion is not well-developed at present, the psychogram gives a hint of emotion which may be developed. And there is my lone Fc which, while dwarfed in the presence of 13 Fs, indicates a rudimentary level of sensitivity which may be developed.

How much do the record of Student 6 and those of Students 7 and 8, which follow, deviate from the accepted norm? To answer this we have to look not only at the published norms from the original Rorschach contributors, but also at an unusual phenomenon which came to light during the 13 years of accumulating students' records within the framework of the insight-instruction method of teaching.

If we look at some published norms we find Klopfer (1954) considered an acceptable $F\%$ to be between 20% and 50%. Alcock's (1963) findings placed her $F\%$ figure between 30% and 50%. Harrower and Steiner (1951) found that 224 student subjects showed an average of 36% while for older adults the percentage was 54. Piotrowski (1957) did not concern himself so much with the average range but considered below 20% to "indicate serious mental disturbance."

The current studies on which this book is based ran from 1962 to 1975. During that time a marked decrease in the $F\%$ was found in our student groups.

Sometime ago I expressed this trend as follows:

I have felt for some time that the lowered $F\%$ in the college age group nicely parallels the "zeitgeist," the disregard of formal dress, the antagonism toward established modes of behavior, and the intense individualism displayed.

In the "old days" one used to be taught that an $F\%$ of 50 was acceptable norm. Over the 8 years in which I have taken student records, each year the $F\%$ has come bumping down, keeping pace with the general disregard for formalities that one sees all around. Last year it hit, for my records, an all time low of 13% for a group of 30 students. It seems to be slightly on the rise this year, although still in the low twenties.

I find this a sufficiently intriguing idea so that I have instigated a more systematic study with over 3,000 Rorschach records of theological students, taken since 1953. It would appear from preliminary scanning that this same trend is evidenced. Last year, also, was the peak year for low $F\%$, anti-establishment stories in the TAT, and cracks at the established order in the Comprehension subtest on the Wechsler (Harrower, 1971).

THE HIGH *F*
RORSCHACH RESPONSES, PSYCHOGRAM, AND SELF-EVALUATION OF STUDENT 7

The psychogram of Student 7 is very similar to that of Student 6. Like 6, he concerned himself with the absence of spontaneous expression of emotions and was able to come to the conclusion that he was actually afraid of his feelings.

However, he was not only aware that his intense love of music was a direct avenue for expression of his feelings but saw that his pleasure at reading the score of the music while listening, demonstrated his ever present intellectual needs—an excellent observation.

Student 7 was happier "inside" than 6, which shows up in his more numerous and freer M responses, for example, the motorcyclist. His introversion is more marked and, therefore, gives an alternative orientation to the objective viewpoint of his high F score.

Seven saw himself as becoming an effective therapist, a field in which he has now become competent. A follow-up, written 10 years later, is given after his self-evaluation. Student 7's Rorschach record appears in Table 4–2, and psychogram, in Figure 4–2.

TABLE 4–2
Rorschach Responses of Student 7

Card I

1. Butterfly	W	FM	A	P
2. Map of a state with four lakes, some islands	WS	F	Geo	
3. A flying animal; squirrel or bat	W	FM	A	P

Card II

1. Female pelvis	W'	F, FC	At, sex	P
2. Horseshoe crab	D	F	A	
3. Feet (lower red)	D	F	Hd	

Card III

1. Two natives playing drums or bending over a pot. I'm not sure if they are female or male. They have breasts; do have penises but highheels	W'	M	H	P
2. Pair of lungs in middle	D	F	At	

Card IV

1. Big hairy dude on a motorcycle from *behind*	W	M	H	
2. Godzilla from the back playing leap frog over a tree trunk	W	FM	(A)	

Card V

1. Butterfly	W	FM	A	P
2. Man in a bird costume	W	M	H	

Card VI

1. Bearskin rug	D	Fc	A	P
2. Erect penis	D	F	sex	
3. Mine shaft (lightened areas to each side)	D	F, C'	obj?	
4. Some sort of indian thing on penis part	D	F	obj	
5. A zipper	di	F, C'	obj	

TABLE 4–2
(Continued)

Card VII				
1. Two girls with pigtails blowing in the air looking at each other	*D*	*F*	*H*	
2. Two thumbs hitchhiking	*D*	*F, m*	*Hd*	
3. A very fat woman	*WS*	*M*	*H*	

Card VIII				
1. Two lizards crawling up something	*D*	*FM*	*A*	*P*
2. A corset which is being tight to fasten	*D*	*F*	obj	

Card IX				
1. Penis in a vagina	*D*	F	sex	
2. Man driving away on a motorcycle, red exhaust	*W*	M, *CF*	*H*	

Card X				
1. Rabbit with green plant strands coming down from eyes	*D*	*F, CF*	*A*	*P*
2. A goblin voodoo face with a flying creature above (or on forehead)	*W'*	*F*	*(Hd)*	
3. Man descending with a parachute	*D*	*M, F*	*H* & obj	

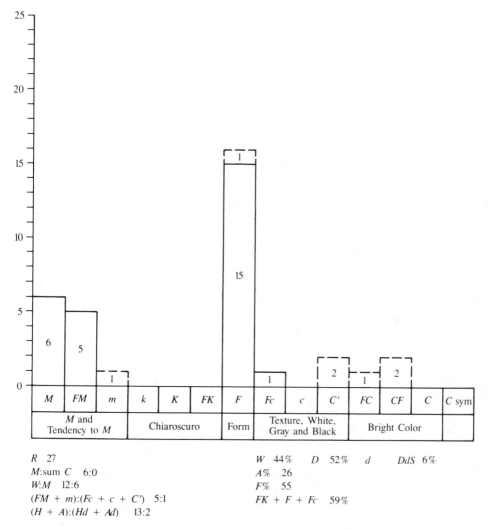

M	*FM*	*m*	*k*	*K*	*FK*	*F*	*Fc*	*c*	*C'*	*FC*	*CF*	*C*	*C* sym
6	5	1				15	1		2	1	2		
M and Tendency to *M*		Chiaroscuro				Form	Texture, White, Gray and Black			Bright Color			

R 27

M:sum *C* 6:0

W:*M* 12:6

(*FM* + *m*):(*Fc* + *c* + *C'*) 5:1

(*H* + *A*):(*Hd* + *Ad*) 13:2

W 44%   *D* 52%   *d*   *DdS* 6%

A% 26

F% 55

FK + *F* + *Fc* 59%

FIG. 4-2. A psychogram of Student 7

Self-Evaluation of Student 7

It seems to me that, in many regards, my Rorschach record is consonant with the way I and others see myself. Most people see me as being calm, objective, and highly logical, perhaps to an extreme. Consequently, emotional expression is a relative rarity. This is not to say that my emotional reactivity is nonexistent, only that for me, emotions are felt rather than expressed.

The high *F* as revealed in the psychogram indicates that I operate in a controlled, highly rational way. Perhaps the low number of overall responses further indicates an inability to deviate from form-determined responses. The high *F* may also be related to having a fairly large number of popular responses. I take this to be an outgrowth of my earlier development, in which I assimilated a regard for what is and what is not "proper." In recent years, I have recognized this aspect of my "life script" and have attempted to become more loose, spontaneous and creative. I see myself still in the process, I suppose the continuous process of finding myself, my individuality, as opposed to what others would like for me to be.

The nonexistence of color responses is rather striking to me. I have realized in the past that the state of my emotions are of concern to me. In fact, in a journal that I keep, I have noted that my emotional life needs to be worked on and that I may be afraid of my emotions. This is perhaps best represented in my record as two additional *C'* responses. It is possible that this expresses a desire for emotional expression, yet some apprehension or fear of that expression. I feel that I am presently working toward better emotional expression. Some indication of this may be observed in my additional color responses.

I do not feel that the lack of color responses indicates an inability to react emotionally. It does seem true, though, that I have difficulty in expressing emotions. Probably the most intense emotional experiences I have are in "being in Nature" and in music. These experiences often invoke awe; I have previously felt that the feelings arising from these two areas are religious experiences and bring me as "close to God" as I have ever gotten. I have felt strong emotion in singing in various choral groups as well as in playing organ and piano. Interestingly enough, in listening to music (particularly Bach), the experience is often enhanced by simultaneously reading the music score. This represents a melding of intellectual and emotional experiences, something that seems to be consonant with the Rorschach record. The case for such a representation in the Rorschach might be better if the quality of the *M* responses was enhanced. Not that the *M* responses are unhappy; they are just not particularly striking.

The slight emphasis on *W* responses also seems to be consonant with the degree of rational, intellectual control. I'm a fairly theoretical person and like the synthesis of ideas and information that theories attempt to create. Also, when confronted with a problematic situation, I am well able to view the situation as a whole and not become overconcerned by any of the component parts.

The *M:C* ratio indicates, correctly I believe, my basic mode of functioning as an introvert. Subjective states typically hold more interest for me than do external events. Friends sometimes comment on my "introspective," quiet nature. I typically like to ponder things, including responses to being addressed. In my record, this may be indicated by my rather lengthy average response time (2′). My slowness in responding to others is also a function of wanting to be tactful and sensitive in the things that I say. Perhaps some flavor of this may be picked up in my *Fc* response. I place a great deal of importance in being sensitive and tactful toward others.

Certain aspects of my sexual life seem to be expressed in my responses. Although ambiguity concerning the sex of the figures in Card III is presumably often expressed, my personal response may be reflective of conflicts I have felt in the past about expressing affection toward males. My expressed uncertainty as to the figures' sex may represent an ongoing conflict in this area. Perhaps my two sex responses indicate the degree of satisfaction and activity I am currently experiencing in a very fulfilling heterosexual relationship. These responses indicate an active sex life which is personally meaningful after a rather prolonged abstinence.

It seems that several assets are revealed in my record which would contribute toward making me an effective psychotherapist. My rational and objective qualities as well as the ability to generalize and see situations in their totality are essential equipment for the clinician. I possess sensitivity and tact which are also important qualities. Some work is needed in the emotional area to round out my rational nature and to become more comfortable in dealing with and experiencing others' emotions. A more highly differentiated emotional development along with a strong logical and objective base would interact well in assisting clients toward rational approaches to dealing with their problems in living.

Student 7 was one of those who took the Instruction–Insight course some 10 years ago, but welcomed the task of updating his experiences in the light of his former self-evaluation. Seven prefaced the following personal history with the statement: "You have given me an introspective challenge which will provide a wonderful opportunity to take stock." His stock-taking is as follows:

Occupationally, for the last 6 years, I have been working at a community mental health center doing therapy largely with kids and families. I have cut down to a half-time position, primarily as Internship

Coordinater while also doing a lot of intern supervision and consultation to the Youth and Seniors Day Treatment programs. Incidentally, I have been fascinated in doing some family therapy where the "identified patient" was the oldest person in the family. My direct service energies are conserved for private practice, largely focused on families and couples. I believe that this mixture is a psychologically perfect situation for me in meeting my needs for stability (paycheck, benefits, collegial relationships) and excitement (higher risk and challenge, greater financial reward with private practice). A recent development which fell my way has been a consulting position at a Nuclear Power Plant doing interviews and interpreting MMPI's to assess employees for emotional stability. This has been challenging and necessitated tough decisions on potential dangerousness vs. denying someone employment.

Since leaving U.F., I had a wonderful internship at Palo Alto V.A. Medical Center with specialized training in family therapy as well as an excellent inpatient rotation. My experience on the Family Study Unit of the V.A. really changed my way of thinking of clients and I've adopted much more of a systemic, interactional view. I've rather strayed from my previous predilection for intrapsychic/psychodynamic conceptualizations. Although I'm not much of an astrologer, I am the perfect Libra, weighing and balancing both sides of a situation, which I think helps me in working with couples and families. I find that if a client presents a certain perception of his situation, I automatically am looking for another way of framing "the facts" which may help the client to feel, think or behave differently which in turn would influence the response from others, which in turn would, etc. . . . I believe that relatively small changes can set in motion significantly different interactional sequences. As I have become more interested in systems theory, I have found myself thinking in behavioral terms of S-R chains which comprise "interactional loops" whose punctuation is arbitrary (e.g., does husband withdraw because wife nags or vice versa). I have come to find individual therapy to be something of a bore and feel at a disadvantage in helping others if there are not significant others to include in the therapy, at least partially.

I continue to struggle with the need to be in control vs. spontaneity/risk taking in personal and professional areas. My musical directions reflect this as I have concentrated my efforts in playing jazz piano vs. singing classical choral music.

I have needed to remind myself and make an effort with the interns I supervise to be positive and nurturant, building on their positive qualities. It is easy to point out suggestions for improving and not always be as supportive as I "know" would be facilitative. This is true also with clients, as I tend to operate in a relatively detached way. Until a couple years ago, in fact, I had the sense that clients didn't cry in sessions with me as much as I heard and imagined other clients did for other therapists. I was aware, in some cases, of helping the client to avoid or minimize affect and have struggled, with success, in reducing this barrier. I now feel that I have the flexibility to choose whether or not to facilitate affective expression, depending on what I see as the client's need at the time. I recently joked to a colleague that the interns I supervise at some point either cry in supervision (if female) or confide that they're gay (if male).

Even though I have enlarged my repertoire of being more emotionally available to clients, I still prefer to function in a relatively detached way. To be honest, it is sometimes an effort to convey empathy in a heartfelt way. My relative detachment seems to work well for me in family therapy in not being pulled into the family's system. To be effective, I must remain outside the system. Actually I conceive of myself as moving back and forth, needing to be accepted by each family member but remaining detached so that I don't become immobilized by the interactional rules and constraints that govern the family's interaction. Often, I will detach myself even further toward the end of a session to gather my thoughts before making a behavioral prescription for the family or individual to carry out before the next session.

I like my work currently, though occasionally, I have questioned how valuable psychological services really are (generally and compared to other less-trained mental health professionals). But then, I feel that 80% of physicans' services aren't very valuable either. Nevertheless, sometimes the intangible aspects of psychotherapeutic work are frustrating, but as long as it stays reasonably lucrative (and I need to work at all), this ain't such a bad way to make a living.

RORSCHACH RESPONSES, PSYCHOGRAM, AND SELF-EVALUATION OF STUDENT 8

The third illustrative case in the response pattern of the high $F\%$ shows an even stronger introversive component than Student 7. Moreover, the energy and drive reflected in his strong FM score and the pure C response give a more dynamic picture overall.

Student 8 needed his relatively high F column to protect himself from a pressureful inner world. His record shows powerful drive and intense experiences. He also had more demand from his extroversial needs than did Students 6 and 7. Thus, while initially, the three psychograms may appear similar, the dominant *F* plays a different role in each.

Student 8 wrote an extremely full and detailed self-evaluation. We have chosen to include two sections, one in which he speaks of himself as Bill and analyzes Bill's responses to each of the 10 Rorschach cards. In the other section, speaking of himself as "I," he related personal experiences which are pertinent to his overall Rorschach output. Student 8's Rorschach record appears in Table 4–3, and psychogram in Figure 4–3.

TABLE 4–3
Rorschach Responses of Student 8

Card I			
1. Two hands	*d*	*F*	*Hd*
2. Two people in nightgowns [sleep-walking]	*dS*	*M, C'*	*H*
3. Woman's body—hips, legs, breasts, hands [The arms are raised, the head bent back out of sight.]	*D*	*M*	*H*, sex
4. Perched birds—heads, wings, body	*D*	*FM*	*A*

Card II			
1. Two black tribesmen dancing and patting hands—eyes, mouths— they are yelling [frenzied]— I see spit or sweat—and are wearing tall hats	*W'*	*M, C', FC*	*H*
2. Blood—perhaps they are dancing in it?	*D*	*C*	blood

Card III			
1. Two women around a cauldron talking [African]—there are breasts, shoes, chins, etc	*W'*	*M, C'*	*H*, sex
2. A fanny	*d*	*F*	sex
3. A monkey or other animal hanging by his tail (Two of them)	*D*	*FM*	*A*

Card IV			
1. A squashed beaver [I saw this card once before right after seeing a National Lampoon picture of a squashed beaver—had the same shape.]	*W*	*Fc*	*A* obj
v 2. A monster insect	*W*	*FM*	*A*
v 3. The head of an insect coming out of something [a shell or cocoon]	*W*	*FM*	*Ad, A* obj

TABLE 4–3
(Continued)

Card IV

4. Two profiles	*de*	F	*Hd*
5. Swans' heads	*d*	F	*Ad*

Card V

1. A bat [Seen as the shape of a bat or perhaps a picture or representation of a bat]	*W*	F	*A*
v 2. A Butterfly—wings, antennae [Same comment as above]	*W*	F	*A*

Card VI

v 1. Two eagles' heads	*d*	F	*Ad*
v 2. Two breasts	*d*	F	sex
v 3. A ravine with mountains on each side	*D*	F, FK	N
4. A Klingon warship	*W'*	F	obj
5. It reminds me of a totem pole—the outcroppings on the sides [Looks like a black and white picture of the way one would be painted]	*D*	F	obj
6. A Christ figure with arms to the sides and extra arms. It's like Da Vinci's drawing of Christ with three sets of arms [a sketch with arms horizontal, at its sides and at a 45° angle]	*D*	F	*H*obj

Card VII

1. Two Indian girls—feathers, faces in profile and small bodies	*D*	M, Fc	H
2. The edges are very rough	*W*	F–, Fc	abst
3. Looks like everything is made of smoke	*W*	K, C'	smoke

Card VIII

1. A bear walking—one on the other side, too. A red polar bear? [I saw polar bears that were a distinct green once in a zoo—these remind me of them—wrong colored bears.]	*D*	FM	A
2. Ice—like a glacier	*D*	Fc	N
v 3. A person seen from the back—legs, large rear end and back melds into	*dr*	M	H

TABLE 4–3
(Continued)

Card VIII			
surroundings, then I see hands upraised. [Head is missing, but it is more like it is obscured than that it is not there.]			
v 4. Muscles—like an anatomy drawing that you would see in a book	*di*	*FC*	*At*
5. Two feet	*d*	*F*	*Hd*
6. Some type of engineered structure balancing through the "bear's legs" and the central "Y." [It's well engineered not to collapse with such small support.]	*W*	*F*	Arch

Card IX			
1. Two wizards casting lightening at each other.	*D*	*M, C*	*H,* fire
2. Two Fetuses in the red part.	*D*	*FC*	*H*
3. A big animal or person chasing a little one [They are people.]	*D*	*M*	*H*
4. Two instruments being played.	*d*	*m*	obj

Card X			
1. Two blue crabs [Color as locator]	*D*	*FM*	*A*
2. Two green unicorns—Jumping	*D*	*FM*	*(A)*
3. Two orange sheep	*D*	*FM, Fc*	*A*
4. Orange testicles	*D*	*F*	sex
5. A wishbone	*D*	*F*	*At*
6. Plant stamen	*d*	*F*	*Pl,* sex
7. Topagraphical map or photo of Costa Rica or some island—two of them —mountains and flatlands.	*D*	*k*	Geo
8. Two "smile faces"	*d*	*F*	art
9. Two insects eating the "stamen thing"	*D*	*FM*	*A*
10. Two pipes	*D*	*F*	obj

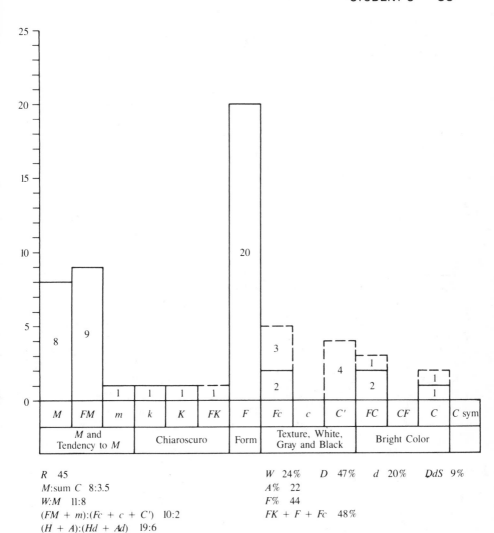

FIG. 4-3. A psychogram of Student 8

The psychogram data (from the figure):

	M	FM	m	k	K	FK	F	Fc	c	C'	FC	CF	C	C sym
	8	9	1	1	1	1	20	3 / 2		4	1 / 2		1 / 1	

M and Tendency to M	Chiaroscuro	Form	Texture, White, Gray and Black	Bright Color

R   45
M:sum C   8:3.5
W:M   11:8
(FM + m):(Fc + c + C')   10:2
(H + A):(Hd + Ad)   19:6

W   24%   D   47%   d   20%   DdS   9%
A%   22
F%   44
FK + F + Fc   48%

TABLE 4-4
Student 8's Comments Card by Card

Next, it may prove fruitful to go through the blots one by one and examine both the sequence of responses and the content of them.

Card I

Bill fails to see the whole response on this card, though on others he has no problems in seeing wholes. Instead, his first response to two hands, which, although he does not say this, are upthrust and I wonder if they are reaching for anything. It seems as if Bill rejects

TABLE 4–4
(Continued)

Card I

---

the more obvious *D* or *W* response and retreats to the safety of a *d* response—he constricts in the face of an anxiety-provoking situation. By the end of the card he has relaxed this somewhat and allowed himself to see a sexual response in the woman's body and the more obvious side detail. Bill specifies that he sees breasts as part of the woman's body—this seems somewhat important in light of later responses. Also, this woman's arms are raised.

Card II

Bill sees this card as a whole, as two black tribesmen. He integrates the red color into the pictures, and his second response (blood) again integrates with the rest of the card. By the end of the first two cards, we note that Bill has two additional *C*s and that his use of color has rather sinister connotations. It may very well be that his adverse reaction to the color caused him to only make two responses to this card and then move to the next one—it will be interesting to note the tonal quality of his future color responses. The men are frenzied—I wonder what Bill does with his frenzy or anger?

Card III

Bill sees the popular people as women, and again, specifically mentions their breasts—he seems drawn to the breasts in both of these people in identifying the bodies. The *M*s so far have been well organized, with one pair of them frenzied or angry (men) and the others passive, with their bodies described (women).

If fannies are sexual to Bill this is another sex response. Here Bill responds to the color stimulus, seeing it as monkeys. They are not seen by their color, but the shape of them—it is as if, so far, Bill's only color response is sinister, and aside from this, he is using only the shape of the colored portions of the blot.

Card IV

Responses to this "father card" have often been thought to relate to the subject's relations with authority figures. Bill sees three rather sinister forms at first, a squashed beaver, a monster insect, and the head of an insect emerging from his cocoon. From there, he moves from seeing wholes to seeing an edge detail, and it seems that perhaps the whole was an anxiety producing stimulus for Bill. Although with no more evidence than this, I might wonder fleetingly about his relationship with his parents and/or with authority figures.

Card V

Bill goes through this card quickly, giving two popular responses using the whole card, and then looking for other percepts and not finding any. It seems almost as if this card might have been a relaxation for Bill after Card IV.

Card VI

The interesting thing about Bill's response to card VI is that he gives no texture responses to this, the most usually seen texture card. Instead, again he retreats back into two *d* responses, and then into a *D* response which is an internal *D* with some distancing

TABLE 4-4

(Continued)

Card VI

involved. Only after four responses can Bill respond to the phallic symbol, and he does so by a "totem pole." Bill sees two more breasts on this card, and I might wonder if there is any sexual repression operating. The Christ figure could symbolize some religious thing for Bill, or might merely be seen as a piece of art.

Card VII

Bill does not respond well to this card—he has one *F*–, a *K, C'* and two *Fc*s that are badly formed. I would suspect that this card was another anxiety-producing situation for him. The *M* response he gives, however, is a good *M,* including most of the card and detailing the response.

Card VIII

In Card VIII, the first color card, Bill has six responses. Of these, only one is an *FC* response, the others do not use the colors. VIII-6 is perhaps the most interesting response in the record: some type of engineered structure, "It's well engineered not to collapse with such small support." Is Bill well-engineered not to collapse with such small support? I might hypothesize that with the low *Fc* with additional potential *Fc,* Bill may feel an affectional need which he represses; perhaps this might be something behind the blockage of emotional expression we note in the psychogram. Again in this card Bill sees hands upraised—could these be reaching for something? Someone? Affection?

Card IX

The first *M* in this card is two wizards casting lightening at each other. Both Bill's Cs have been sinister—blood and lightening. These two people, presumably men, are in opposition, conflict. The other two men before were frenzied. Bill's women have been neutrally staring at each other, or else only their bodily posture has been described. Again, we might wonder about this: Are women seen primarily in terms of their bodies?

One other interesting response to this card is the big person chasing a little person. Again, this may fit in with the affection need and relations to parents—is someone chasing Bill? (Again, it should be noted clearly, I am proposing many more hypotheses here than I would eventually suggest in the final assessment in order to share with the reader my analysis of this record as it progresses.)

Card X

Bill has many responses in this card, 10 total. Again, he has no color responses, using only the shapes of the details to form many different animals and objects. This shows a weakness and strength of his—he will not allow himself to respond to the color (or emotional aspect); but he does show a lot of versatility in the different content categories of his responses.

Student 8 Now Speaks
of Himself as "I"

Overall, I think that the assessment I made using the Rorschach is pretty close to my personal assessment of myself. As far as the positive side of the record goes, I *am* in fact interested in many things—I play the guitar and piano, do calligraphy, read extensively, play chess, do karate and most other sports competently (although I do not spend much time with them anymore), type, swim, etc. I find myself a "jack of all trades" in terms of doing a lot of activities fairly well, rather than one or two excellently. I think that the greatest strength that I see in myself is that I have the ability to learn new things—to adapt myself to different tasks and situations, very well.

As far as areas I find problematic, I have found both relationships with women and expression of certain emotions problematic for myself over the past couple of years, and these are things I *do* work on in therapy. I do not find that I only treat women as sex objects as indicated by the Rorschach, but lately in therapy there have been hints of this underneath—that is, I do not *experience* women as sex objects, but there has recently been a suggestion that to some extent I may be doing so subconsciously. I *do* experience women very sexually, and I must admit that I do fixate on breasts (rather than on legs, etc.) in seeing a woman sexually. The way I have experienced the problem with women so far is basically as a series of unrequited love affairs, with my getting hung up on women who are physically, personality-wise, and intellect-wise very attractive (and usually involved with other people) and who usually are attracted to me only as "friends," so whether there is some excess sexual frustration here as the effect of this or as an underlying cause is up in the air.

I find that I have a lot of problems in expressing negative emotions—in fact, I find it *very* difficult to do so. Positive emotions are something else—I can tell someone I like them or love them, express good feelings toward them, but I have a lot of blockage in expressing negative emotions—I have a lot of shoulds in my head saying "You really shouldn't get angry—don't you see his side—it isn't right to be upset—you're being really childish . . . ' which really block me from allowing myself to be angry, upset, etc. My expression of positive emotions can often be more intellectualized than I desire—I suspect that I have a lot of controls in *being* joyous, *being* happy, although I do find it easy to *say* that I am joyous, etc.

In the last quarter, I have been in individual counseling at the infirmary. I have been in group therapy or growth groups for the last two years, and both of these have been done less because I find coping with the world hard and more because I want to be psychologically growing and becoming more integrated—I see this as almost my main purpose while at Florida. I think that the image of "well engineered to stand there with such little support" or upraised arms does in fact characterize a lot of the root of my problematic areas. I quite often do not have a center within myself—as Perls would say, I require a lot of environmental support rather than having self support. This comes out in my being unwilling to assert myself and allow myself anger and other negative emotions; and it comes out in a real affectional need. It is definitely true that I am OK when someone I am attracted to is attracted to me (for then I feel attractive, worthwhile, etc.), while when my "love life" is going badly—that is, no one I am attracted to is returning this sentiment—then I am not OK, I can get depressed, unhappy, and focus my energies on finding someone to be attracted to me and make me OK.

5

The Low *F* Experience

RORSCHACH RESPONSES, PSYCHOGRAM, AND SELF-EVALUATION OF STUDENT 9

What comes to mind when we consider a low *F%?* We are obviously dealing with a less-than-usual proportion of psychic energy being utilized in the service of control.

This may mean, but not necessarily so, that the individual is impulsive, too quick off the trigger, unable to postpone gratification of one kind or another. But another interpretation could be that the more rigid forms of control, the built in taboos on certain kinds of behavior, and the "thou shalt nots" of childhood have been discarded in favor of a more idiosyncratic way of adapting behavior.

As far as Rorschach scoring goes, when a low *F* is accompanied by a towering column of *FM,* absence of both *FC* and *M,* high scores in *CF* and *C* and some *F* minus responses, we will find clinically validated cases showing lack of rational control. For instance, in a study of first offenders in the Children's Court of Manhattan we found this to be characteristic of dangerously aggressive adolescents (Harrower, 1955a).

One also finds lack of control, low *F,* in what can be described as the "old fashioned hysterics," where emotional problems find expression on a rather naive level through bodily symptoms.

The low *F* scores in our student population do not show these extreme patterns. The two psychograms, Rorschach responses and self-evaluations from Students 9 and 10, which we give as illustrations, show control through adapted emotional responses, lack of explosive experiences, and human movement responses, which are rich and alive.

What characterizes both of these self-evaluations is the willingness to let the reader into the more strictly personal side of their lives. In Student 9 we have an abrupt shift from the third person to a very intimate "I." Her self-evaluation starts with comments such as "This person's psychogram is ..." or "This person has an adequate number of *FM*s," but almost immediately more intimate illustrations are given: "I get my feelings hurt very easily and also cry very easily," "I have very little control over my crying." Returning to the third person she may sum up such vulnerable comments with the statement: "She may have some difficulty in controlling her emotional impulses."

Discussion of this self-evaluation in a post examination interview called attention to the fact that the "I" was actually much less in control than she had admitted and that her crying was a good example of the low *F*% taking its toll. Student 9's Rorschach responses appear in Table 5-1, and psychogram, in Figure 5-1.

TABLE 5-1
Rorschach Responses of Student 9

Card I				
This looks like a big moth or butterfly with white spots on it. Its edges look as if they have been burned or torn which make them very ragged. It has two very small antennae and a tail. Parts of its wings are falling off around the edges. It could be that the moth is very old and its wings are deteriorating.	*W (S)*	*FM, m*	*A*	*P*
Card II				
This looks like two roosters fighting. They look like roosters because of the red combs on their heads. Their beaks are wide open and they look very angry. It looks as if sweat is coming off their heads. They look like they're standing up almost like humans and are kicking each other	*W*	*FM, FC, m*	*A*	*P*
which has caused a lot of bleeding at the bottom.	*D*	*C*	blood	
The white part in the middle looks like a space ship blasting off. The red is the fire from the explosion which propels it into the sky.	*S (D)*	*F, C, m*	obj fire	
Card III				
This looks like two African natives playing bongo drums. They have big red feathery	*W (D)*	*M, F,*	*H* (obj)	*P*

TABLE 5-1
(Continued)

Card III

headpieces and big wide bands around their necks. They look like females as they have large bosoms. The red in the middle looks like a fire in the distance. This is probably a tribal dance and celebration.	(D) (D)	Fc C, FK	(fire)

Card IV

This looks like a very big, old tree. Its leaves have grown so big and heavy that its limbs bend over and reach the ground. This tree looks very strong and beautiful and looks as if it could never be destroyed.	W	F	Pla

---

Card V

This looks like a butterfly in flight. Its wings are in the downward position of flying. It has large wings which come down to a point of a different color. It has two fat antennae.	W	FM	A	P

Card VI

This looks like a mountain that has many cliffs and jags. Someone has climbed the mountain and put a marker on top. The marker looks like a totem pole, with a head on the top and several arms sticking out of it.	W (D) (D)	F (F)	Ntr obj
The top part looks like an Indian maiden with her arms spread out and looking up at the sky as if she were praying to her God. She has a woolen shawl around her with fringe around the edges.	D	M, Fc	H

Card VII

This looks like two cancan girls dancing. They have feathers on top of their heads and have their hair up. They are turned away from each other with their heads turned around looking at each other. They are bumping their rears together. It is a very funny dance and everyone enjoys watching it.	W	M, Fc	H	P

TABLE 5–1
(Continued)

Card VIII				
This looks like a pine tree growing out of some rocks. There is a bear on each side of the tree. They are standing on their hind legs, looking up into the tree, trying to find something to eat.	W (D) (D) (D)	FC, FM, F	Ntr, A	P

Card IX			
This looks like a person with a green and orange halloween mask over his face. You can see his eyes in the middle of the mask. The mask has two orange points coming out of the top of the mask which look like devil's horns. It is a very ugly mask and he is trying to frighten people at the party.	W	M, C/F	H, obj

Card X			
This looks like the grand finale of a fireworks display. There are all colors of beautiful light in the sky, which make the sky very bright. It is also very noisy as each firework makes a huge bang. It is very exciting but also sort of sad because it means that the fireworks are over.	W	CF, FK	obj
The yellow parts look like two little baby canaries with big eyes. They are very soft and cuddly.	D	FC, Fc	A

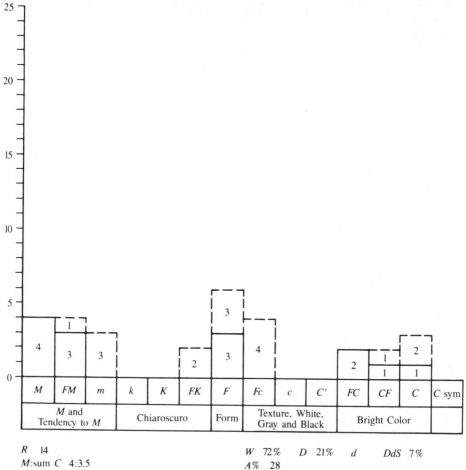

FIG. 5-1.   A psychogram of Student 9

Self-Evaluation of Student 9

This person has an extremely high percentage of *W*s and an underemphasis of both *D*s and *d*s. This suggests a person with a theoretical bias, who is not practical and not interested in details. However, upon examination of the *W*s, some are built up from several *D*s and also include some *d*s. For example, in the *W* response to Card I, every part is brought in, the antennae *(d)* and tail *(d)* and also parts of the wings falling off (*ddd*). In the first response to Card II, *ddd*s are also included in this *W* as sweat coming off of the roosters' heads. The *W* response to Card III is made up of three *D*s, the *W* to Card VI is made up of two *D*s, and the *W* to Card VIII is made up of three *D*s. Thus, although this person's manner of approach is basically abstract and and theoretical, she is able to relate to practical concerns and small details.

Before I took the Rorschach, I never thought of myself as a theoretical person. In fact, I always thought of myself as a very practical person, who was always concerned with details. I keep lists of things that I need to do and always plan my activities down to the smallest details, such as what time I'll do each thing. I never really enjoy the theoretical aspects of psychology, but always want to know how they actually relate to people and how they can be applied. However, this relates to my color side of the psychogram. But now that I have considered it further, I can see my overemphasis of *W*s as my compulsion to organize and relate everything to each other. I can never begin to write a paper until I have the whole thing clearly laid out in my mind and also outlined on paper. I can't stand for something to be out of place or included in a group of things in which it doesn't belong. For example, my whole trailer is decorated in blues, greens, and purples. However, for wedding presents, we received many different colored towels and an orange pillow. I refuse to use any of these things. Thus, I see my *W*s as a sign of my compulsiveness.

The number of responses in this record are fourteen. This is considered reduced output rather than high productivity. There are also six populars which is 43%. However, the small number of responses is largely due to the preponderance of *W*s. Most of these *W*s are fairly rich in content and often combine several responses into one. The rather high percentage of populars shows a desire to be like everyone else and also a lack of originality.

The reduced output is very characteristic of me. Whenever I write a paper I always feel that it is too short. Perhaps it is due to my excellent organization and conciseness. The high number of populars were safe answers which I felt would not show me to be weird or different. I tend to want to be like everyone else around me, especially in my clinical psychology class, so that I feel that I belong.

This person's psychogram is fairly well balanced, with no extreme abnormalities. The *F* ratio is 21.3% which is the lower end of normal, with three additional *F* responses. All of the *F*s are of good form. Thus, the person does seem to have a firm hold on reality, but is not rigid. She does have a logical, rational aspect of life. The two aspects of the psychogram which might tend to detract from this are the

number of *Fc*s and *C*s. The relatively high amount of *Fc*s suggests a
degree of sensitivity and the number of total *C*s, consisting of blood
and fire, seem to call for a higher *F* ratio.

Before taking the Rorschach, I also thought of myself as being very
controlled. By this I mean that I never break any rules, even the
smallest insignificant ones, I very rarely lose my temper, and I always
live up to my standards of what are right and wrong morally. But I
think the basis for this control is my high desire to be accepted and
approved of by others. I am very sensitive and self-conscious. I get
my feelings hurt very easily and also cry very easily. However, I feel
that I am also sensitive to others' feelings as well and am able to
understand them quite well. Because of this, I am always tactful and
try not to hurt anyone. I have very little control over my crying. If
someone, even if I don't know the person, is mean or rude to me for
no reason, I often break down into tears. I cry at every movie I see,
whether I'm happy or sad, no matter how hard I try to hold it in.
Thus, I can now see that I'm not nearly as controlled as I thought I
was, especially in the emotional area.

In examining this person's *M:*sum *C* ratio, she seems to be what
Rorschach called ambi-equal. The ratio is 4:3.5 which is at the lower
end of this category. One can conclude that she has both a rich inner
life and emotional contacts. The adequate number of *M*s suggests
that she has a personal inner life with a good deal of fantasy and
imagination. In looking at the content of her *M*s they include two
African natives playing bongo drums, an Indian maiden, two cancan
girls dancing, and a person with an ugly Halloween mask on. These
all are lively *M*s and mostly on the pleasant side. The man behind
the Halloween mask could pertain to her concern with role playing
and a desire to hide behind a mask. However, this mask is ugly and
frightens other people.

In looking at her color side of the psychogram, she has an adequate
amount of emotional content. The *FC* and *CF* are in adequate
proportion to each other which shows that she is capable of having
relevant and genuine emotional relationships with others. What
relationships she does have are very meaningful to her. However, she
does have a high pure *C* column in relation to the *FC*s and *CF*s.
Although two are additional, they are all rather explosive—blood, a
fire, and fire from a space ship. She may have some difficulty in
controlling her emotional impulses.

I think that my *M,* sum *C,* and *M:*sum *C* scores on the Rorschach
describe me quite well. I do think that I am ambi-equal, having both
an inner life and a concern for other people and my relationships
with them. In regard to the *M*s, I do tend to see the world in relation

to myself and in terms of my own values and needs. I am often swamped with ideas and thoughts running through my mind until I can't accomplish anything or sometimes can't go to sleep. These thoughts and ideas often pertain to what I did that day or what I plan to do the next day or even fantasizing about the future when I'm finished with school. I often escape from my worries and the pressures on me by having daydreams. I often fantasize that I'm on the beach with the sun blazing down on me and the sea breeze blowing. This is my favorite method of relaxation. I also have many sexual fantasies where I see myself always being pursued by many men, and often I am unfaithful to my husband, but sometimes I'm not married in my fantasies.

In regard to my emotional relationships with others. I am very selective. I have very strong and fulfilling relationships with my husband, my family (my parents and younger sister) and only one very close friend who is a male and has been a mutual friend of both my husband and myself for many years. On top of this I have two relatively close friends in my class who I feel close to due to our similar interests and problems. Besides that, there aren't too many people that I dislike or feel very strongly about. In my closest relationships, especially with my husband, I am very dependent and demanding. I demand a lot of consideration and affection, which he has always shown. I have stayed very close to my family and we all get together very often. As I mentioned before, I am very emotional and have trouble controlling it, but mostly in the form of tears and sadness rather than anger, as it would seem from my Cs.

This person has an adequate number of FMs which shows her acceptance of her more primitive impulses, such as sexual drives. This also suggests an adequate amount of drive and energy.

I do feel that I accept my sexual drives and more primitive impulses. I have a very satisfying sexual relationship with my husband and don't have any hangups in this area. I also have a large amount of drive and energy which are necessary to be a graduate student in clinical psychology.

The $W:M$ ratio of this person is very close to 2:1 with a slight emphasis on the W (10:4). This suggests that she is fairly well balanced in her amount of psychic material and intellectual approach to life. She does have a tendency to intellectualize too much.

I'm not as sure of myself in this area of the Rorschach as the others. I sometimes feel that I am being too intellectually ambitious for my capabilities. However, when I stop and think rationally about it, I have always done well in everything I've tried and there is no real reason that I can't do whatever I want. I think a lot of my doubt is the cause of the ms in my record or perhaps vice versa.

There are three additional *m*s and two additional *FK*s in this
record. This is a sign that this person is feeling pressures and tensions.
However, she is struggling with them rather than succumbing to them.
The *FK*s show that she is able to withdraw from the situation and
look objectively at the source of her anxiety.

This part of my record certainly describes me well. I am feeling a
lot of pressure from school. I am very concerned about doing well
and about finishing everything in time. I am getting tired of going to
school and am ready to get out and practice what I've learned. My
husband is also in graduate school, in history, and we are having quite
a few financial struggles. We both have federally insured loans and
have borrowed from our parents. I am anxious to get started working
so we can pay back all of these debts.

The content of this persons' responses shows a bipolarity in the
person, some are pleasant and some unpleasant. However, there is
no outstanding depressive or morose quality in this record. The first
response about a butterfly with burned or torn wings is somewhat
sad. Her reference to his being old and deteriorating shows some
concern about herself and possibly about getting old someday. This
comes up again in her response to Card IV, a big, old tree, which is
strong and looks as if it can never be destroyed. The response to Card
II, the roosters fighting and the blood, is a somewhat aggressive
response. However, her *M* response to Card III is a tribal dance and
celebration, which shows a happy side of life. The response to Card
VIII is also a gay one, two cancan girls dancing and everyone enjoying
it. Both responses to Card VI are signs of hope and ambition. In the
first response, someone has climbed the mountain and put a marker
on top. In the second one, an Indian maiden is praying with arms
outstretched. The first response to Card X perfectly exemplifies the
bipolarity of this person. She describes a beautiful, exciting fireworks
finale, but at the same time it is sad because it means that it is the
end of the show.

I often do feel this two-sidedness of myself. I am often extremely
happy or extremely sad. And, when I am happy or doing something
that I enjoy, I am very sad when it is over.

From both the psychogram and the content of the record, it can
be concluded that this is a well-adjusted person with some conflicts,
but no overwhelming problems. She is dealing with what is bothering
her and also has an inner life and strong emotional attachments which
help her in this struggle. She does not see her world as a threatening
or unhappy place.

THE LOW *F*
RORSCHACH RESPONSES, PSYCHOGRAM,
AND SELF-EVALUATION OF STUDENT 10

Student 10 proceeded in an orderly way by first discussing her Manner of Approach, finding real-life instances of her wholistic emphasis in various situations.

Turning to the psychogram, however, the impact of the low *F* struck her, as it did each of the three members of the low *F* group. "The first thing I noticed about my psychogram (and to be honest, it concerns me) is the relatively short *F* column and the low *F%*— 15%. Theoretically, this puts me in a very vulnerable spot in terms of the adequacy of my self-control and relationship to reality." What is interesting here is that she reported further, "At a deeper level I feel strong and able to cope with anything. Obviously this sense of control must come from somewhere, and I assume it is a combination of inner resources (*M* responses), reality-bound emotions (*FC* responses), and organizational ability (*W* responses)." This valuable self-acceptance, one might say, is a kind of control in itself.

Student 10's self-evaluation is full of revealing material. She was able in many instances to relate her own life as examples of Rorschach tenets. Her Rorschach answers show a blend of color and movement responses, which to Piotrowski, bespeaks artistic qualities. For example: "I see a man in an elaborate costume performing on stage with a blue sparkler in each hand. He is Oriental—he has a tall, black topknot typical of eastern hair fashion. His robe is a rich rose-colored brocade with multicolored designs." That Student 10 mentioned her special interest in art is another of those occasions of Rorschach confirmation which makes blind diagnosis from the responses alone possible.

Her delightful and appropriate frankness about her deep feelings enables the reader of her self-evaluation to come close to the real person.

The Rorschach responses, psychogram, and self-evaluation of Student 10 follow in Figure 5-2 and Table 5-2.

TABLE 5-2
Rorschach Record of Student 10

Card I				
1. I see a woman's body with no head. Attached to this body are great appendages like wings. It reminds me of an elaborate costume for a stage play. (The shape is the determinate. There is an	*W*	*F*	*Hd,* Clo	*P*

TABLE 5–2
(Continued)

Card I

ambivalent feeling of life here.)			

Card II

1. I see two creatures facing one another with their hands together in a patty-cake position. They appear to be dancing and singing. (The creatures are more animal than human.)	W	FM	(A)	P

Card III

1. I see two people (women because-they appear to have breasts) standing across from one another. Their hands are on the rim of a round, hand-molded and artistically-decorated clay pot.	W	M	H	P
2. They look as if they are getting ready to lift up the pot.	(D)	(F, Fc)	obj	
3. A red butterfly has flown between them, and two monkeys are hanging from their tails on each side.	(D)	(FM, FC)	(A)	
4. The women look African because of their shaven heads, and this scene is taking place in the jungle.	(D)	(FM)	(A)	

Card IV

1. I see a man dressed up in a furry gorilla suit. He has great big feet and his arms are outstretched as if to be playfully frightening. (The furriness of the suit is important.)	W	M (Fc)	H
2. I also see an animal who appears to walk low to the ground with almost a rug-like body. He has a kind face and is not as ferocious as first appearances suggest.	W	FM (m)	A

TABLE 5–2
(Continued)

Card V

1. I see the bodies of two rabbits joined at the neck so that one head is behind the other, and consequently, we see only the front head. A hunter has brought these rabbits home. They are posed on a table—ready for an artist to paint them as part of a 17th-century Flemish still-life composition.	*W*	*F*	*A* obj art

---

Card VI

1. I see a cat sitting on a fence happily meowing and singing the night away. His head is up so we see the underside of his chin and his throat.	*W*	*FM*	*A*

Card VII

1. I see two delightful little Indians. (They remind me of the indian girl in J. M. Barry's play *Peter Pan*.) These two little Indians are doing a dance.	*W*	*M*	*H*	*P*

Card VIII

1. I see two pink bears climbing up a mountain. They are reaching the top because the warmth of the lower slopes (pink and orange) is giving way to the icey-blue chill of the summit.	*W* (D)	*FM* (FC, C Symb	*A* (Ntr)	*P*
2. The whole inkblot reminds me of an elaborate oriental headdress worn by an ancient Chinese emperor.	*W*	*F/C*	obj	

Card IX

1. I see two seahorses facing one another. (Color is important here—the orange of the seahorses coming	*D*	*FM* (FC)	*A*

TABLE 5–1
(Continued)

Card IX

---

out of the green sea.)			
2. I see a fanciful creature with an orange forehead and ears, wide green cheeks, and a ruffle of pink around its neck.	*W*	*FC*	*(Ad)*

Card X

---

1. I see a man in an elaborate costume performing on stage with a blue sparkler in each hand. He is Oriental—he has a tall, black topknot typical of eastern hair fashion. His robe is a rich rose-colored brocade with multicolored designs.	*W*	*M* *(F/C)*	*H*

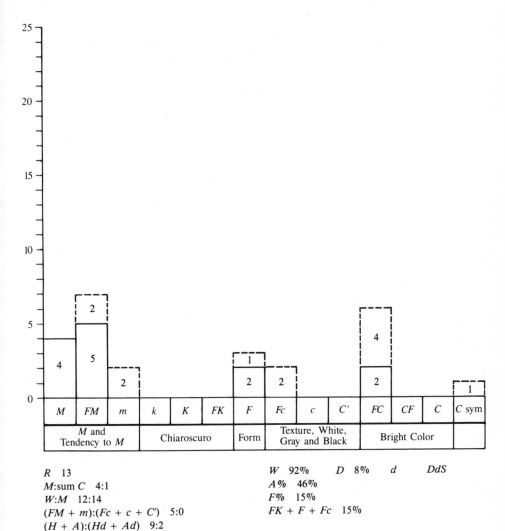

	M	FM	m	k	K	FK	F	Fc	c	C'	FC	CF	C	C sym
	4	5 (2)	2				1 (2)	2			4 (2)			1
	M and Tendency to *M*		Chiaroscuro				Form	Texture, White, Gray and Black			Bright Color			

R 13

M:sum *C* 4:1

W:*M* 12:14

$(FM + m):(Fc + c + C')$ 5:0

$(H + A):(Hd + Ad)$ 9:2

W 92%   *D* 8%   *d*   *DdS*

A% 46%

F% 15%

$FK + F + Fc$ 15%

FIG. 5-2. A psychogram of Student 10

Self-Evaluation of Student 10

Manner of Approach

I am obviously a big *W* person to a very marked degree. While I could easily find big *D*, little *d*, and various *Dd*s responses on request, such a performance would essentially seem trivial and not worthwhile to me. While taking the test, I got great pleasure from organizing the blot as a whole into one well-integrated perception.

. . . I am aware, however, that my way of dealing with details is very different from that of a little *d* person. My ultimate goal is to fit all these details into one well-functioning whole and not to seek attention to detail as an end in itself.

Being a big *W* person has its drawbacks for me. Many of the routine tasks in life send me into a frenzy of frustration. (When it comes to doing the laundry I'll never figure out what goes in cold water, what in warm water, and what in hot water, which detergent goes with which, and when you put the fabric softener in!) Also, other people's obvious enjoyment of very simple things sometimes leaves me envious and with a sense of missing out on some of life's pleasures. Graduate school has exacerbated this problem; my time is so limited now that only major issues get dealt with.

Finding out that I am a big *W* person is a relief to me also. I've always loved theory and loved putting things into broad perspectives. During the Christmas holidays I attended an art exhibit in Washington with a friend who knows very little about art. When he asked me a question about a particular painting, I answered him with an explanation covering man's social, aesthetic, and philosophical evolution. He was a bit nonplussed and gave me that very quizzical look I've seen all too often on the faces of family and friends. And now I know why—it's all that big *W* coming out.

Psychogram

The first thing I noticed about my psychogram (and to be honest, it concerns me) is the relatively short *F* column and the low F%–15%. Theoretically, this puts me in a very vulnerable spot in terms of the adequacy of my self-control and my relationship to reality. Subjectively I often feel the need to "hang on tight" just to keep going, but on a deeper level I feel strong and able to cope with most anything. Obviously this sense of control must come from somewhere, and I assume it is a combination of inner resources (*M* responses), reality-bound emotions (*FC* responses), and organizational ability (*W* responses).

The second-largest number of my responses fell into the *M* category. Theoretically, this suggests an active imagination and inner life. I do find that I need a considerable amount of time alone (it refreshes me), that I enjoy my solitary pursuits and projects, and tend to guard my privacy. As a child, I was left to my own devices a great deal of the time and was happy writing stories and poems, painting and drawing, reading, making up games, etc. by myself. I can live without personal attachments for awhile when necessary and prefer having a few very close friends to a number of acquaintances. I do not interpret this aspect of myself as involving a rich "fantasy" life as much as just being comfortable inside myself and enjoying my own talents and thoughts. I trust my own inner abilities a great deal.

As I mentioned before, another control factor may be my *FC* responses, the only color responses I gave (except for one additional color symbolism response). This scoring category denotes a blending of emotions with reality. In no way do I feel that my restriction of color responses to the *FC* range suggests superficial emotionality. Often my emotions are extremely intense, and I am truly surprised that I had no *CF* or *C* responses. (As an hypothesis, perhaps without much *F* and a high *FM* I can't afford too much *CF* or *C?*)

The greatest number of my responses fall into the *FM* category. Coupled with my low *F,* this could suggest a tendency for primitive impulses to carry me away. I think, however, it denotes two things. First, when something is important to me, I can find an almost unlimited amount of energy and drive to go after it and persevere in my attempts to achieve it. Secondly, I enjoy my sexuality and have a tremendous urge to marry and bear children. Because of various circumstances, I have chosen to try to keep a lid on these latter drives until I finish or almost finish grad school. It's not easy, and perhaps the struggle is inflating the *FM* category and is also reflected in the two potential small *m* responses.

It's nice to see the two potential *Fc* responses. As a future clinical psychologist, I need to be sensitive to others (and to myself). At this point in time, I am aware of being able to "turn on" or "turn off" at will this sensitivity; it doesn't press to be "on" all the time.

. . . I will now make some comments about qualities in the record that strike me as interesting.

There is a marked contrast between my first response (Card I) and my last response (Card X). The first one makes me anxious, especially because of the difficulty I had in deciding whether the woman is alive or not. Perhaps the lack of a head (intellectual control?) and the overbearing size of the wing-like appendages (constricting the body or overpowering it?) make me uneasy. The blot doesn't seem complete. My last response (Card X) feels totally pulled-together, very much alive, and beautifully functioning. It is interesting that both responses involve "an elaborate costume for a stage performance."

Card I and Card V affect me in a similar manner to some degree. They are the least interesting cards to me, they draw my only *F* responses, both of which involve the theme of death in some manner. Perhaps the rather uniform blackness of these two cards and their similar overall shape pull the same qualities from me.

Cards IV and VI, designed to pull attitudes toward sexuality, give a lovely chronology of my sexual development. In Card IV, the "playfully frightening" and "he has a kind face and is not as ferocious as first appearances suggest" remind me of my attitude toward sex in my early 20s—a little scared but aware that there really wasn't anything to be scared about. My response to Card VI reflects my present, more seasoned, attitude which accepts sex on a fun, even earthy level and finds it pure joy.

The quality of my *M*s and *FM*s are neither thunderous nor static. There seems to be a lot of "singing and dancing" and general contentment.

It is interesting that my only big *D* response came to Card IX which is the most difficult to deal with intellectually. I generally prefer the cards with color to those without.

Summary

To sum up, I would say my assets are good inner resources, a great deal of energy and drive, and realistic emotions. My liabilities involve impulses which press for immediate gratification and may cause some conflict as well as a certain insularity caused by my big *W* approach. The task ahead of me is to constructively deal with these liabilities in a way that furthers my personal growth.

THE LOW *F*
PSYCHOGRAM AND SELF-EVALUATION
OF STUDENT 11

As we have seen in the case of Students 9 and 10, persons with low *F* percents are drawn to the question of where their control comes from. Student 11's insightful self-evaluation is another good example of this concern. He wrote in the third person, speaking of himself as "Z," but in the final paragraph he added an important "Personal Inside Assessment."

Again like Students 9 and 10, who have the same personality structure, he was able to experience directly what is meant by "low formal control." He was very aware of his vulnerability and the fact that he could be easily hurt and could not rely on readily available defenses. Student 11 was also concerned with where the existing control could come from. For him, the major source of control was an "inner control indicated by *M* responses," but this was no final solution. He became anxious, for instance, by his response of the headless woman: "It might be said that he is 'wrapped up in his own head.' " Thus, the loss of the head threatens a loss of the self.

Student 11 yearned for a freedom to be creative, which did not seem to be a problem for Students 9 and 10. Eleven felt, for instance, "I do feel I am somewhat creative yet disorganized. . . . I have not really found the way out of myself to my satisfaction."

The case of Student 11 has been used as an example in a former publication (Harrower, 1971). His Rorschach responses themselves are not available for inclusion in *The Inside Story*. The psychogram and self-evaluation of Student Eleven follow in Figure 5-3, including a summary of some of the important ratios.

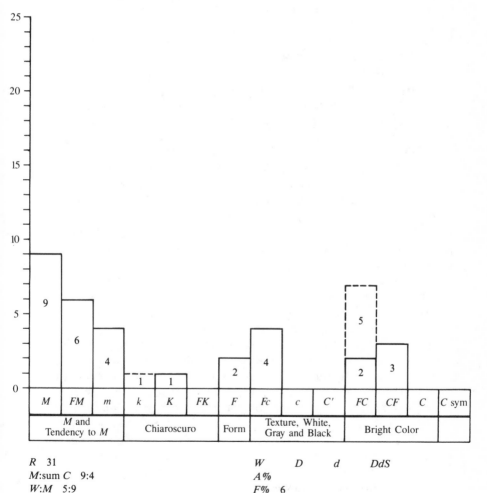

M	FM	m	k	K	FK	F	Fc	c	C'	FC	CF	C	C sym
9	6	4		1	1	2	4			5	2	3	

| M and Tendency to M | | Chiaroscuro | | | Form | Texture, White, Gray and Black | | | Bright Color | | | |

R   31

M:sum C   9:4

W:M   5:9

(FM + m): (Fc + c + C')

(H + A):(Hd + Ad)

W   D   d   DdS

A%

F%   6

FK + F + Fc   23%

FIG. 5-3. A psychogram of Student 11

Self-Evaluation of Student 11

Though other aspects of Z's record will indeed be emphasized, the most striking element is the conspicuously low percentage of form responses (F = 6%). This indicates in itself, that he is lacking in self-control, and may have conflicts with authority along with difficulty accepting societal norms. The question raised by this is, "Upon what resources does Z rely for control and structure in life?"

For the answer to this question, we will look first to Z's inner life. It is evident that he is in possession of rich inner resources and fantasy life (M = 9). This quality leads him to experience his world in an immediate, personal way rather than as formalized prescriptions for living. Thus, he has the capacity to direct his life from within, in terms of his own needs and values (M:sum C 6:3).

Though Z is not very responsive to the formal aspects of societal controls, he is sensitive to others (Fc = 4, 4 add.). He is aware of his needs and feelings and those of other people, and has the capacity to be responsive to them. Thus, the "social control" that he experiences is of a very personalized nature, in terms of interpersonal interaction, rather than of impersonal norms and strictures. A danger in this is that he may at times be too easily hurt by others—a possibility that wouldn't be as likely to occur if he had the protection of more formalized modes of control. This possibility may be potentiated by a strong need for affection, which may also motivate interpersonal action ($FK + Fc$:F = 5:2).

Though Z's inner life is rich, he has not found a satisfactory outlet for creativity (W:M = 5:9). He will find difficulty organizing and carrying out his projects, as his style of approach to problems is factual and analytical as opposed to integrative (W = 5, D = 24).

Overall, Z is introversive (M:sum$C$ = 9:4). That is, he directs his life primarily from within. It might be said that he is "wrapped up in his own head." A concern for the head is shown in the content of his two responses, the headless woman in Card I, and the headless rug in Card VI. This concern is also indicated by his Most Unpleasant Concept—a guillotine—and his "draw a person" pictures. In these, the head is emphasized. Even the pressure of the pencil on the paper shows this emphasis and therefore possible tension related to the head. Indentations can be felt on the reverse side where the pencil was pressed heavily while drawing the head.

All this may reflect an inner tension resulting from forces perceived as outside his control (m = 4, 1 add.). We may speculate that their source could be in social and cultural mores with which he may be in conflict (from low $F\%$). If Z's answer to the incomplete sentence, "Few children fear me," can be taken as his own fear, it is supportive of the speculation that he is greatly concerned with the preservation and growth of his own inner resources. It hints of the existential anxiety one feels when faced with the aloneness, and yet the challenge, of knowing that his own resources, his own values are all he has at his disposal to make his way in the world. In other words, Z fears what he could do to himself and that is, in the figurative sense, lose his head, his main source of life experience.

Personal "inside" assessment: I am surprised at the low $F\%$ on my record, though I didn't expect it to be very high. This has led me to introspect about my sources of control. The inner control indicated by M responses sat well with me and conformed to my self-ideal. The interpretation derived from the higher Fc than F seems to have validity. I will accept it tentatively as an insight. I can recall a number of people in the past few years telling me that I was too sensitive, that they were afraid of hurting me. I was aware of such needs for care and affection, but to have them play a major role in directing my life is something I would not like in myself. I do value having interpersonal relations play a role in determining my values, but not if they are tempered so by what appears to be a need deficiency.

I do feel I am somewhat creative yet disorganized. This showed up clearly in my $W{:}M$ ratio. I have for some years enjoyed creative expression in music and somewhat in writing, but have not fully committed myself to either. Therefore, I have not found outlets that are completely satisfactory.

That my record shows introversion is not too surprising. I have thought of myself as ambi-equal originally, but, on reflection, I am aware that what has been happening is that I want and need to be stimulated and sustained by others, but have not really found the way out of myself to my satisfaction.

6

Introverts Assess Themselves

In this chapter we consider the inner worlds of four psychologists in training . . . all of whom are "introverts" in Rorschach's sense of the term. As seen by Rorschach, the introvert is a resourceful individual with a rich and imaginative inner life who may or may not be shy and withdrawn, as is popularly assumed. The psychological marker of the introvert lies in his or her ability to envision numerous scenarios, numerous possibilities, numerous hypotheses about the world around him or her before reacting overtly to it. At best, this involves an enriched understanding of relationships implicit in reality. At worst, distortion occurs.

In contrast, the inner world of the extrovert—or extratensive individual as called by Rorschach—is populated by color, by feelings, by emotions. It involves an immediate responsiveness to the environment in terms of emotional expressiveness and warmth. After describing a spectacular trip to Europe, an introversive friend once secretly confided that the planning of the trip and imagining what might be seen was as spectacular as the trip itself. Such would rarely be experienced by the extrovert.

In quantitative terms, the introvert's Rorschach world is populated by Ms—and these Ms exceed the introvert's color responses by at least a 2:1 margin. The "true introvert," of course, is one who gives no color responses at all. Such individuals were rare indeed among our psychologists in training.

THE TRUE INTROVERT: STUDENT 12

We begin by first meeting an individual, Student 12, who comes closest to being a "true introvert." Only one color response, a pure *C,* is given among 74 answers. In presenting this material, we give the Rorschach record in its entirety, the self-evaluation and the psychogram, shown in Table 6–1 and Figure 6–1, respectively.

This self-evaluation, written in the third person, is one which shows considerable in-depth awareness of her own difficulties, and it is a courageous attempt to come to grips with her problems.

TABLE 6–1
Rorschach Responses of Student 12

Card I

1. Two witches flying through space	D	M	H
2. Shadow of two ladies	D	M, Fc	H
3. A hand grabbing with a mitten on	d	Fm	Hd
4. An open mouth	d	F	Hd
5. Lady's head with mouth open	de	F	Hd
6. Seal	de	F	A
7. Jagged rock	D	F	obj
8. Face, pouting	de	F	Hd
9. Person with long cape on	S	M	H
10. Person with long nose	d	F	Hd
11. Head with mouth open	de	F	Hd
12. Back of a man with hands up	D	M	H
13. Shadow of the back of the bottom half of a woman	D	M, Fc	H

Card II

1. Footprints	di	Fc	
2. Two hands clapped together	d	F	Hd
3. Two animals walking	D	FM	A
4. Moth	D	F	A
5. Two turkeys	D	F	A
6. A face	de	F	Hd
7. Sea shell	S	F	nat obj.
8. Two figures playing patty-cake	W	M	H

Card III

1. Two Africans mixing a large pot of boiling water	W	M	H
2. Bow tie	D	F	Clo
3. Bone	D	F	anat
4. Two snakes doing a dance to a flute	D	FM	A
5. Two fingers pointing	dd	Fm	Hd
6. X-ray of the chest	D	k	X-ray
7. Icicles	dd	Fc, C'	Nat

TABLE 6-1
(Continued)

Card IV

1. Bear rug	W	Fc	A-obj.
2. Snake	d	F	A
3. Old lady with hunch back	D	M	H
4. Back of a cat with ears perked up	D	FM	A

Card V

1. Bat	W	F	A
2. Lamp post	d	F	obj
3. An open claw	d	F	Ad
4. Worm	di	F	A

Card VI

1. Bear rug	W	Fc	A-obj
2. Lady with a pot on her head	dd	M	H
3. Two birds	d	F	A
4. Bust of a woman with no arms	dd	F	obj
5. Old man hunched over with a sack on his back	d	M	H
6. Flying insect	D	FM	A

Card VII

1. Face of a lady with a feather in her head	D	F	Hd
2. Lobster claw	W	Fc	Ad
3. Lady sitting down—no head	D	M	H
4. Caterpillar	d	F	A
5. An arm with no hand	dd	F	Hd
6. Rock	d	Fc	nat

Card VIII

1. Panther crawling across rocks	D	FM	A
2. Two statues	dd	F	obj
3. Small rug	D	cF	obj
4. Bones of a fish	D	F	A-anat.
5. Puddle of water	dd	K	nat
6. Bridge	dr	F	obj

Card IX

1. Two witches with pointed hats	D	M	H
2. Two long fingers	d	F	Hd
3. Embryo—two heads	D	Fc	Anat
4. Person leaning with his arm against the wall	dd	M	H
5. Two deep holes	d	FK	nat
6. Cat with a long tail	dd	FM	A

TABLE 6–1
(Continued)

Card IX			
7. Head	*de*	*F*	*Hd*
8. Profile of a tall person, arms at the side of body	*D*	*M*	*H*
9. Face profile	*de*	*F*	*Hd*

Card X			
1. Crab	*D*	*FM*	*A*
2. 2 boxers boxing	*D*	*M*	*H*
3. Sea horse	*D*	*F*	*A*
4. Wishbone of a chicken	*D*	*F*	*A*
5. Sea horse	*D*	*F*	*A*
6. Man with arms above his head . . . held in air by a clamp	*D*	*F, m*	*H*
7. Blood spot	*dd*	*C*	blood
8. Bamboo pole	*D*	*F*	obj
9. Spider	*D*	*FM*	*A*
10. Animal jumping into space	*D*	*FM*	*A*
11. Cloud	*D*	*K*	cloud

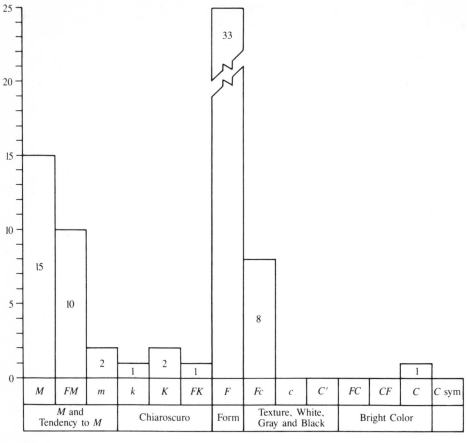

M	FM	m	k	K	FK	F	Fc	c	C'	FC	CF	C	C sym
		2	1	2	1							1	
15	10					8	33						

M and Tendency to M		Chiaroscuro			Form	Texture, White, Gray and Black			Bright Color			

R 74

M:sum C 15:1.5

W:M   6:15

(FM + m):(Fc + c + C') 12:8

(H + A):(Hd + Ad)   33:16

W 8%   D 44.5%   d 17.5%   DdS 30%

A% 26

F% 46

FK + F + Fc   58%

FIG. 6-1. A psychogram of Student 12

Self-Evaluation of Student 12

The Rorschach record portrays a withdrawn individual preoccupied with an inner life of fantasy. Although withdrawn, this individual is extremely sensitive to the reactions of other people toward her. She is overly dependent on the affection of others and consequently fears rejection. It is precisely this fear which causes a withdrawal in the face of emotional challenge.

This dependent orientation is shown in the Rorschach in terms of oral content and Fc emphasis $(8 + 12)$. This emphasis suggests an awareness of an exaggerated need for affectional responses from others. From the existence of this need, it can be hypothesized that there was probably some deprivation of affection with a consequent feeling of rejection in primary familial relationships. Evidence for this hypothesis is seen in the extreme imbalance of achromatic to chromatic responses. Deprivation in affectional relationships resulted in a withdrawn adjustment. There is considerable responsiveness in terms of feeling, however, little responsiveness can be expressed or acted out. This imbalance in the psychogram implies that the need for affectional response from others is so great that the individual is inhibited in her overt reactions for fear of being hurt. This results in over-cautiousness in emotional contacts and a reluctance to establish emotional ties with others.

Responses to Card I further confirm the subject's oral dependency with relation to mother-child relationships. A certain degree of hostility toward the mother figure is seen in the first two responses. The third response—"a hand grabbing"—is an expression of aggression, probably directed at the mother. The next response to the same location—"an open mouth"—shows the aggressive impulse to have an oral component. The fourth response—"a lady with mouth open"—is further evidence of an oral dependency. Juxtaposed to a strong need for affection from the mother, one recognizes a concomitant feeling of hostility and aggression. The expression of this hostility is impossible because of the threat it would pose to the highly valued dependency relationship. The oral aggression shown by the "hand grabbing–open mouth" response is the hostile component of an ambivalent mother-child relationship.

The implications of this relationship, if understood, would be too painful. The emphasis on small details (d, de) shown in this card can thus be recognized as a defense against the anxiety caused by the impact of affectional relationships. There is a need to fragment—to stay on the fringes of the situation in order to avoid its full impact. Connections between her isolated perceptions would cause her to become too deeply involved and thus to become overwhelmed by anxiety.

In Card II, the first reaction is an Fc response to a colored area in the blot with no corresponding use of the color. The disregard for color, in this case, seems to indicate a retreat from situations of emotional challenge with reference to affectional needs. The subject is aware of a *need* for affections (indicated by a high Fc column), however, unaware of the *situation* touching off the difficulty around the dependency need. Because of this absence of awareness, any successful attempt at control of these disturbing feelings would necessitate a retreat from all social contacts of an emotional nature. If awareness were present, only those social contacts that caused a disturbance would have to be avoided. Discrimination in the realm of social and emotional relations seems to be impossible.

This same lack of awareness is present with regard to disturbances of an instinctual nature. This individual's instinctual life seems active and alive indicated by the presence of 10 *FM* responses. There is, however, a complete inability to act out or give behavioral expression to this active instinctual life as indicated by an absence of any *CF* responses. In light of this high degree of frustration, a lack of awareness has certain implications. In Card II there are three animal responses made to the colored areas of the blot disregarding the blatant and striking red. The first animal was seen in movement, the other two were not, indicating some attempt at repressing the impulse. The complete disregard for color here again implies a retreat from situations involving emotional challenge. This occurs whenever the instinctual life is involved or associated in any way with this challenge. This retreat is enacted with little awareness of the source of discomfort. There is a need to repress the instincts: If the repression fails, the only alternative for the subject is withdrawal. Ignorance of the situation causing the disturbance produces a greater withdrawal from emotional contacts than would be necessary if the awareness were present.

Anxiety with regard to the instinctual life can be further exhibited if content and sequence analysis is considered. In general, whenever an *FM* response is given the following response or set of responses indicates extreme anxiety implied by the need to kill off the original impulse. In Card III the response "two snakes doing a dance to a flute" is followed by "two fingers pointing," an "X-ray of the chest," and "icicles." Here one can recognize the inability to accept any active sexual impulses, the unsuccessful effort to deal with the anxiety through intellectual means and, therefore, the necessity for killing off the feeling completely. In Card VIII, the first two responses show a similar killing off of sexual feeling. The next four responses to this card indicate diffuse anxiety associated with an infantile craving to be held and fondled and a longing for childlike dependence on others. The individual is conscious of the anxiety, however, unaware of the specific source. There seems to be some hope of discovery indicated by the response of "a bridge."

The analysis of quantitative proportions shows an extreme imbalance in the *M:C* ratio of 15:1.5. Here is further evidence of the extremely introverted and withdrawn nature of the adjustment. The subject is more dependent on her own needs and fantasies in perceiving her world, than on the actual stimuli presented.

The only color response given to the test was a pure C, which would indicate some lack of emotional control. Perhaps this individual's lack of overt reaction is her only means of controlling emotion of an explosive and violent variety. This explosive emotion is understandable in light of the world the subject has created. It is a world in which her thoughts and feelings cannot be channeled outward. They remain bottled up inside, ready to explode. Control is maintained only through withdrawal from involvement with others. Preoccupation with her own thoughts and fantasies, a compulsion to rework reality, becomes so great that it *necessitates withdrawal.* She is compelled to seek solitude because her "inner world" is much more important than any possible involvement with others.

The over-emphasis on Dd gives one the impression of an individual who is clinging desperately to limited areas of certainty for fear of becoming overwhelmed by anxiety. She is defending herself against insecurity by remaining only within the realm of the certain and the known. Uncertainty brings too much anxiety because there is that everpresent fear of rejection.

The exaggerated stress on $Dd + S$ (30%) at the expense of W seems to indicate a hesitancy in drawing general conclusions, rather than a lack of capacity for integrated perception. This is indicated by the production of six Ws. However, the fact that they are all popular responses may indicate that the subject is afraid to tie her perceptions together unless she is *sure* of being correct. Fear of error is probably associated to such an extent with her fear of rejection, that she is inhibited from utilizing her capacity for integrated perception.

The striking imbalance in the $W{:}M$ ratio of 6:15 demonstrates that the subject is incapable of utilizing her creative potential for fear of what would happen should her integrations and organizations of detailed perceptions be unlike those of others. Originality presupposes nonconformity; since she is terrified of rejection, any possible creativity is frustrated.

THE WELL-BALANCED INTROVERTS
STUDENT 13

We now turn to the inner world of three other psychologists in training. We have grouped these individuals together because they epitomize variants of what we would consider the "well-balanced introvert." Inner pulls, as reflected in their high *M*s, clearly dominate their experience.

We begin with Student 13, who, like our previous "introvert," also has a sum *C* of 1.5. These two "introverts" differ, however, in some very important ways. Most salient is that two very different patterns of emotional reactivity can be gleaned by considering their respective *FC:CF:C* ratios. For Student 12, her sole color response was a pure *C,* whereas Student 13 gave three color responses, all *FC*. In reading the psychogram, Rorschach record, comments and psychogram of Student 13 (Shown in Table 6–2 and Figure 6–2), the reader might consider other ways in which their experiences differ as well as ways in which they are alike.

TABLE 6–2
Rorschach Responses of Student 13

Card I			
1. Butterfly	W	FM	A
2. Hen (can see feathers, especially in tail)[1]	D	FM, Fc	A
3. Elephant	D	FM	A
4. Woman on tiptoes, hands raised (looks like you can see through her skirt to the outline of her legs)	D	M	H

Card II			
1. Two bears touching noses (they look furry)	W	FM	A
2. Crab (red is important)	D	FC	A
3. Profile of face	de	F	Hd
4. Donkey (just head; eyes and nose are shaded; can see fur)	di	Fc	Ad
5. Two warriors with red faces pushing each other (red at bottom not included)	W	M, CF	H
6. Space rocket (the red could be fire where it is taking off)	S	Fm, FC	obj

Card III			
1. Two women dancing (they are African Negroes; the middle part is a pot)	W	M	H
2. Butterfly (color not important; not necessarily alive)	D	F	A
3. Two birds (in sitting position; color not important)	D	FM	A

[1]Comments reflecting an Inquiry have been included in parentheses in this Rorschach record.

TABLE 6-2
(Continued)

Card III			
4. Ballet dancer with head back	D	M	H
5. Fish swimming (fins and tail are prominent; scaly quality to outline)	D	FM	A
6. Two hands pointing toward each other	d	F	Hd

Card IV			
1. Woman and child	D	M	H
2. Profile of face	de	F	Hd
3. Two lizards ready to jump	d	FM	A
4. Man and woman facing (light shadows inside; they are standing up and holding hands)	di	M	H
5. Profile of woman wearing hat	di	F	Hd
6. Profile of man	di	F	Hd
7. Woman touching toes (as if she were exercising)	d	M	H

Card V			
1. Two men in opposite directions (just head and bust; heads are bald)	d	F	Hd
2. Person eating (a fat man raising fork to mouth—can't see all of body but activity is important)	D	FM	H
3. Profile of face	de	F	Hd
4. Two snakes	d	FM	A
5. Butterfly (the inside of the body is prominent; can see head and antennae)	W	FM	A
6. Alligator head	d	F	Ad
7. Man with beard (profile)	d	Fc	Hd

Card VI			
1. Two women, talking or singing	d	F	Hd
2. Bird flying (wings look feathery)	D	FM, Fc	A
3. Two eagles (just the heads)	de	F	Ad
4. Person playing violin	D	M	H, obj
5. Woman in long dress	S	M	H
6. Two faces	W	Fc	Hd

Card VII			
1. Two women facing	D	Fc	Hd
2. Indian with headdress	d	Fc	Hd
3. Elephant head	D	Fc	Ad
4. Two dancers	W	M	H

TABLE 6–2
(Continued)

Card VIII			
1. Two bears walking (color important but secondary)	D	FM, F/C	A
2. Two profiles facing (can see hair and eyes)	D	Fc	Hd
3. Hand	d	F	Hd
4. Woman kneeling	S	M	H
5. Chinese man with beard (faces)	D	Fc	Hd

Card IX			
1. Woman running after child, who is also running	D	M	H
2. Two heads, facing forward (can see beards)	D	Fc	Hd
3. Baby, sitting down (pink color is important)	D	M, F/C	H
4. Woman lying down	di	M	H
5. Two women reaching up—one is in foreground so she looks bigger	D	M	H
6. Profile	de	F	Hd
7. Grasshopper (green is important)	di	FM, FC	A
8. Two dragons	D	FM	A

Card X			
1. Two faces	D	F	Hd
2. Eels (color is important)	D	FC	A
3. Woman	D	M	H
4. Old man	D	M	H
5. Two faces	D	F	Hd
6. Bird	S	FM	A
7. Lion (color makes a difference)	D	FC	A

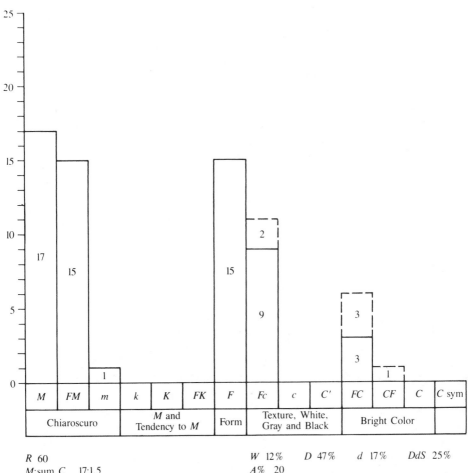

R 60
M:sum C 17:1.5
W:M 7:17
(FM + m):(Fc + c + C') 16:9
(H + A):(Hd + Ad) 22:14

W 12%   D 47%   d 17%   DdS 25%
A% 20
F% 25
FK + F + Fc   40%

FIG. 6-2. A psychogram of Student 13

Self-Evaluation of Student 13

I have divided this discussion into two parts. The first will deal with my record in the third person as if it were a report and the second with my personal comments and observations. I have included an inquiry in this presentation.

Part One

This subject produced a total of 60 responses, suggesting a relatively high level of productivity compared to the general population and normal for her education. The quality of these responses indicates some original trends (15, or 25% $Dd + S$), but, at the same time she gives the typical "how-do-you-do" responses to the cards, indicating a concern with the social amenities.

The frequency of M and FM (17 and 15, respectively) shows a high concentration on inner experience and fantasy coupled with an equally high level of "animal," or biological drive.

The proportion of F (25%) is within the acceptable range for her peer group. There is evidence that the average F% for the younger population groups is declining, in line with current social changes and movement toward individual freedom and nonconformist thinking. The $FK + F + Fc$ ratio is 40%, which indicates an additional reserve of control. So, her capacity for accepting social norms is appropriate but not hampering. There were no $F-$ responses, indicating a high degree of control over the inner experiences. There is a good level of $Fc,$ indicating sensitivity.

Her main color responses were somewhat diminished, although with the additional FC and CF she had 7 and 1, respectively. This suggests that the emotional arousal is there and can be drawn out. The emotional expression is appropriate to the situation, perhaps a little too much so. The low CF and absence of C indicate that her emotional equipment is controlled by her intellect and is not impulse-ridden or explosive. Her proportion of responses to the colored cards was 30%, which indicates that her arousal in the presence of emotional stimulation is at the expected level, neither excessively high nor low. The $M:$ sum C ratio of 17:1.5 indicates a dependence on inner life rather than emotion evoked by others (Rorschach's use of the term *introversion*), and a high degree of self-containment. A comparison of the ratios $M:$ sum C and $(FM + m):(Fc + c + C')$ shows that they are in the same direction, toward the introverted, and that she was the same as a child as she is now. Or, alternatively, this comparison could show that there is a relative lack of conflict between the inner and outer experience in the present. Of course, no interpretation is based on any one set of ratios, and the low proportion of color responses is offset by the sensitivity in $Fc,$ the appropriateness of the content of the color responses, and the additional responses.

The $W:M$ ratio of 7:17 suggests that she has more ideas than she has capacity to organize and bring them to fruition. However, the high FM

is indicative of a high level of drive which offsets the previous interpretation to some extent. She appears to be stimulated and aroused by an inner life which does not always get translated into action.

Her first response is the butterfly, the socially amenable response, and her last is a lion. This could indicate that she lets her impulses to be "king," perhaps to dominate, come out after the initial period of acquaintance.

Part Two

My reaction to the findings of my Rorschach analysis is that they are generally true with a few exceptions. I was at first astonished by the accuracy of what the $W:M$ ratio told me, as it is absolutely true that I have some difficulty in organizing the ideas I have and getting them translated into action. And, I agree with the interpretation that I am introverted (in Rorschach's sense of the word) but not as much so as the record indicates, I think.

The interpretations related to color and emotional expression leave me with mixed feelings. I do not feel that I have as much difficulty with emotional expression as the responses indicate. But I do agree that I cannot let go and get angry without a great deal of provocation and do not "blow off" unless absolutely backed to the wall. I have learned something significant from this—that I probably should "let go" a little more and not be as afraid of losing control of emotions.

In my interactions with friends I find a great deal of emotional satisfaction. Also I have a need to be alone a lot, to read or to think, and just generally be away from people sometimes. But when I am with people I enjoy it. However, in one area I feel that I am overcontrolled and inhibited. I begin to tighten up and withdraw in the presence of overt hostility directed at me, especially yelling. But, even there I feel there has been progress in handling these feelings. Ten years ago I was totally freaked in such a situation. Now I am able to stand my ground a lot better at least in outward appearances, in order to defend myself. Still, I intensely dislike initiating such hostility or having to deal with it. And I have made progress in accepting this trait as not necessarily bad, or abnormal.

In the last 10 years I feel I have changed a great deal in my capacity to experience warmth for others and to express it and accept it. When I began in psychology I was an experimentalist and was most interested in studying learning in rats, partially as a defense against personal involvement or closeness. Since then I have changed my goals and interpersonal orientation radically and feel now much more open and involved with people. I have been steadily becoming more "extroverted."

> The finding that I had the most difficulty incorporating was the low W (7%, or 11%). I see myself as a theoretical person and I enjoy playing with ideas and try to see whole pictures as much as possible. I feel that the high M is corroborative of my self-perception.
>
> In summary, I found the insights from the Rorschach to be valuable to me and the total picture it presented was, I felt, mostly accurate. No one ratio or finding is an interpretation in itself (for example, as control is indicated by several different components); and in the total configuration the inconsistencies have resolved themselves for me.

Student 13 left a unique imprint on her production and assessment of herself in several ways.

She was able, for instance, to show how the Rorschach Inquiry—usually questions asked by the examiner—can be integrated into a self-administered test. She called attention to her perceptual components within each response. The hen is not only seen as a live animal (FM) but shows why an additional response of Fc is needed: "I can see feathers [texture] especially in the tail."

The extent to which color enters in is carried by comments such as "Green is important"; "Color is important"; or "Color makes a difference" when "lion" is scored FC.

The F for the butterfly in Card III is explained by the statement, "Color not important; not necessarily alive," denying her use of FM and FC in this case.

Another interesting feature is her comparison of her ratios and major scores with those of the "person" epitomized in the class record. For example:

Scores

1. My record has much more M responses (17 to 9)
2. My record has no FK, while "hers" has 3 main and 1 additional FK
3. My record has no c, while hers has 1 main and 1 additional c
4. The color responses on my record are fewer than hers
5. My record has a much lower percent of W (11% to 36%), more D and d and slightly more $Dd + S$.

Ratios

1. My $(H + A):(Hd + Ad)$ ratio is 3:2 while hers is 3:1
2. My sum C is 1.5 while hers is 6

3. My $M:$ sum C is 17:1.5 while hers is 9:6
4. My record is slightly lower with respect to total responses to Cards VIII, IX, and X.
5. My $W:M$ ratio is 7:17 while hers is 14:9.

Her high M score, her strong introversive trends, are evidenced even more clearly than from the psychogram alone in calling attention to the fact that "My record has much more M responses (17 to 9)." She also highlighted some of her inevitable difficulties in certain tasks with the statement that her ratio of W to M is 7:17 while the class average shows the reverse, 14:9.

It is this student, incidentally, whom we quote in our Introduction, who gave rise to the facetiously expressed excuse of not getting work in on time because of the lack of the optimum $W:M$ ratio.

Student 13's record is one which I have found characteristic of several other psychologists not within this program; namely, the high scores for M *and FM,* inner life plus drive.

RORSCHACH RESPONSES, PSYCHOGRAM AND SELF-EVALUATION OF STUDENT 14

Student 14 is a good example of one of our scoring categories seen in chapter 1, (p. 4), namely, a scale varying from sparse to rich (her Rorschach record appears in Table 5-3 and psychogram in Figure 5-3). We are using the word *sparse* for a single-word answer; and *rich* to denote answers which evoke much amplification in order to satisfy the experience of the perceiver—answers such as:

Card II, 2: Two people or animals fighting, the right half versus the left half; their arms are meeting up at the top and their knees and claws at the bottom. They look like they are squawking a lot and jabbering nonsense. They are being very silly about it. Their faces are red because they are getting so flustered and carried away. They are not bleeding though. They are more like people than animals.

Card V, 3: A seductress, though in the inkblot she has the nose of a unicorn, you can see her hair, eye, mouth. She is reclining with her back to us, with her legs stretched out. She is holding a cigarette holder in her hand.

Card VIII, 1: The two pink parts at either side resemble some kind of amphibian walking up, out—reminds me of evolutionary pictures where earlier forms of life "move up" and evolve new features like the Escher prints, where animals are moving and changing.

TABLE 6–3
Rorschach Record of Student 14

Card I			
1. The face of a man on the left side of the blot with a large nose and protruding chin	D	F	Hd
2. A mystical-magical human figure in the center lifting her arms up with mouth open, saying something; perhaps invoking spirits. Her hands are raised over her head.	D	M	H
3. The top white sections within the blot look like two men sleepwalking	S	M	H
4. Small faces on the right and left sides calling out. Their mouths are open.	d	F	Hd
5. Head of an animal—like a wolf	d	F	Hd

Card II			
1. The bottom part with the red resembles the vagina during menstruation with the blood flowing out, though it usually doesn't flow that much	D	CF	sex
2. Two people or animals fighting, the right half versus the left half; their arms are meeting up at the top and their knees and claws at the bottom. They look like they are squawking a lot and jabbering nonsense. They are being very silly about it. Their faces are red because they are getting so flustered and carried away. They are not bleeding though. They are more like people than animals.	W	M, FC	H

Card III			
1. Two women—they have breasts—facing each other involved in some type of activity together. There is a feeling of movement as if they are spinning around together.	W	M	H
2. Bow tie	D	FC	clo

Card IV			
1. A view from the bottom up of some looming animal/man figure—the lines from the eyes going down seem			

TABLE 6-3
(Continued)

Card IV

---

to be the power to see and perceive deep within. The larger, floppy features at the lower sides are oversized circus-type feet. It has a soft, rather furry body. The center column in the blot might very well be an exaggerated penis, by its location. He is not an evil or sinister person, rather just comical/grotesque. Looks as if he were free floating in the air, so that the lower half of his body is more immediate as in photography when the view is fore-shortened	W	FM, Fc, FK	A
2. The lower half in the lighter shaded part resembles the lions sitting in front of the 42nd St. Library. Where his front paws should be, though, do not fit, they have merged with something else.	D	F	A obj
3. A duck or bird with elongated neck bending down. His foot is touching his throat.	d	FM	A
4. Two small profiles looking up at the sky at the top of the blot	de	F	Hd
5. A witches face/profile with pointed hat and a large, crooked nose	d	F	Hd

---

Card V

---

1. A bat, with its wings soft and flowing rather than stiffly arched upwards. There are ears and small feet.	W	FM	A
2. The little legs are funny—they remind me of the bandy legs of some comical, slightly pigeon-toed man. For some reason, they could not be the legs of a woman, or not as easily imaged.	d	F	Hd
3. A seductress, though in the inkblot she has the nose of a unicorn, you can see her hair, eye, mouth. She is reclining with her back to us, with her legs stretched out. She is holding a cigarette holder in her hand.	D	M	H

Card VI

---

1. The dark portion within the top part

TABLE 6–3
(Continued)

Card VI

---

of the blot resembles a totem-pole type figure of a woman. The lighter out-flowing part reminds me of wings of freedom or movement and being alive. I don't know. Maybe the woman is trapped within this freedom of the winged creature. She seems so rigid with her hands tight to her side. There is relaxing and flowing in the wings.	*D*	*M, Fc, m*	*H*
2. The textures in the middle remind me of watermelon, where the center is more pithy and lighter colored, with many seeds, and the outside is more fleshy and solid	*Di*	*Fc*	food
3. Looks like a sleek black cat in a top hat and white bowtie—kind of a Dr. Seus character	*D*	*FM, C'*	*A*
4. A crab with its two front legs showing emerging from out under a rock	*d*	*FM*	*A*
5. On both sides, two stone or marble busts of a man	*d*	*F*	*H* obj

Card VII

---

1. Two sylph like creatures, almost half elf and half female. Their asses are together and their torsos apart. Their heads are are turning to face each other. Their arms resemble the front legs of animals when raised on their hind legs. Their hair is standing straight up.	*W*	*M*	*H*
2. A grotesque, leering face with bulbous nose and open mouth showing teeth	*D*	*F, m*	*Hd*
3. On the left side there is a rabbit with its ears perked straight up, sitting still with its body all full and soft and fluffy	*d*	*Fc, FM*	*A*
4. On the right side, the vertical part is the upspread wing of a bird about to take off	*d*	*FM*	*A*
5. Two people in long flowing robes on their knees facing each other. Their hands are joined at chest level	*di*	*M, Fc*	*H*
6. A little frog sitting still, looking out			

TABLE 6–3
(Continued)

Card VII

---

sideways or backwards, with his eye open wide	di	FM	A
7. This looks like the very soft and gentle face like a lamb or cow—a kind of sweet and passive look	d	Fc	Ad

---

Card VIII

---

1. The two pink parts at either side resemble some kind of amphibian walking up, out—reminds me of evolutionary pictures where earlier forms of life "move up" and evolve new features like the Escher Prints, where animals are moving and changing	D	FM	A Sym
2. The pink and orange bottom reminds me of female genitalia	D	CF	sex
3. Hands reaching out—they seem to be reaching out and touching and/or holding the amphibian's hands. Perhaps they are helping them climb up, guiding and offering assistance.	D	F, m	Hd
4. A small female totem-like figure	d	F	H obj
5. Two figures with their inside arms raised high as if stretching, or in the position as when a winner is declared in boxing	d	M	H
6. A figure with its arms stretched out in front of them, diving down	de	M	H
7. Two boots handing down from somewhere	dd	F	clo

Card IX

My first reaction to this card was that it was messy and not very pleasant. I did not like where the green and orange colors mixed			
1. I keep seeing totem-type figures— this one is male, facing to the left. He has a smooth head; there is the center axis through him in yellow	D	F, Fc	H obj
2. There are hands reaching down in the blue-green being met by hands from the pink. We can seen the thumb and open palm of the pink hand	di	m	Hd

TABLE 6–3
(Continued)

Card IX

3. Something appears to be rising in the blot from out of the depths. Perhaps it is the totem figure who is rising out of the union of the green and pink. It seems to be pushing the orange/red apart, getting closer to the light and air. Above the head there are no restrictions or enclosings—there is sunlight	W	m, CF, F/C	Sym
4. A figure of a heavy man with a jowly face wearing a pointed hat and a big nose. Kind of frowning, pointing his finger toward the center with a kind of dismay or indignation	D	M	H
5. Someone's head peeking up from behind a fence or hedge peering through very open eyes	D	F, CF	Hd
6. Lonely figures looking outward	dd	M	H
7. The head of an alligator or crocodile. You can see his long mouth and eye and part of his body. It appears to be leathery and scaly.	di	Fc	A
9. The head and body of a big bear. It has the shape and big lumbering body of one. His head is lifted as if looking ahead	D	FM	A

Card X

1. Two animals or bugs arguing with each other. Two hard shell bugs. They are standing on their hind legs	D	FM	A
2. The antennae of these bugs look like wild flowers in meadows	d	F	pla
3. A rabbit face with long ears. The darker green is flowing from the eyes. The extension of his being through his eyes. Not evil or frightening, just there. Like a magical being	D	F, K	Ad
4. Two grasshoppers	D	FC	A
5. These look like some kind of spidery creatures	D	F	A obj
6. These remind me of deer, very rapidly and agilely leaping into the forest	D	FC, FM	A
7. This part looks like some goofy cartoon character with a big nose, mouth, eye, funny hat. He seems to			

TABLE 6-3
(Continued)

Card X			
be kind of dangling/walking, just loping along. A comical happy-go-lucky sort	D	M	H
8. The dark green on the bottom also resembles shrimp or snakes with their heads on top and their tails curled up	D	F	A

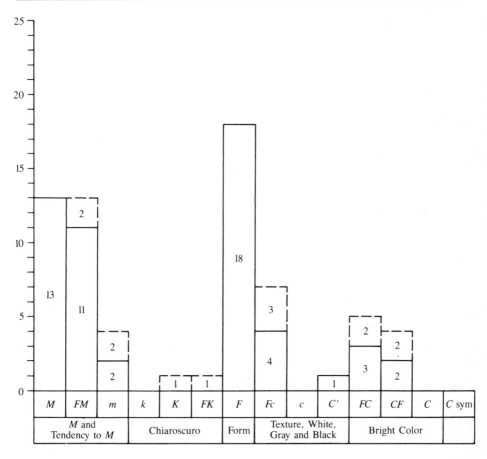

R 53
M:sum C 13:3.5
W:M 6:13
(FM + m):(Fc + c + C') 13:4
(H + A):(Hd + Ad) 28:13

W 11.3%   D 45.3%   d 22.6%   DdS 21%
A% 33
F% 34
FK + F + Fc 41%

FIG. 6-3. A psychogram of Student 14

Self-Evaluation of Student 14

My first response while doing the analysis of my Rorschach was, "how much of this is just another projective." I think I was very much struck by what the psychogram revealed to me, and the meaning it had for me, that it became fascinating as I found myself finding these themes in many responses, and in the manner of approach. It appears as if the responses to each card as a card, not to mention for the whole record, form "gestalts" or a meaningful unit of responding to a particular card in toto, or the ideas evoked by the card.

The appearance of a lot of *M* responses was expected. I am very much guided by my own set of values, which I almost stubbornly adhere to. I have always enjoyed spending time with myself, and more so, have come to realize that I need to spend time with myself, and be in touch with my feelings, and thoughts, and to allow myself to know myself.

The high *FM* column did not surprise me much either. Although I do not believe that this represents a "drive" which is channeled into great productivity per se, I am a high energy person, and am considered that by most people who know me. I enjoy the use of my body in physical activity. Moreso, some of my *FM* is related to the almost joyous energy which is part of "my child," so to speak. When I am being my child and when I am happy, I dance around the house. I love to run down long hills, and when I am in a rather cheerful or spry mood I usually do.

What surprised me was the sparse amount of color responses. I would have expected, particularly if the Rorschach tapped long range orientations, that I would have come out introverted, although much closer to being ambi-equal. I am often considered to be very outgoing and friendly. However, further inspection of my approach to color provided the needed clues. The implication from the number of responses I gave to the last three cards is that I do have the potential to respond with greater emotion to the environment, but that presently I am not consciously doing so. This made a lot of sense, for I have been rather withdrawing into myself. I have found myself becoming much "tighter," less spontaneous, and enjoying the company of people less. Yet the absence of my spontaneity was not comfortable, and I longed to be in touch with my *joie de vivre,* so to speak.

The responses concerned with rebirth, with changing, and emerging all reflect the commitment I have made to work through some of my conflicts, and regain a new sense of balance with myself (and therefore probably my psychogram as well, I suppose).

I found my responses to Card II interesting, in my denial of blood resulting from the argument of the two men. It was very definite in my mind that blood did not belong in the picture, although it could have easily been incorporated into the response. This may be seen as the denial of pure emotional response. It also reflects my general means of coping with anger and hostility, which is to withdraw. Withdrawal, or distancing is a coping device of mine, as can be seen in the *FK* response in Card IV. Intellectualization and rationalization, which are other forms of withdrawal or removing yourself from the situation, is another one of my defense mechanisms. These appear in the protocol along with amorphous answers, or responses, which are later modified. My coping is adequate, however, and certainly not out of control. The defenses do not attempt to, or succeed in blocking many responses. Nevertheless, they are there. Do people give complete protocols without revealing, or using their defenses at all?

Many students voiced concerns about their "intellectual" approach to the Rorschach, particularly when a *W* approach was not dominant. Frequently, this was misinterpreted as indicating that they lacked in abstracting, theoretical abilities. Such a concern is reflected in the following comments by Student 14.

The rather low *W,* when interpreted as reflecting my abstract capabilities caused some dismay, and also some puzzlement. I am quite fond of theorizing at times, and enjoy seeing things in a grand perspective. My approaches in intellectual endeavors are often interdisciplinary. However, I also know that it is often some little nuance, or more so, series of nuances or interesting facts or insights which start me on this exercise in theory. I am, by nature, an inductive reasoner.

The *D*% was about what I would expect; I am pragmatic but not overly so. At first I was a little surprised at the percentage of *d* responses, for I have never considered myself to be very careful with details, particularly as it concerns my everyday life. Possessions are being misplaced, found again, etc. However, I do use the concreteness of small details as a means of coping. Cleaning the house, straightening up my room, cooking, small *d* tasks are used as a means to get myself centered again, to deal with, and channel anxiety. It is the concreteness and the ability to cope efficiently with these small details that make this a good coping device for me. It is rather

interesting that this same coping device appeared in the protocol—
the retreat into small details after certain important responses. Rather
than compulsivity, though there is probably that element too, I think
my emphasis on small details and *DdS* responses also stem from my
criticalness. When one is critical, one looks at small details, particularly
to see if they negate the image of the whole. I have a tendency to be
very critical of myself.

RORSCHACH RESPONSES, PSYCHOGRAM, AND SELF–EVALUATION OF STUDENT 15

Our final psychologist-introvert—Student 15—differed in some important
ways from the others. First, she took an organizing *W* approach to her
perceptual world, showing this with a *W*% of 50, as opposed to the 8%,
11%, and 12% of the other students—a marked difference. The common
denominator, incidentally, in terms of mental approach for Students 12, 13,
and 14, is *DdS*. Secondly, Student 15's *W:M* ratio comes close to the ideal
of 2:1 that makes for easier functioning. She was not one to become bogged
down by her good ideas, not one of those who had to struggle to turn their
papers in on time.

Finally, her emotional responsiveness was governed by the most controlled
of the color responses, *FC*. Thus several avenues of control were available
to her; she did not need to rely on a high *F*%. Otherwise stated, her *F*
column does not need to be higher than those of all other determinants.

In examining her record (Table 6–4), psychogram (Figure 6–4), and
self-Evaluation, consider how Student 15 exercised the type of formal
control that is usually associated with a dominant *F*%.

TABLE 6–4
Rorschach Record of Student 15

Card I			
1. Whole figure . . . a bat in flight as seen from overhead	W	FM	A
2. Two hooded figures with raised arms	D	M	H
3. Upside down . . . a large bear, standing on something	D	FM	A
4. Center portion . . . a figure of a woman without a head	D	M	H

TABLE 6-4
(Continued)

Card II

1. Two dancing human figures, crouching and dipping heads together or holding a torch	W	M	H, obj
2. Upside down—top red part, a large insect with antennae protruding on top	D	FC	A
3. Upside down—the backs of two people sitting and watching something in front of them	W	M	H
4. Red part on bottom—a butterfly	D	FC	A

Card III

1. Two cannibals stirring a cauldron on the ground between them, with skulls or dead animals hanging from the ceiling	W	M, F, m	H, obj
2. Two women making a basket of their arms in order to catch something (red part in between figures)	W	M	H
3. Upside down—opening of a cave as seen from outside looking in	W, S	FK	nat
4. Upside down—two faces looking away from one another	D	F	Hd

---

Card IV

1. Very old tree with withered branches and shrubbery to the sides	W	Fc, F	pla
2. Two snakes	d	F	A
3. Upside down—two roosters sitting on top of fences with clouds beyond	D	FM, K	A, clo
4. Upside down—dissected frog spread open	W	F, m	anat

Card V

1. A bat with wings spread out	W	FM	A
2. A rabbit standing on hind legs—ears sticking up	W	FM	A
3. A dancer on her toes with long stole or blanket draped across her shoulders and on the floor on both sides of her	D	M, Fc	H, clo
4. Upside down—butterfly in flight as seen from above	W	FM, FK	A

TABLE 6-4
(Continued)

Card VI

1. Totem pole with special carving of bird on top		D	Fc, F	obj
2. Bearskin rug		W	Fc	A
3. Upside down—two gorillas sitting back to back with paws outstretched		D	FM, FC	A
4. Upside down—two men sitting with their backs to a pole, with cigar stubs in their mouths, their arms outstretched holding glasses		D	M, F	H
5. Penis		D	F	sex

Card VII

1. Two little girls with their hair standing up in pigtails—dancing back to back, with heads turned around and facing one another		W	M, Fc	H
2. Two French poodles standing on hind legs with paws held up		W	FM	A
3. Upside down—two women bent slightly forward with their backs facing one another, wearing large hats		W	M	H, clo
4. Upside down—two elephant heads with trunks		D	F	Ad

Card VIII

1. Sideways on top—an animal stalking its prey		D	FM	A
2. Map—blue represents water, other colors are land masses		W	F, FC	geog
3. Dissected animal with organs spread apart		W	F, m	anat
4. Crab		W	F	A

Card IX

1. Two witches with pointed hats, arms raised, holding wands		D	M	(H)
2. Upside down—two parrots sitting on perches seen from the back		D	FM	A
3. Upside down—a beach umbrella		D	FC	obj

Card X

1. Underwater scene with crabs, snails, sea horses, underwater plants, and various other underwater life		W	FC, FM	A, Pla

TABLE 6-4
(Continued)

Card X			
2. Two grasshoppers	D	F	A
3. Two worms	D	FC, FM	A
4. Fireworks exploding	W	CF, m	obj

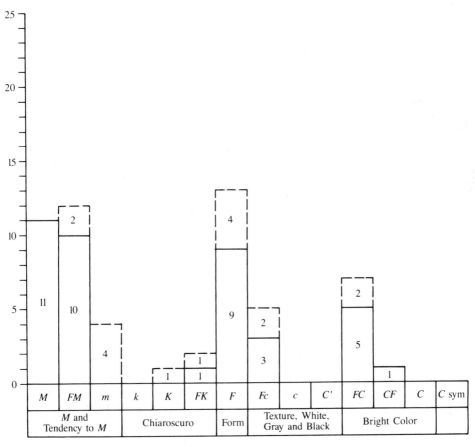

R 40

M:sum C 11:3.5

W:M 20:11

(FM + m):(Fc + c + C') 10:3

(H + A):(Hd + Ad) 29:2

W 50%   D 18%   d 22%   DdS

A% 48

F% 23

FK + F + Fc 33%

FIG. 6-4. A psychogram of Student 15

Self-Evaluation of Student 15

This is a fairly well-balanced record, except for the fact that F (9 responses) does not dominate and, in fact, is surpassed by M (11) and FM (10). This would ordinarily indicate a lack of control or self-discipline and one might question whether enough emotional control is present. However, this factor is somewhat balanced by the FC score (5, +2) which indicates that this person is reacting in an emotionally appropriate way. (Frankly, I am puzzled by the low F score. I tend to be overly self-disciplined and perfectionistic, setting impossibly high standards for myself. I also have a tendency toward compulsivity and tenseness and I suffer from occasional mild migraine headaches. However, I am very much aware of this problem at present and have achieved some success at combatting it. Could this be the reason for the low F?)

The good M score in this record indicates the presence of a vital and meaningful fantasy life, capacity for empathy, and ability to experience herself as a person. The FC:CF:C ratio (5:1:0) shows that appropriate emotional responses are attached to appropriate objects, and this young woman is able to relate to other people in a rich and meaningful way without explosive emotionality. The FM score in this record indicates an awareness of basic animal instincts, without repression of them, and a goodly amount of drive.

The rather high Fc score (3, +2) in this record indicates a capacity for sensitivity and tactfulness, and an ability to look at the finer nuances of life. However, the high d scores also demonstrate a tendency toward over–self-awareness and self-consciousness, and it is likely that this person depends on others for self-approval and can be easily hurt by others. (This last part is a fairly accurate description of me. I do crave approval from others and my self-image has not tended to be very favorable. In the last year or so I feel I have improved in this respect and have come to trust much more in my own abilities. Hopefully, I will be able to use this abundant sensitivity constructively, rather than turning it against myself).

The Rorschach record shows no evidence of any strong anxiety, although some feelings of discomfort are experienced by the subject ($m + 4$).

The abundance of popular responses indicates a tendency to perceive things in the usual way. It may also indicate a certain lack of originality, although I had no way of determining which responses were original. (I feel that I do, at times, demonstrate a lack of originality and this is probably due to an unconscious stifling of original and creative ideas because of my apprehensions about the reactions of other people and my own feeling that I should not say something unless I am sure it is correct).

In summary, this Rorschach record reveals a fairly well-balanced personality structure with a good potential for future development and self-actualization.

7

The High *FM*

In this section Rorschach "look-alikes" are presented whose inner worlds are dominated by high *FM* scores.

What role, we may ask, does the *FM* play in one's psychological functioning? At best, it reflects a high level of energy, a playfulness, and a *joie de vivre*. It also denotes an acceptance of one's more primitive urges. At worst, it can reflect a drivenness, an unchecked acting-out of impulses, a narcissistic posture in the world.

The direction or manner in which the *FM* is channeled can be seen in its relationship with other Rorschach components. Most important is how *FM* relates to *M,* but the relationship to *F* and to color responses is also informative. The kind of animals and the kind of movements in which they engage are also of great importance.

All three psychograms in this section show that the *FM* scores are conspicuously higher than those of human movement—the *M*. It is this relationship, or this quality, that evokes the need for a special category, a special recognition of the power of the *FM* drive.

Two psychograms (16 and 18) show almost identical scores with *FM* and *F.* At no point do these *FM* scores soar above the central column of logical control. One would have to admit, however, that Student 17's psychogram comes closer to an *F*-dominated record. We would have to say that there is a rivalry between *FM* and *F* here, though neither establishes total preeminence over the psychogram as a whole.

Turning now to the relationship of *FM* to color scores: The *FM* is unquestionably the dominant note in psychograms 16 and 17 but Student 18 has rich color scores, thereby changing the flavor of the record dramatically.

Small *m* seems to play a slightly greater role in these three psychograms than do some of the other categories, but not to such a marked degree as to be considered characteristic or a necessary ingredient in high *FM* scores.

The most interesting comparison comes in terms of the choice of animals and the choice of the activities in which these animals engage. For simplicity's sake, we introduce a chart showing five kinds of options by which the perceiver can envisage his animals in action.

1. Animals are scored by the student as *FM* because they are seen as "alive." One has to trust each individual perceiver in this scoring choice (*F* or *FM*) because only he or she can know which best describes, for example, the answer "Bat."
2. Animals engage in actions which epitomize them "doing their own thing." Fish swim, bats fly, many animals run. These can be modified in some cases by statements such as "a butterfly trying to emerge from the caterpillar." Such nuances are helpful in self-understanding for the student, and of course for the therapist using the Rorschach profile in sessions related to more active self-understanding.
3. Animals can express activities that are pleasureable. They may not be actually pleasurable to the animal, but are perceived by the subject in terms of enjoyment: "cats prancing," "bears dancing," "dogs smiling," "creatures playing patty-cake."
4. Conversely, movement can be seen to be not so pleasurable, or in some cases to express aggression: "fighting," "confronting," "raging." And finally,
5. Movement can be expressed as a passive attitude: "looking," "sitting," "gazing," "sniffing."

Our chart (see Table 6–1) shows some interesting differences in our *FM* dominant small group. For Student 18, animals, though "doing their own thing," also carried symbolic messages of reassurance as to the outcome of events. For example, the "butterfly *trying* to emerge from the caterpillar," the "butterfly *flying south,*" possibly to less harsh conditions; animals "walking in a forest into which the sun shines," the clumsy hippo "rears up," the "dying horse" somehow gets his foot to the ground.

Student 17 allowed animals to be what they are and do what they do. The birds, for example, hatched eggs; the water animals swam and floated.

TABLE 7–1

	Alive	Doing Their Thing	Active: Pleasurable	Active: Aggressive	Passive Movements
Student 16	Crabs	Fish swimming	Bears dancing	Raging (*little* animals)	Horses looking

TABLE 7-1
(Continued)

	Alive	Doing Their Thing	Active: Pleasurable	Active: Aggressive	Passive Movements
Student 16 (Continued)	Bat Cats Crabs	Butterfly flying Seahorse swimming	Cats prancing		
Student 17		Bat flying "Attempting to fly" Hatching eggs	Bear dancing Dog smiling Animal running Bears climbing	Poodles confronting ("not too vicious")	Steer looking Seahorse looking Dog sitting Hens looking Vultures gazing Terrier sniffing
Student 18		Microorganisms swimming Octopuses floating slowly Butterfly trying to emerge from caterpillar Horse touching ground with forefoot Butterfly flying forward Butterfly going south Bears walking (in sunlight)	Scorpion grasping Elephants teasing Creatures playing patty-cake Hippo rearing	Seahorses fighting	

RORSCHACH RESPONSES, PSYCHOGRAM, AND SELF-EVALUATION OF STUDENT 16

Student 16 was far less passive than Student 17. Only his horses are seen as "looking." But 17 had hens, seahorses, and a steer "looking," dogs "sitting," vultures "gazing," and terriers "sniffing."

Student 16's one aggressive attitude, namely "raging," is modified by the fact that it is done by very *little* animals. Student 17's entry, "poodles confronting each other," is similarly modified: "but in not too vicious a manner."

With these pointers in mind as to what the choice of animals and animal action may mean, the reader may be interested to look at the many other animal examples which appear in various Rorschach records and Inside Stories throughout the book.

The Rorschach record, psychogram, and self-evaluation of Student 16 appear in Table 7-2 and Figure 7-1.

TABLE 7-2
Rorschach Record of Student 16

Card I			
1. Two Santa Clauses facing each other holding onto a flag pole, spinning on a revolving pole	W	M, m	(H)
2. A female with a dress on, facing backwards, without a head	D	M	Hd

Card II			
1. Two dancing bears, putting one of their paws together with each other	W	FM	A
2. A stingray or mantis (fish)	S	F	A
3. A jet airplane	S	F	obj
4. Two prancing cats wearing two red stocking hats	D	FM, CF	A
5. Two sets of rabbit ears	dd	F	Ad

Card III			
1. Two male puppets in full dress suits, moving about	W	F, m	(H)
2. Butterfly, red and flying	D	FC, FM	A
3. Ribs, sternum, lungs	D	Fk	anat
4. Two little raging animals hanging next to the heads of the two puppets	D	FM, F, m	A
5. Two horses looking over their shoulders	D	FM	A

Card IV			
1. Some sort of hairy insect or bug	W	Fc	A

TABLE 7-2
(Continued)

Card IV			
2. Two feet	D	F	Hd
3. Two cartoon animal heads	d	F	Ad
4. Two swans' necks hanging over	d	F, m	Ad

Card V			
1. A bat	W	FM	A

Card VI			
1. A rug made of animal skin	W	Fc	A
2. Some sort of insect	D	F	A
3. An Indian totem pole	d	F	obj

Card VII			
1. Two little children, girls, with their hair standing up	D	M, F, m	H
2. Two pig's heads, furry	D	Fc	Ad
3. Two fish swimming toward each other	D	FM	A

Card VIII			
1. Two animals in the cat family	D	FM	A
2. A bat, flying	D	FM	A
3. An old fashioned corset pulled apart at the laces	D	Fc, m, F	clo
4. A cactus plant	d	cF	plant
5. Spinal column X-ray	D	k	anat

Card IX			
1. Two witches	D	M	H
2. Two stomachs	D	F	anat
3. Two sets of claws	dd	F	Ad

Card X			
1. Two crabs	D	FM	A
2. Two maps of Italy	D	F	map
3. A chicken wishbone	D	F	A anat
4. A foot, covered with old rags tied to it	dr	Fc	Hd
5. Two sea horses, swimming	d	FM	A
6. Two heads with open mouths	D	F, m	Hd

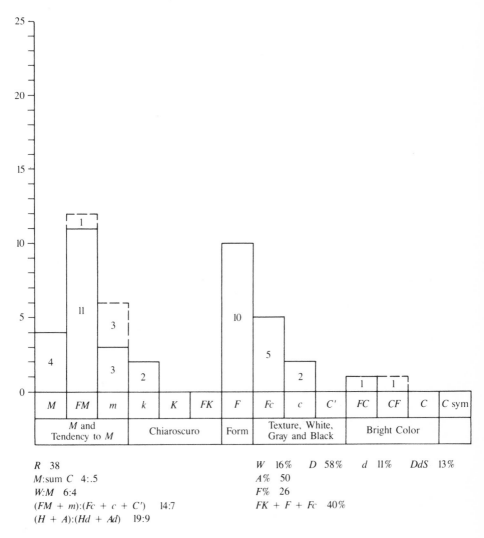

M	FM	m	k	K	FK	F	Fc	c	C'	FC	CF	C	C sym
M and Tendency to M			Chiaroscuro			Form	Texture, White, Gray and Black			Bright Color			

R   38
M:sum C 4:.5
W:M   6:4
(FM + m):(Fc + c + C')   14:7
(H + A):(Hd + Ad)   19:9

W   16%   D   58%   d   11%   DdS   13%
A%   50
F%   26
FK + F + Fc   40%

FIG. 7-1. A psychogram of Student 16

Self-Evaluation of Student 16

One thing that impresses me when looking at my psychogram is the low *M*s, and its relationship to the high *FM*s. It is suggested that a well adjusted adult has at least three *M*s or more, and since my protocol has the least amount suggested, I think it is a worthwhile factor to investigate. Even though good quality Ms and high numbers are signs of high intellectual capacity, according to Klopfer, I believe that my very minimum amount of Ms may be due to an emotional factor, which Klopfer also mentioned as a reason for low M productivity. This emotional factor may interfere with my empathy with other people and the utilization of imaginal resources necessary to see human figures. Because my M responses are (H), content, it is believed that the individual uses his imagination to escape reality situations instead of integrating imagination with reality to change a situation. Also the Ms with (H) content may indicate hostile and critical tendencies, both toward myself and others, which tend to obstruct free-flowing empathy and indicates a self-preoccupation that interferes with warm interpersonal relationships.

These hypotheses seem to fit very well my impression of myself as that which came about by introspection in my own personal psychoanalysis and in my experiences in a group analytic situation. One of the main issues that the group always confronts me with is my outward and inward hostility, and my inability to form warm interpersonal relationships with others.

Another outstanding feature of my psychogram is the high FM column and also its relationship to the low M column. The FM responses also represent an enlivening of the blot material, and the hypothesis is that it indicates an awareness of impulses to immediate gratification. It does not necessarily mean that the individual indulges his impulses to immediate gratification, but rather that he feels them, whether or not he expresses them in action.

Also a high FM, where CF responses are absent (in my case very low, one main response and one additional response), implies frustration, because the person does not act out his impulses. To feel impulses without acting them out implies frustraction.

Another ratio that is quite revealing in this respect is the $M{:}FM$ ratio. If the FM is greater than twice the Ms (in my case $FM = 4M$), the individual is ruled by an immediate need for gratification, rather than by long range goals. But because of the lack of color emphasis in the record, it cannot be said that the person tends to act impulsively. There is preoccupation with egocentric needs, but these are not overtly manifested in impulsive behavior.

I can readily recognize, as myself, the picture drawn by the preceding hypotheses. I have a great need for instant gratification, which I fulfill with material things, and the presence of tension and of anxiety is frequent, especially when I am unable, emotionally, to act on my impulses.

One ratio that I find indicative of my own personality is reflected in the ratio $M: (FM + m)$. In general, $FM + m$ should not be more than one half of M (in my case $5M$). A greater number of $FM + m$ indicates that the tensions are too strong to permit the person to utilize his inner resources for the constructive solution of his every day problems of living. I find this to be very apparent to me in my dealing with certain problems of living.

I have tried to show the aspects of myself that I recognize from my psychogram. These aspects are very well known to me because I am dealing with them in my own psychoanalysis. These areas are dealing with anxiety, need for gratification of my impulses, dependency, and need for improvement in my interpersonal relationships.

RORSCHACH RESPONSES, PSYCHOGRAM, AND SELF-EVALUATION OF STUDENT 17

We now introduce our second high FM student, Student 17, whose Rorschach record (Table 6-3), psychogram (Figure 6-2), and self-evaluation follow. A look at Table 6-1 will show that the quality of 17's FM responses tends to be more passive than that of the two other students within this category. It is not that he lacked some active movement, but the emphasis on "looking" suggests a more contemplative use of some of his drives.

TABLE 7-3
Rorschach Record of Student 17

Card I			
1. The entire blob looks like a head of a fox	W, S	F	Ad
2. Two large stoned majestic birds standing in the entrance way of an Egyptian palace	D	F	(A)
3. Woman's breasts	di	FK	sex
4. An orchestra conductor with his arms raised, ready to begin work	D	M	H
5. A woman from the waist down facing away from me, dressing behind some silk screen	D	M, Fc	H
Card II			
1. Two Russian Cossacks doing a dance	W	M	H

TABLE 7–3
(Continued)

Card II			
2. Two Russian bears doing a dance	W	FM	A
3. Some form of sea life like a stingray	D	F	A
4. Two hands, with long gloves, held up in prayer	d	m	Hd
5. Two poodles confronting each other, but in not too vicious a manner	D	FM	A
6. A Christmas tree decoration	S	F	obj
7. Two misshapen sea horses looking at each other	D	FM	A

Card III			
1. Two women fighting over a man, the man being presented figuratively by his chest cavity and his bow tie	W	M	H, anat
2. A science fiction "insect monster" one sees in the motion pictures	W	F	(A)
3. A dog sitting and looking back on his very long tail	D	FM	A
4. Profile of a man with a long nose	D	F	Hd
5. A Shantung bow tie	D	Fc	cloth
6. Two Congolese tribesman standing back to back	D	M, C'	H

Card IV			
1. Vagina	d	FK	sex
2. The head of a pooch, smiling, perhaps a fox terrier	W, S	FM, m	Ad
3. A crown	D	F	obj
4. Two hens at the feed box looking at each other	DS	FM	A
5. The head of a vulture gazing down, perhaps on prey	d	FM	Ad
6. The head of a steer looking straight ahead	D	FM	Ad

Card V			
1. A bat taking off in flight	W	FM	A
2. Bugs Bunny attempting to fly	W	FM	A
3. Alligator, coming out of hiding, head protruding	D	FM	A
4. The hind leg of an animal with a tail, running into a thicket after food	D	FM	A

Card VI			
1. A bear skin hung up on a wall	W	Fc	A obj

TABLE 7–3
(Continued)

Card VI			
2. Top man on a totem pole	D	F	obj
3. Penis	D	F	sex
4. A bell	D	F	obj
5. Profile of Cyrano de Bergerac	D	F	Hd

Card VII			
1. Two of Santa's little helpers, trying to determine where he went . . . each pointing in opposite directions	W	M	H
2. A nice comfortable arm chair	W, S	F	obj
3. A scot terrier sniffing	D	FM	A
4. The head of an angry bear	D	F, m	Ad

Card VIII			
1. Two bears climbing a rock ledge to go to the top	D	FM	A
2. Some theatrical character reaching out at someone	D	M	H
3. Two birds hatching eggs	S	FM	A
4. A buffalo head	D	F	Ad

Card IX			
1. The head of a dinosaur	di	FK	Ad
2. Horse's head with nostrils	DS	F	Ad
3. Color of ham	D	CF	food

Card X			
1. Crabs, blue crabs	D	FC	A
2. Rabbit	D	F	A
3. Caricature of man with moustache and glasses	D	F	Hd
4. Sea horses	D	F	A
5. Two WWI soldiers singing "Over There"	D	M	H
6. French poodle	DS	F, Fc	A

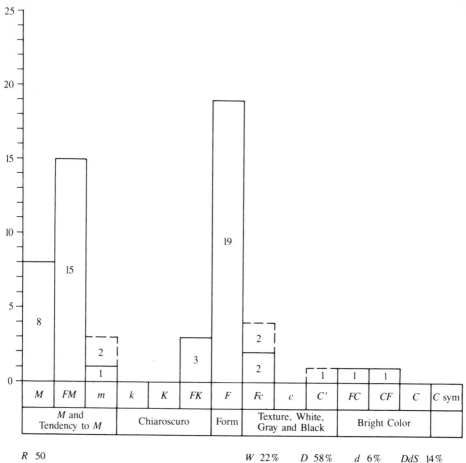

8	15	2 / 1				3	2		2	1	1	1	
M	*FM*	*m*	*k*	*K*	*FK*	*F*	*Fc*	*c*	*C'*	*FC*	*CF*	*C*	*C* sym
M and Tendency to *M*		Chiaroscuro				Form	Texture, White, Gray and Black			Bright Color			

R 50   *W* 22%   *D* 58%   *d* 6%   *DdS* 14%
M:sum *C*   8 :1.5   *A*% 36
W:*M*   11:8   *F*% 38
(*FM* + *m*):(*Fc* + *c* + *C'*)   16:2   *FK* + *F* + *Fc*   48%
(*H* + *A*):(*Hd* + *Ad*)   26:12

FIG. 7-2. A psychogram of Student 17

Self-Evaluation of Student 17

The overall pattern of the psychogram shows a high number of *FM*s (15) that represents an abundance of impulse. In relation to *FM*, the *M* (8) responses form a ratio of 8:15 which indicates an ability to cope with the impulsivity by means of inner resources. The *F*% shows use of intellect to exercise control. The sum *C* of 1.5 shows little emotional responsiveness to the environment. The number of responses on the last three cards equals 26%. Of these 13 responses, however, only two were color responses. This would tend to show an unemotional reactivity to the environment.

Turning to content, the record indicates unfulfilled aggressiveness which is illustrated in Card I, response 4, where an "orchestra leader has his arms raised, ready to begin work" and Card VI, response 2, with "top man on a totem pole." The conductor symbolizes the desire to be a leader of men as does the response of being top man on the totem pole. Both show the desire to excel over others, but as indicated in the psychogram, because of limited reactivity to the environment (sum C = 1.5), the aggressiveness does not reach fruition. Thus, in further examination of the conductor response, the conductor is seen as prepared to lead, but does not, in fact, lead.

Aggressiveness is further controlled by the utilization of passivity and can be seen in the responses showing the animals in postures of just looking or staring. On Card IV, response 6, the head is that of a steer looking straight ahead, and on Card VIII, response 4, it is a buffalo head stoically looking. Although the steer and buffalo are potentially powerful animals, they are depicted as passive. Card III of the TAT may offer some indication as to one of the sources for this passivity. The story is one of a mother who frowns upon her son's desires to be a fighter as it is in opposition to her own wishes to have him become a violinist. Aggressiveness may thus have a negative valence because of the mother's inherent values against aggression, or it may be curtailed whenever it is an expression of self-interest that is in opposition to someone else's interests.

Another set of responses shows only the animal heads without the bodies, and this may be interpreted as a preference for the intellect (the head) as opposed to the emotions (the body). At the outset of the record, the use of intellect is established with the initial response of the 'entire blot looks like the head of a fox.' The choice of a fox compounds the idea of being smart, of being 'foxy' and quantitatively, this preference for the intellect is borne out in the many F responses.

Overtly, the aggressiveness appears as friendliness and is seen on Card II, response 1, where the two Russian Cossacks doing a dance are an image of comraderie, as are the WWI soldiers on Card X, response 5, singing "Over There." Implicit, however, is the symbol of combat, as both men are soldiers, and by extension, we may further hypothesize that this attitude relates to male authority figures, especially the father.

On Card II, response 4, where two hands are held up in prayer and on Card VII, response 1, where Santa's helpers are seeking Santa, the theme of dependence on the father is presented. In juxtaposition to the aggressive feelings, the dependency creates an ambivalence which, as this record indicates, resulted in a lopsided solution of suppressing the aggressive needs so as not to endanger the dependent needs. The result has been an impoverished emotional response to the world.

Turning to the figure drawings, the first one depicts a man surmounting hurdles and the third is of a man in transit. Both reflect a current attempt at achieving a fuller life through psychotherapy which too is a period of overcoming obstacles and of transition. In light of my Rorschach record, the direction of the therapy should be in the channeling of me outward into more reactive and emotional involvements with outer reality. To counteract the passivity and stimulate more emotional responsiveness, group psychotherapy would be most beneficial.

This profile coincides very closely with what I know about myself.

RORSCHACH RESPONSES, PSYCHOGRAM, AND SELF-EVALUATION OF STUDENT 18

The *FM*s of our third student, a clinical psychology major, serve a very different purpose from those of Students 16 and 17. As she commented with considerable insight, her *FM*s may perhaps replace distorted *M* responses, which she interpreted as reflecting a distorted body image. Very different concerns were experienced by this student, whose mature emotional responsivity to the environment helped channel much of the energy implied by her *FM* responses. Such was not available to Students 16 and 17, whose color responses were few.

The Rorschach record, psychogram (Table 7-3), and self-evaluation (Figure 7-3) of Student 18 follow.

TABLE 7-3
Rorschach Record of Student 18

Card I			
1. A scorpion with its claws extended for grasping	D	FM	A
2. Two baby elephants on either side teasing the scorpion with their trunks	D	FM – M	A
3. A woman from the neck down standing very stiff and straight	D	M	H

TABLE 7-3
(Continued)

Card II

---

1. Human lungs covered with dripping blood	D	CF, m	anat
2. Looks like two creatures with ugly red faces playing patty-cake while standing on their hind legs—the faces have beaks like hawks	W	FM – m, F/c	A
3. A stingray with a man-of-war he's just stung to death	S,D	Fm,m	A

Card III

---

1. Two kidneys	D	FC	anat
2. Overall figure looks like two human figures that have been separated into pieces:	W		
• head and upper torso are intact —figure looks like two black African women		M, C'	H
• lower part of the body—pelvic area is under the figure but separated from it		F	anat
• each woman has only one leg with a bony bony and a high heeled shoe		F, Fc	clo
• the kidneys belong in the body along with the stomach and esophagus . . . many parts of the bodies are still missing and they can't be made whole without them		FC	anat

---

Card IV

---

1. Upper end of a caterpillar	D	Fc	Ad
2. On either side are boots getting ready to smash the caterpillar with their heels	D	F, m	obj
3. A butterfly is trying to emerge from the caterpillar before it gets stepped on	d	FM	A
4. Looks like a dying horse's head, very elongated as with tremendous sadness, touching the ground by its front leg . . . like a statue of Don Quixote's horse, but real	d	FM	A

TABLE 7–3
(Continued)

Card V

---

1. Looks like a large bat flying forward with its legs outstretched behind; protrusions at the top of the head are sending and detecting ultra sonic wavelengths to keep it on path	W	FM	A
2. They don't really fit on the bat's head—they look more like rabbit ears perked up listening for intruders	d	F, m	Ad
3. The feet really look more like rabbit feet	d	F	Ad
4. The figure could also be a flying rabbit, if such things exist	W	FM	(A)

Card VI

---

1. Upper part looks like it's springing from the head of the rest of the figure . . . like Apollo springing out of Jupiter's head (in mythology)	W	(M)	(H)
2. Lower ¾ looks like a ghost with very close set eyes . . . its arms are very low on its body and therefore not very useful for him . . . the darker line down the middle is his spinal cord visible because his body is not solid but rather opaque; he has a thumb on each shoulder pointing up to the sky	W	(M), k, C'	(H)
3. Coming out of his head is a totem pole with the face of cat with whiskers . . . it is covered with a gown of flowing silk blowing freely in the breeze . . . this figure is much freer and less restricted than the ghost which produced it . . . might represent the inner wish of the ghost to be free	D	F, Fc, m	obj

---

Card VII

---

1. Land masses cut by a canal	D	FK	geog
2. Pieces of bodies floating at sea, clinging together after a plane wreck at sea . . . each having one or two arms . . . two are touching the land, representing their desire to be back on land and alive	W	F, m	Hd
3. Could also be a butterfly going south for the winter	D	FM	A

TABLE 7–3
(Continued)

Card VIII

1. Whole figure looks like an ecology picture of the North woods . . . grizzly bears walking through the forest, with trees and the ground of the forest . . . there is sunlight coming through the trees and a threat of a forest fire . . . which could also be the sunset	*W*	*FC, FM, CF C, C* sym	nat, pla, fir
2. The bears are touching a human hand	*d*	*F*	*Hd*
3. Mountain peaks	*d*	*F*	nat

Card IX

1. Fire breathing sea horses fighting with each other	*D*	*FC, FM, C*	*A,* fire
2. Ill-defined person riding a hippopotamus that is rearing up	*D*	*M, FM, FC*	*H, A*
3. Human lungs	*D*	*CF*	anat
4. Human hearts	*D*	*CF*	anat

Card X

1. Looks like a view of dirty water under a microscope . . . many microorganisms swimming around	*W*	*FC, FK FM*	water, *A*
2. Two bulls lifting up a concrete post that locks a gate—their cows are running to join them to get out	*D*	*FM, FC*	*A*
3. Octopuses floating slowly through the sea	*D*	*FM*	*A*
4. Smear of blood	*D*	*C*	blood
5. Yellow poodles with large red hearts, very loving	*D*	*FC, CF*	*A*
6. Brown crabs	*D*	*FC*	*A*
7. A giant green wishbone	*D*	*F/C*	obj

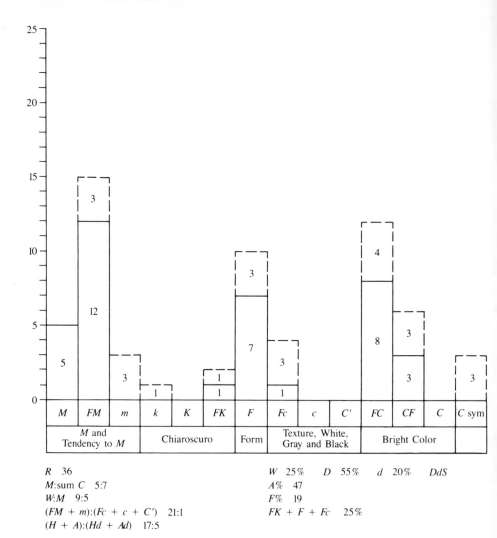

FIG. 7-3. A psychogram of Student 18

R   36
M:sum C   5:7
W:M   9:5
(FM + m):(Fc + c + C')   21:1
(H + A):(Hd + Ad)   17:5

W   25%   D   55%   d   20%   DdS
A%   47
F%   19
FK + F + Fc   25%

Self-Evaluation of Student 18

For me, the most striking feature of my record is the quality of my
M responses. One is a headless woman, one, 2 women whose figures
are separated into pieces, another a ghost, one is vaguely seen as
suggesting mythological figures, and the final one is an ill-defined
person suggested by its location on the back of an animal. The only

other human figure I saw (but not scored as an *M*) were parts of bodies floating together clinging to each other but dead. Thus, all of my human figures are distorted in some way and do no not look like real people. Because of the meaning of *M*s in general, this part of my record seems inconsistent with where I am and what I'm doing.

In trying to figure out what the *M*s in my record mean, several possibilities came to mind, although I do not know whether there are specific things represented by distorted *M*s. The two woman responses with parts of the body missing would appear best to indicate a distorted body image which for me could be related to my own physical deformity which I have not completely accepted. The other *M*s perhaps reflect a certain lack of self-acceptance and clear identity. These are things which to my own awareness are by no means paralyzing although they may perhaps at times get in the way of other things I may be trying to do.

Another aspect of my record deserving some attention is the large number of *FM* responses (1/3 of the total). It is in these responses that I felt more of myself, and perhaps to some extent, this is indicative of immaturity and maybe even of my desire to work with children. Although my *FM*s are high, they do not appear to reflect the kinds of things discussed by Klopfer when *FM*s greatly exceed *M*s. Certainly I do not feel swamped with instinctual urges unless this is somehow occuring at a level I am unaware of. I would speculate that to be where I am, I probably need all the *FM* I can get. One other aspect of myself that may be related to the high *FM* is my need for physical activity. Perhaps my distorted *M* has been able to sublimate my excess *FM* in this way.

Related to the *FM* responses is the large number of animal responses I gave (47%), which is a very high average. The meaning of this may be related to a certain immaturity (or even childlikeness) because of a lack of a wide variety of other responses. However, this restriction of interests is probably more an indication of a purposeful and necessary restriction due to the demands of school.

In looking at other aspects of my record, there is evidence of a good range of psychic reactivity with a fairly balanced *M:* Sum *C* of 5:7 and a lack of explosive color. Two of my CF responses are very benign while the other main *CF* is explosive—blood. My additional *CF'*s range from very quiet to fairly strong, but there is plenty of control in the *FC*s to handle the *CF*s and there are no *C*s to control. The other aspect of the color side of the psychogram is the three additional color symbolism responses which are indicative of intellectualizing and theorizing, which is something I definitely do with emotions. In general, the color side of the record presents a favorable picture with respect to my emotional life and perhaps offsets the problem with my *M*s to some extent. One aspect of the emotional side, which may be suggested by the many *FC*s and few explosive responses is almost an over-control. While this part of the record may possibly suggest this, content-wise this becomes more evident.

A few other things can be said before getting into content. One is that my *W:M* is a good one for the optimal use of the resources I possess. Although my *F%* is low, there are compensating forms of control in the record such as the *FC*s. Still, this may cost me some of the kind of support available from a good solid *F%*.

In looking at the content of my record, there are several things that are apparent. One is the theme of aggression which can be seen in several responses (scorpion with claws extended for grasping, sea horses fighting, boots about ready to smash a caterpillar). Related to this is the theme of death (bodies floating at sea after a plane wreck, a stingray stinging a man-of-war to death and a dying horse). To some extent these themes represent anxiety about death, but they are probably influenced by the fact that a person I admired very much was killed in a plane crash at sea just before I took the Rorschach. Another theme which I picked up was one of constriction versus freedom as seen in several responses (the woman standing very stiff and straight, the butterfly emerging from the caterpillar, and the totem pole representing the inner wish of the ghost to be be free, and the bulls and cows trying to open the gate to get out). This theme reflects a definite conflict within me and may be related to the need for emotional control seen in my color responses and my *m* responses.

In summary, there are both strengths and weaknesses reflected in my record and several things which I could only explain because of my knowledge of myself. The kind of picture I would have gotten of the person who gave this record blind could not possibly have been so complete, as there would have been many more places where I could only have laid out several speculations about possible interpretations. This makes me realize the value of having other material about the person besides his Rorschach available, especially at this level in my skillfulness.

There is some interesting additional evidence available to us in the consideration of these three students with the strong *FM* orientation. Student 16 took the Instruction-Insight course at age 39, when he was established in a career of "business executive." Student 17 was also a business major, aged 35, engaged in employment interviewing. Student 18, after full-time psychologist-in-training experiences, first pursued a clinical career; but later added to this by becoming part owner of a holistic health center. Thus, opportunity for organization and administration seems to have been needed in these cases where a strong aggressive drive was reflected in their test findings.

There is also another student (Student 24), who, as we shall see later, had one of the highest *FM* scores in the group; and who shifted from psychology to administration in the academic world, becoming first dean, and then president, of a community college.

8

The Ambi-Equal Classification

"The normal ambi-equal type represents the ideal result of the development of the experienced type." So says Rorschach.

In more familiar wording we might add that the availability of a developed inner life, in combination with satisfying emotional experiences, results in the richest kind of psychological awareness and living.

In discussing the records of our student population whose scores meet these requirements, we are confronted with a problem regarding the *degree* of equality that is needed to achieve this ambi-equal classification.

Nowhere does Rorschach state that the ambi-equal scores must be numerically exact (for example, a 6 *M* to 6 *C,* or a 10 *M* to 10 *C* distribution). He does consider 3 *M* to 3 Sum *C,* however, not sufficiently important to meet the classification of ambi-equal.

Rorschach's charts also show that his "normal" subjects were artists and "very talented people." Among his artists we find he made a division between those he described as "abstract artists" as opposed to "theoretical artists." The abstract artists have an *M:C* ratio in which "the *M*s predominate *greatly* over the *C*s." The theoretical artists have an *M:C* ratio in which "*M* predominates a *little* over *C*s." But greatly and little are not spoken of quantitatively but are indicated by the signs >> "greatly" and > "little."

In the very talented subjects, the *M:C* ratios are described by an *x* standing for many *M*s and many *C*s (*x M:x C*).

Again we must ask are these "many" *M*s and "many" *C*s identical? This is where Rorschach failed to give a quantitative statement of what the ambi-equal's score must mean.

It must be remembered that Rorschach's weakness—from our point of view—is that he was less interested in studying normals either in large

134

numbers or in detail, although he did point out how valuable it would be if such large studies were made (Rorschach, 1942). This is because the thrust of his work lies in differentiating the normal from a variety of psychiatric categories, namely, psychodiagnosis.

Thus, when speaking of the ambi-equal—a type of person he obviously admired, it is more to contrast the symptom-free individual with a variety of psychotic types. The M and C responses in his tables give the scores of "normals" in order to contrast them with the schizophrenic, the manic depressive, the epileptic and the organic cases. He further differentiated between types of hebephrenics, the simple and the querulous, between the demented, the mild catatonic and the severely catatonic. He was also interested in differentiating between the well-preserved paranoid and the productive paranoid, all of these with specific differentiating scoring.

But there is little help when we come to the point of differentiating between "the many M" and the "many C" normal person.

If one expects absolute equality of M and C endowments in order to be described as ambi-equal in the strictest sense, then the number of cases in such a group would be minimal. This statement can be made on the basis of published studies with 162 medical students, 112 disturbed adolescents and 55 psychotic patients (Harrower, 1955b). Subsequent studies of 150 theological students and 65 nurses give the same findings.

Absolute equality of scores is not found in the record of any of the medical students, nor in the records of the psychotic patients. It was found in only 6% of the Unitarians, 4% of the nurses, and 3% of the disturbed adolescents.

Obviously, we are not including those smaller $M:C$ ratios, such as $M:C = 2:2$ or $M:C = 3:3$ described as belonging to the coartive group by Rorschach. With this in mind, the minimum ratio for absolute equality would be $M:C = 4:4$.

Figure 8-1 demonstrates the distribution of $M:C$ ratios for 166 medical students (Harrower, 1960).

This chart is relevant to discussions on ambi-equal records, since it shows that in this population not a single individual showed an exact ambi-equal score. For example, we do not find $M:$sum $C = 8:8$, or $M:$sum $C = 6:6$, or even $M:$sum $C = 4:4$, although student 12, with an $M:$sum C of 7 : 8, came close to it. (Rorschach did not consider an $M:$sum C of 3:3 as ambi-equal.)

This chart also reveals, in the case of Student 24 (see chapter 10), how rare extroverted records are. Assuming that a record must show at least a sum C of 4 or over to be considered extroverted, we find only a few scattered examples of extroverts (for example, Students 129, 91, 54, 11, 94, and 139), while basically M greater than C is found in this population.

RORSCHACH INTROVERSION-EXTROVERSION RATIOS EXPRESSED GRAPHICALLY

C Responses

M Responses	0.	.5	1	1.5	2	2.5	3	3.5	4	4.5	5	5.5	6	6.5	7	7.5
0	151 128			29	157	149										
1	130 159 71	156 57	72 59	82	64 114 158 115	152 103 92	39		139				129			
2	136 102 55 150 / 120 145 37	3 160 143	41 121 93	15 95 7 35	73 70	68 125 113	104 101	124		54	91					
3	141 107 88 142	6	97 117 62 75 77 / 161 56 38 99 67	108 42 135 53	46 61 19	18	40 153 144	12 60A		111						11
4	85 27	133 69 123 22	58 146 48 50	78 106 134 105	20 52 31 87 / 21 118 109	1 110	14 31A	47								
5	45	36 148 44	60 122 132 / 51 28 4	155 154 147	26	140 131 127	76 16		79 25							
6	8 83	63 116 33 / 18A 5 81	32 86	90 100	126 43 84		23	80			119					
7	105A	74	96 138		137	30					24	17				Mr. X
8					65	98										
9		49		89 50A			9	10								
10-11							34 13 66		2							
14				Mr. M.												

EXTROVERSION SCORES

INTROVERSION SCORES

FIG. 8-1. From Molly Harrower, P. Vorhaus, M. Roman, & G. Bauman, *Creative Variations in the Projective Techniques*, 1960. Courtesy of Charles C. Thomas, Publisher, Springfield Illinois.

136

CONSIDERATION OF FIVE STUDENTS
OF AMBI-EQUAL TYPE

We now begin our presentation of ambi-equal student records (Table 7-1), psychograms (Figure 7-2), and self-evaluations with that of Student 19 whose $M:C$ ratio comes closest to absolute equality, namely 8:6.5. This student also contributed a follow-up statement about her current life after 15 years.

TABLE 8-1
Rorschach Record of Student 19

Card I

1. Head or face of an animal like a fox; it's smiling or leering	W	F, m	Ad
2. A Halloween mask, with ears, eyes, smiling mouth	W	F	obj
3. A pair of hands	d	F	Hd
4. Breasts	d	F	Hd, sex
5. A woman's figure, with her arms up	D	M	H
6. A man's head with a hat on—no, it's more than just a head . . . a whole man with an arm extended and legs in motion, like prancing	D	M	H
7. Owl eyes	di	cF	Ad
8. Lots of faces and heads (3 in particular)	de, de, de	F	Hd

Card II

1. Two women dancing with their mouths open, hands touching, feet kicking, and hair piled high on their heads; my first impression was that they were happily dancing; then I thought it could be interpreted as anger and they are fighting, but the hand position looks more like dancing (as in square dancing)	W˙	M	H
2. The red blot at the bottom looks like a sand crab or some sea animal (a poorly formed red lobster?)	D	F/C	A
3. 2 baby Koala bears or a rabbit stretching out; see the ears and nose, fur	D + d + d = W	FM, Fc	A
4. A toothless face with a jutting jaw and hook nose	de	F	Hd
5. A skeleton of a reptile head (like alligator bones, same as women's hands but upside down)	d	Fc, FC	A obj

TABLE 8–1
(Continued)

Card II

6. Teeth	d	F	Ad
7. A manta ray	S	F	A

Card III

1. Two females with skirts on, high heeled shoes, big breasts and noses, doing exercises	D + d + d = W	M	H
2. A duck's bill (same as the skirt flap above)	d	F	Ad
3. An erected penis (same as the duck's bill)	d	F	sex
4. Their hands are on a head or a mask, a kind of grotesque caricature of a face with deep eye sockets	D	Fc	(Hd)
5. The red blot between the women is a butterfly	D	F/C	A
6. The red outside upper blots are ovaries with fallopian tubes	D	FC	anat
7. A cartoon-type face	D	F	Hd
8. "The Monster that Devoured Cleveland"—a Hollywood-type giant insect with upraised claw-legs, grinning; has huge eyes like a fly.	W˙	FM, Fc, m	(A)
9. Lungs	D	FC	anat

Card IV

1. A bat with its wings out, poised for flight	W	FM	A
2. Hairy, bristly head of a fly	d	Fc	Ad
3. Small head and body (slimy gray)	D	FC, c	A
4. A foot with a crumpled boot on	D	Fc	Hd, obj
5. A cartoon face with a huge nose and a hat on	D	F	(Hd)
6. Three profiles, one with shaggy hair	de de S	F Fc F	Hd Hd Hd
7. Shadings of gray, looks like X-ray film	di	k	obj
8. Pea pod	d	F	pl
9. Also Fallopian tubes again, attached to uterus	d	F	anat
10. A hydra (same as snail upside down)	D	Fc	A
11. Fur or feathers above the boots (the interior shadings)	D	c	A obj

Card V

1. A bat in air, distinct head, wings, feet	W	FM	A

TABLE 8-1

(Continued)

Card V

2. A wet snail head	*d*	*Fc*	*Ad*
3. Handles to a cutting instrument, like a rongeur, which opens when the handles are squeezed	*d*	*F*	obj
4. Legs, like chicken drumsticks	*d*	*F*	*A* obj
5. Butterfly	*W*	*F*	*A*
6. Profile of a face with a beard	*de*	*F*	*Hd*
7. A burning candle	*d*	*F, m*	obj
8. Bird (head only) screeching with its mouth open	*d*	*FM*	*Ad*

Card VI

1. Bearskin rug	*W`*	*Fc*	*A* obj
2. Reptile or turtle head	*d*	*F*	*Ad*
3. Whiskers	*d*	*F*	*Ad*
4. Wings with delicate feathers	*D*	*Fc*	*Ad*
5. Side view of two fat persons with arms and legs extended (mouth open, breasts, hair)	*W`*	*M*	*H*
6. Front end of a crab	*d*	*F*	*Ad*
7. Penis	*D*	*F*	*Hd*, sex
8. Indian medicine man in feathered robe standing with arms out on top of a burial mound chanting	*D*	*M, Fc*	*H*

Card VII

1. Two girls with pony tails up flying in the air and arms outstretched	*W`*	*M*	*H*
2. A pig head	*D*	*Fc*	*Ad*
3. Chain of islands	*W*	*FK*	nat
4. A sea animal swimming—a skate or a ray	*D*	*FM*	*A*
5. A Scottie dog touching noses with a Bedlington Terrier (each half of blot—4 dogs)	*D + D = W*	*FM, Fc*	*A*
6. An elephant's trunk	*d*	*F*	*Ad*
7. An open mouth with jagged teeth; looks like dentures opened up rather than a real set of teeth	*de*	*F*	obj
8. Labia majora or minora	*di*	*Fc*	*Hd*, sex anat

Card VIII

1. Large cat stalking (pink)	*D*	*FM/F/C*	*A*
2. Old-fashioned woman's corset opened out with bone stays and	*D*	*Fc*	obj

TABLE 8–1
(Continued)

Card VIII

loose lacing (blue)			
3. A cartoon head with gray beard, sideburns, and toupee	W	F, FC, Fc	(Hd)
4. A gray squid with tentacles out	D	FC	A
5. A bizarre-looking, cartoon-type deep sea (blue) monster about to bite the gray squid	D	FM, F/C	A
6. A sweet pea blossom	D	FC	pl

Card IX

1. Pelvis	D	F	anat
2. Another cartoon head in profile; it is puffy and has a funny smirk (green)	D	Fc, m	(Hd)
3. A mythical creature with a long nose and pointed hat on a round body with a protruding stomach—laughing	D(ddd)	F, m	(A)
4. Hippopotamus head with little ears and a big snout	D	F	A
5. A femorton! We used to draw them as kids. It looked like a funny creature with a big nose that always hangs over a fence or wall (gray-green middle area)	D	Fc, FC	(A)
6. Sea horses dueling with their noses	D	FM	A
7. Claws	d	F	Ad
8. The embryo from *2001: A Space Odyssey;* it has a tail and umbilicus and is almost pinkish	D(dd)	F/C	H

Card X

1. Blue crabs catching green snails	D	FM, F/C	A
2. Gray crabs	D	FC	A
3. Yellow amoeba	D	F/C	A
4. 2 ovaries with Fallopian tubes leading to tiny uterus	D	F	anat
5. A tiny human figure flying with hands over its head	d	M	H
6. A stained cell with a nucleus	D	CF	anat
7. Orange wishbone	D	F	obj
8. Sea horses sipping sodas	D	FM	A
9. Australia	D	F	nat
10. Gray angelfish held by crabs (angel fish is seen head-on, very skinny)	D	FM, Fc	A

TABLE 8-1
(Continued)

Card X			
11. Island seen from the air	D	FK	nat
12. Yellow roses	D	FC	nat

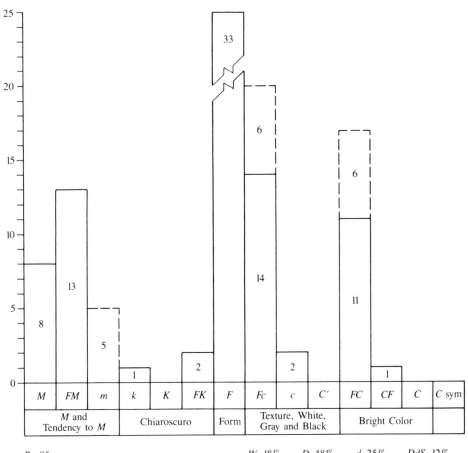

M	FM	m	k	K	FK	F	Fc	c	C'	FC	CF	C	C sym
8	13	5			1	2	33 / 6 / 14		2	6 / 11	1		

| M and Tendency to M | | | Chiaroscuro | | | Form | Texture, White, Gray and Black | | | Bright Color | | | |

R 85
M:sum C   8:6.5
W:M   15:8
(FM + m):(Fc + c + C')   13:16
(H + A):(Hd + Ad)   33:30

W 18%   D 48%   d 25%   DdS 12%
A% 45
F% 39
FK + F + Fc   58%

FIG. 8-2.   A psychogram of Student 19

Self-Evaluation of Student 19

I will first write about "the person who gave this record" as though it were someone I don't know but whom I've tested. I'll follow that with an account of it from a first-person point of view, recognizing that I am the subject.

This appears to be a person who tends to perceive more in terms of small and unusual details rather than larger details or wholes. This does not seem to be excessive, however, considering that it is balanced by a $W\%$ that is almost low normal and a $D\%$ that is well within the normal range. As a graduate student, she may tend to be a little less theoretical than her peers, being more interested in the application and usefulness of research results than just research for its own sake. Her $W{:}M$ ratio of 15:8 gives evidence of organizing ability in good balance with inner resources and ideas, so a W on the low side in this case does not necessarily imply lack of ability to theorize, organize, or do abstract thinking. It is at her disposal, but she may prefer to attend to details or pursue a more uniquely individual way of looking at the world. Her higher than average $d\%$ may indicate a need for certainty or comfort in latching on to small items, which are manageable. The higher than average $Dd + S$ may have been somewhat achieved at the expense of W (but not of D), but she may simply be a very responsive person or enjoy the unusual.

This is reinforced by the high number of Fcs, indicating high sensitivity approaching hypersensitivity. This person probably can be a stickler for details, though not to the point of being pedantic. The $Dd + S\%$ combined with the high Fc may point toward artistic tendencies or creative potential. The proportion of *de, di,* and S is 8:3:2. Concentration on edge details may indicate caution; this may be a person who enters slowly into new territory, preferring a wait-and-see attitude to impulsive rushing-in.

The number of responses is considerably higher than average. While in some this indicates a need to cover all possible ground or achieve closure, in this subject the responses were easily and enthusiastically given with obvious pleasure in the task. Her attention to smaller details contributed to elevating the (R); considering the high Fc, the high R is further indication of perceptual responsiveness and ease of reactivity to environmental stimuli.

Looking at the psychogram, three aspects stand out: a high FM, high Fc, and high FC (though almost 1/3 are F/C). Klopfer indicates that high FM means the individual is aware of impulses to immediate gratification. When CF is low, the person does not act out the impulses but may feel frustration. When FM is not greater than $2M$ (as in this case) it does not imply immaturity and is within the normal range (Klopfer). This person is not impulsive (low CF, high de) but probably has a high drive level and is very active. Considering that there are at least 4 sex responses, a high level of sexual interest may be hypothesized. The quality of FMs is high, and they are somewhat balanced by the 8 Ms, so an infantile personality cannot be concluded.

A high number of Fc responses may imply extreme sensitivity either to self or others, which in the case of a clinical psychologist concentrating on psychotherapy is good unless it approaches paranoid proportions. This person seemed to derive enjoyment out of tactile responses; she remarked that she enjoys touching, which may be an expression of her need for affection and belonging or response from others. The fact that Fcs dominate pure c answers indicates a control imposed on her sensitivity or affectional needs so that they are channeled. It is possible she is overly dependent on others for affection or responses to her, or, considering her profession, it may have been deliberately developed to increase sensitivity to clients and people in general. The quality of the Fc responses is very good; that the number of F responses is more than twice the number of Fcs indicates a good control system, thus leading to the conclusion that these Fcs reflect healthy sensitivity.

The high FC column reflects both successful integration of color and form (true FCs) and a self-conscious effort to achieve emotional involvement (F/Cs). This person is quite emotional but is careful to control her feeling expressions. This may be another indicator of her caution—she prefers to test the water with her big toe rather than her whole foot. Since FC is considered one of the best signs of adjustment, she appears to be adjusted (whatever that means) or satisfied with her life. This would tend to moderate any doubts about the high FM rate indicating frustration. The 7 F/C responses may point toward some tension in social relationships (Klopfer, 1954, p. 280), perhaps a self-consciousness, as in the conscious attempt to relate inappropriate color to form. In other words, emotionality is recognized and not ignored, but it is not handled with complete ease as in the FC responses.

Eight Ms indicate an active inner life and availability of resources from within. As previously mentioned, the $W:M$ ratio is almost 2:1 so her ideas and intellectual efforts should be successfully channeled. Her M:sum C ratio is fairly balanced (8:6.5), showing a slight tendency to introvertism but with extraversion available.

The $+5$ ms and one k point toward anxiety, but the fact that they are plus ms and not main ms is encouraging. It can be noticed that most of her ms are facial expressions rather than inanimate movements. To be aware of expressions on perceived faces may be another facet of sensitivity to other people, but some awareness of anxiety in relating to these people may be involved. Two FK responses may be another expression of anxiety by handling it with introspection or intellectual distance. Considering that this is a female graduate student in a competitive field (with added family responsibilities) an absence of anxiety indicators may be worse than an expression of them.

Her F% is well within the normal range, indicating solid control without rigidity and inflexibility. She is capable of impersonal analysis and logic without being a slave to it.

Regarding content, the A% is higher than normal (45%, with 20%–35% being considered optimum). There is a wide range of animals and animal details, but many are sea animals. Also several of the "object" answers are animal objects. This could indicate a narrowness of interests (low intellectual capacity is not likely) or an area of anxiety. The frequency of anatomy answers is also evident, especially recurring Fallopian tubes and ovaries. She might have concerns in these areas. In addition to these anatomical references, most of which are sexually related (pelvis, uterus, labia), there are 4 direct sex references (2 penises, breasts, labia). It is possible she is a person with a high sex drive (high FM) and sexually active, or she may have problems in this area. Her sexual references are straight-forward without negative elaboration or images and represent both males and females. Further inquiry is necessary before any conclusion could be drawn. She has several (7) references to cartoon or mythical figures. This reflects fantasy capabilities and a desire to be "correct" or do accurate labeling.

Her cognitive style is verging on richness but doesn't quite make it. Perhaps because of the attention to small details, she does not take off on elaborate descriptions or extremely complex explanations. At the same time there was an ease of progression, a light-heartedness, and maybe a childlike quality (the cartoon figures, femorton, monster that devoured Cleveland). She had 5 populars and some originals.

In summation, her strengths are her inner resources, strong drives, and realistic, rational approach, combined with sensitivity and channeled emotionality. Her weaknesses come from some of the same areas: almost too much drive, requiring a lot of control, hypersensitivity (perhaps painful self-awareness at times) (or social awareness), and a need to monitor and control (over control?) emotions. Specific anxieties are indicated, perhaps about health or in the sexual area. There are three indicators of a well-balanced record: the $W:M$, $M:$sum C, and $(H + A):(Hd + Ad)$ ratios. Succession was rather orderly, with Ws coming first position in 7 out of the 10 cards. Only with the color cards was the lack of integration into wholes evident.

It was very difficult to write about myself as though I were someone else and be unbiased. I don't think I succeeded because there seems to be somewhat of a "halo effect." What I have to do now is fight the temptation to rationalize all the above negative comments and produce logical-sounding explanations for my deficits. Again, I will do the best I can to see myself objectively and rely on comments by people who know me well to supplement my own observations.

I am a small detail person who sometimes can't see the forest for the trees. At other times, though, when I am faced with a task, I can leap into abstract, philosophical, theoretical thinking—but I don't necessarily enjoy it. I really do prefer to attend to details, but I hate routine. I like odd, unusual, surprising details, sometimes little things other people completely miss or don't care about. It may be related to my memory, which other people often comment on as being unusually sharp, especially for details. As an undergraduate I found that attention to details brought high grades, so this channeling of perception was reinforced until now it's habit. Sometimes in reading a textbook I have to remind myself not to obsess on details and overlook the larger organizational structure. The best thing I can say about this is that I'm aware of it and can adjust accordingly. It's my choice. I couldn't be where I am without adequate ability to tie details together and integrate them into cohesive wholes.

The edge detail thing is interesting. I am cautious, but once I make up my mind on something and commit myself I can become quite impulsive. I'm not as cautious as I used to be, as the result of knowing myself better and trusting other people more.

The high R is just the result of my usual way of reacting. I can be enthusiastic to the point of being obnoxious and am very sensitive to cues from the environment, especially social ones. I sometimes become overstimulated and then withdraw or retreat because of overload. There were times I wanted to wring every drop out of the cards, but it was more of a fun challenge than a need or compulsion.

The high FM certainly fits me. I have a great deal of drive and am an extremely active person—partly a reflection of the demands of school and partly just me. Impulses to immediate gratification— yes, but well controlled. I don't know how much FM reflects sex drive/interests/activities. I enjoy sex probably more than the average person my age; I expect to continue enjoying it well into old age, and I consider that a healthy attitude. I'll return to the topic of sex in a later section. I'm glad Jung had high FMs so I'm in good company.

The high Fcs are exactly what I expected. This is something I've developed in the last 4-5 years. Before that time I was hypersensitive in a more negative sort of way, having feelings that were easily hurt and being more sensitive to myself than others. Then partly because of my involvement in psychology and encounter-sensitivity training I began developing externally directed sensitivity, until now I can almost pick up vibrations in the air when people are together, and I've been described as unusually empathic. This will have obvious professional benefits for me. It is true that I have a huge need for affection and response from others, but this need is met and is the greatest source of my happiness.

I think of myself as a very emotional person (on the Myers–Briggs I came out a feeling type, INFP) but certainly not explosive or uncontrolled. My record looks like I would do well to have a little more spontaneity, but in fact I guess I am quite spontaneous in emotional expression, sometimes to others' embarrassment (if I feel like hugging someone out of sheer joy, I'm likely to do it wherever we are). Other people seem to think I'm well-adjusted (got my head together); I think I have moved in that direction, so that now I feel quite secure in my identity. It's a fairly new feeling for me. I'm an old adolescent. Being basically an introvert, I'm not very much at ease in social situations until enough time has passed for me to become comfortable. It takes me quite a while to begin expressing myself in classes, even though I usually have a lot to say. I converse much better in small groups or on a one-to-one basis, when I really feel free to be myself.

I think there are definite indications of anxiety in my record. I am currently living a rather stressful life, and if there were no anxiety responses I would be in trouble. The anxieties are specific: will I get the course work done on time, will I forget something important I had to do, is the family all right? Also my mother died this past year, and now my father is critically ill and not likely to improve. These are all pressures I feel and am aware of.

I don't know why the $A\%$ is so high—my interests are very broad, but they aren't really reflected in the content at all. I am a photographer and before graduate school used to compete in exhibitions; music is one of my passions, and I've always been very active in choirs, choruses, dancing, etc. I'm very art-oriented and would like to try all sorts of expressive media. But—it's not evident. I think the Rorschach record is reflecting a very real fact of my life right now—because of school my other interests have been temporarily put aside, and this hurts; I have become more constricted than I've ever been before. I don't like it, but it's been forced on me by the sheer weight of the load we have to carry here. I really think the narrowness of the content is my way of saying—look at what a little box I'm living in, let me out. Wow—that's really a big discovery; it fits feelings I've been vaguely aware of and didn't confront.

Anatomical anxiety—I had surgery on my ovaries several years ago, and lately I've been having problems again, I'm not terribly concerned about it, but there is an awareness of possible future difficulties. Also I had just been reading the textbook for a course in human sexuality and had been studying the anatomical drawings. I don't think my sex answers point to a sexual problem. I'm very open in this area and am specializing in it within psychology.

The past 6 months I've been doing sex research (open marriage and comarital sex), so it's very much on my mind. That I saw a lot of anatomy and sea animals is not surprising—my husband is a biologist, and I was once a surgical technician.

I'm not sure what my cognitive style is. I know I like to get to the point or heart of the matter quickly and not waste time getting there. In taking the Rorschach I was aware of wanting to put down what I saw and then move on. I am impatient when it comes to exploring new ground; I want to take it all in and not get too hung up at one point. My style wasn't sparse, but I can see it isn't rich either.

Student 19 was one of those whom we asked to write a short statement about her current life, with a view to relating it to her self-evaluation of some 15 years ago.

I thrive on a healthy dose of change, variety, and new experiences and will take risks to pursue alluring ventures. I love learning and discovering and even doing old things in new ways to keep my senses and attention sharp. I'm happiest when things feel in motion (not random motion but purposeful, with direction and meaning in some larger context), unhappiest when I feel stagnant, jammed against the flow of things.

In my life I've moved my home a great deal (to follow opportunities and to try out new places/people) and have worked at many types of jobs (newspaper reporter, laboratory research technician, teacher, clinician). As a psychologist I've worked in a community mental health center, hospitals, colleges, a think-tank, and private practices and enjoyed the variety. For fun my husband and I ride horses, go camping and canoeing, play guitars and sing, do research and writing together, walk and talk.

I've written one book (psychological poetry) and have another one (age-related self-descriptions) underway. I'd like to get back to doing more photography and show my photos in local crafts shows again.

All my life I've been active in vocal ensemble singing and continue musical activities wherever I am. Participation in the expressive arts are obviously a vital outlet of energy for me. Underneath it all I have spiritual concerns and want to devote more time and effort in this area, primarily through meditative practice.

I don't think I'll ever settle into one niche, though as I grow older (I'm 45) I feel more need to focus and deepen my involvements and be more selective. But my curiosity is as strong as ever and will undoubtedly propel me here and there as long as I can keep moving.

RORSCHACH RESPONSES, PSYCHOGRAM, AND SELF-EVALUATION OF STUDENT 20

Of the five students we have chosen to represent this general category we began with Student 19, the case that showed the closest approximation to absolute equality of M and C. We now proceed to make a differentiation between those individuals whose scores tend toward emphasis on M on the one hand, and those with greater color endowment on the other. Specifically, we are presenting the scores of $M:C$ = 8:4.5 and $M:C$ = 12:6.5 on the introversive side and those of $M:C$ = 4:8.5 and $M:C$ = 6:10.5 for the extroversives.

Student 20 is an excellent example of a richly endowed record where color predominates ($M:C$ = 6:10.5). Her Rorschach responses (Table 8-2), psychogram (Figure 8-3), self-evaluation, and an additional up-to-date comment now follow.

TABLE 8-2
Rorschach Responses of Student 20

Card I

1. It looks like a bat.	W	FM	A
2. Or a flying insect with well-defined body and protruding eyes and pincers. The peripheral outlines are not so distinct.	W	FM	A
3. It may have been pressed, like a pressed flower.	W	F, k	pla
4. The picture might also be of a moth with triangular markings. The moth is in flight with wings fully outstretched.	W + S	FM	A

TABLE 8-2
(Continued)

Card II

1. First, I saw the birth canal (in the center white), with blood dripping from the vagina. I can make out a clitoris and labia, and pubic hair also stained with blood. Very beautiful.	W + S	FC	sex, blood
2. I also see a space capsule just firing its rockets, with the smoke and fire from the explosions surrounding the capsule. The rocket could also be in space, traveling through the surrounding darkness.	D + S	F, m	obj
3. Also, an impressionistic watercolor, very sensuous and fluid, with a nice relationship between color and space	W	CF	art

Card III

1. A nice rendering of two African tribal women lifting a basket of wet wash or of goods to sell. They are doing a bit of a dance, leaning toward each other and stretching their spines.	W	M	H
2. The touch of red on the side of the womens' heads gives the picture a festive air. It looks like confetti or fireworks have been thrown.	D	FC, m	obj
3. The red in the center might be flowers just beyond the women.	D	CF, FK	pla
∨ 4. I see an enlargement of the head and thoracic section of a fly, with eyes bulging and feet in front.	W	F	A
5. I see a snow-covered mountain and its reflection in a pool of water below.	W + S	F, FC	ntr, art
< I also see trees at the edge of the water. It's a sort of Japanese line drawing with a touch of color.			

Card IV

1. An ancient, dappled scroll, unraveled	W	Fc	obj
2. A ground view of a troll leaning, or sitting on a tree stump, seen from behind	W	M	H
> 3. A stormy lake scene, with dark clouds reflected in the lake	W	F, K	ntr, clouds
∨ 4. I see a lamp hanging from a ceiling	D	F, Fc	obj

TABLE 8–2
(Continued)

Card IV			
with hook-shaped ornaments and delicately painted bottom-piece.			
5. I see a beak-faced person with stocky legs and big feet and thick tail standing on an iced-over pond. The perspective I have is looking up, from under the ice.	*W*	*(M), FK*	*(H)*

Card V			
1. It appeared to me as a bat or flying creature.	*W*	*FM*	*A*
2. I see the form of a rabbit in motion underneath a shadow of a fallen log or cloud or an arch of a hedge. How about a flying rabbit?	*W*	*FM, K*	*A*
> 3. Oh, it's a large-winged bird in flight with mouth open, calling or ready for attack.	*W*	*FM*	*A*
v 4. I see two female ballerinas, in long tutus, on pointe, en arabesque, facing each other. Their necks are long and they appear almost as swans. They might be dancing Swan Lake.	*W*	*M*	*H*

Card VI			
1. I see the skin of some beautiful cat, outstretched.	*W*	*Fc*	*A obj*
2. I see a monument with sun behind and reflection in a pool, a Taj Mahal.	*W*	*F*	arch
3. I also see a diagram of an erect penis, showing the urethra and testicles.	*D*	*F*	sex anat
> 4. Sideways, it is dusk on a lake, with a glimpse of the last bit of sun setting, and a streaking hydroplane splashing across the right. The left is tranquil with the gentle rocking of the remaining wake.	*W*	*F, FK, m*	ntr, obj
v 5. Upside down, I see a mercury-filled thermometer.	*D*	*F*	obj

Card VII			
1. Two winged cherubs, mounted on a revolving stand. They have their eyes closed and lips extended, as if trying	*W*	*M*	*H*

TABLE 8-2
(Continued)

Card VII

to kiss each other.			
2. Seeing the reverse image in the white space, it is a table lamp against a dark background.	*S + W*	*F*	obj
v 3. Upside down, it is a comfortable; worn old French armchair.	*W + S*	*Fc, F*	obj

---

Card VIII

1. A green mountain with some snow and evergreen trees.	*D*	*FC*	ntr
2. A surrealistic picture with pink rats emerging from a mass of others, attempting to tackle this mountain.	*W*	*FM, FC*	A, ntr
3. A rosebud, not open yet, so that its tips are still bluish.	*W*	*FC*	pla
v 4. A colored-in skeleton, with ribs and backbone showing—a textbook anatomical drawing.	*W*	*FC*	anat
5. A three-staged firecracker, exploding.	*W*	*FC, m*	expl

Card IX

1. A watercolor painted as if taken from a moving car, or in the rain, of a café lamppost in a French city at dusk. It is in the impressionistic style.	*W*	*FC*	art
2. One can see a thin reflection of a human figure in the lamppost.	*d*	*M*	*H*
v 3. Upside down, it's an erupting volcano.	*W*	*FC*	ntr, expl
4. This could also be a waterfall at sunset.	*D*	*CF*	ntr

Card X

1. Looking down on an artist's palette of paints. The colors are gaudy, modern, not very subtle.	*W*	*CF, FK*	art
2. The sort of Wow-Pop-Bang surrealistic hallucination scenes that Ken Russell throws in the movies he makes.	*W*	*CF, m*	art
v 3. Upside down, it's a flower just opening with visible leaves and stem and stamen and pollen. The card makes more sense to me in this position.	*W*	*FC*	pla
4. With the use of almost psychedelic,	*W*	*CF, m*	art

TABLE 8-2
(Continued)

Card X

artificial-hued colors and fine curli-
cue detail and fuller use of the space
on the card, it reminds me of some
of the recently popular "acid-art,"
with flashing lights (yellow) and
forms and colors melting.

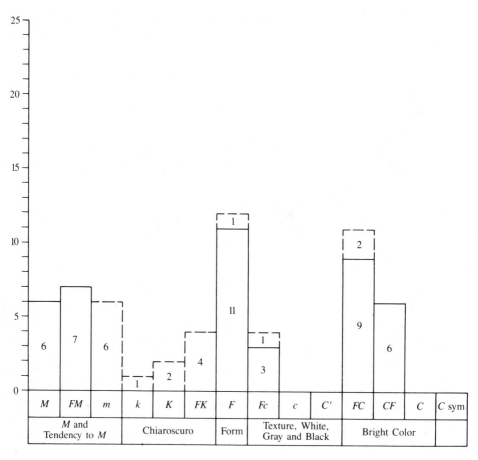

R 42
M:sum C   6:10.5
W:M   28:6
(FM + m):(Fc + c + C')   7:3
(H + A):(Hd + Ad)   14:10

W 66%   D 16%   d 2%   DdS 14%
A%   21
F%   26
FK + F + Fc   33%

FIG. 8-3.   A psychogram of Student 20

Self-Evaluation of Student 20

I remember waiting for the term to begin to take the Rorschach on the first day of classes. I was really looking forward to this hopefully more creative and fun approach to testing. I want to preface my self-report by saying that I was disappointed at having to share my cards with someone who had neglected to bring his. I felt somewhat restricted about when and whether to turn the cards as this person looked on. I thought of this test as a very personal experience and must confess that I was somewhat disappointed.

Over 66% of my responses were wholistically perceived. I think that percepts are naturally seen as wholes. I really saw my task as trying to make a complete gestalt, including appropriate details, of each card, unless some big detail seemed too obvious to ignore (such as the penis in Card VI). Card X especially frustrated me because I couldn't seem to make any sense of the whole thing that really satisfied me. I think this over-theoretical approach led to some rather poor *FC* and *CF* responses on this last card (the 'all-is confusion' sort of psychedelic art responses) and others because I felt the need to make everything in the inkblot "fit" into a grand scheme. My estimated average time per response was nearly 2 minutes. In part, I think this was due to having to share the cards. However, I also enjoyed elaborating and adding a bit of fantasy to some of the more interesting percepts. My *W* orientation may be one reason I have always done well in school as I have always been intrigued and fascinated by theory and the hope of integrating all my interests into an organizational framework. An example of effective *W* orientation, especially during my high school days, was my involvement with many organizations where I assumed leadership responsibilities. I was editor of my yearbook, captain of the cheerleaders one year, vice-president of my service club, etc.

The very lopsided *W:D* ratio may be exemplified by all my fantastic ideas for sewing and art projects, which are still half-finished in my closet! However, this may be sometimes offset by my slight *DdS* emphasis (I have been called very stubborn and will sometimes stubbornly stick to my own very impractical way of doing things) and my very powerful emotional side which finally "explodes" and moves me to action.

The *W:M* ratio is likewise very topheavy. On the negative side, it might classify me as intellectually shallow, spread a little too thin. I feel as though I do have a variety of interests and may tend to flit from one to the other. However. I also believe I can elaborate richly and organize details effectively as can be seen in some of the longer responses. I think it is very interesting that I have many big *D* girlfriends. This may be a way that I seek out good practical influences for myself. Also, I think some of my secondary anxiety responses represent a coping mechanism that I use: Namely, I sometimes need to feel a little pressure and anxiety in order to get tasks accomplished, since I'm not usually a very practical person. This is an example of how anxiety may be facilitative. I also think my secondary *FK* column points to a capacity to reflect ("reflections" in III, 5, IV, 3, VI, 2 and IX, 2) upon myself and become aware of when I get "carried away" in fantasy.

My *F*% is 26% which is optimal and probably quite necessary at times to keep my more impractical, emotional, and personalistic qualities in check. This more "objective" and universal approach can also be seen in the number of popular responses (9) and neutral content (objects = 7 + 1) and the initial formality in response to Card I.

The *FC* to *CF* to *Fc* proportions are in good balance in *FC* towering over my less directed emotions (*CF*) and sensitivity (*Fc*).

What is curious to me is the *M:*sum *C* ratio which is 6:10.5. This might put me in the extrovert category. I'm afraid that even in my cheerleader days I was somewhat shy, and most of my friends would say I'm very warm and friendly once we have become close but on the surface I am hardly what people would call outgoing. If one can put any stock in the (*FM* + *m*):(*Fc* + *c* + *C'*) ratio, it might substantiate my feeling that I have always been more introverted than otherwise. I also think this can be coupled with my secondary *FK* column, which indicates I am able to reflect upon myself and can be introspective at times. I have lived alone now for several years (with two cats) and enjoy very much my time alone to play the piano, to bake, to garden, to read and write. I feel as if I have adequate inner resources and potential to keep myself happy and contented when I am alone. At times, I am lonely and feel the need for close friends to talk with in nonacademic environments. The environment does indeed impinge upon my moods and I see the world as a very colorful place where a 'waterfall at sunset' (IX, 4) or 'dusk on a lake' (VI, 4) evoke tranquil, peaceful feelings and 'a three-staged firecracker' (VIII, 5) and 'an erupting volcano' (IX, 3) seem to charge me with life.

The secondary *m* column may indicate that I am able or trying to deal with problems that arise from the pressures of graduate school and interpersonal conflicts. I suppose I do feel there are many demands placed on me right now from my current research project and graduate school requirements. However, these are secondary and I do believe that I have the resources and the choice to do what I would like to do with my life.

I gave six *M* responses and I notice that the most pleasing and fully developed ones are females who are facing or leaning toward each other, usually dancing. I think this, coupled with the female sexual response at the beginning of Card II, might reflect my increasing satisfaction and awareness of what it's like to be a woman. I am especially intrigued by the sexual birth response, as it may be an indication of what I'm experiencing now in my life. I have also been involved recently with the National Organization of Women's consciousness-raising groups.

My male figures, if they are indeed male, are not as well-developed. The thin human figure (IX, 2) I felt was a male and the troll and beak-faced person in Card IV are certainly questionably-good males. Also, I am 'looking up' at the figure in IV, 5. I don't necessarily want to interpret this psychoanalytically. My male sexual response (an anatomical diagram of a penis) is quite in contrast to my beautiful female sexual birth response. Yet I have some very warm and alive relationships with men; however at the time we took the Rorschach I was feeling disappointed about a particularly emotionally unsatisfying relationship with a male.

Content was nicely diversified with some emphasis on nature, plants, and art. I feel strongly anchored in these areas, but with a variety of interests and potential that is nice to have to rely on.

I would like to close with my next to last response instead of the last one on the last card. This was a flower just opening with visible leaves, stem, stamen and pollen. I would like to interpret this as seeing the possibilities for personal growth as rich, alive and pregnant, realizing that possibilities become reality only through action.

From the perspective of a decade subsequent to taking the course and writing her own self-evaluation, Student 20 contributed the following:

In reading over my self-assessment of 10 years ago, I was struck by the continuing common themes in my life. In addition, however, I wondered whether I would continue to be so strongly ambi-equal if I was to take the Rorschach for the first time now.

Developmentally, I do feel I was encouraged at an early age by my father, both by his words and example, to be "well-rounded" and adventurous. He has always had what I would describe as an optimistic and adventurous outlook. However, I also feel that he has had difficulty in feeling really satisfied from the inside about much of his work, and that was something I saw in him that I wanted to overcome in myself. So I now feel that while I continue to be involved in many activities, my focus has become at least a little narrower, and I realize that for me to feel satisfied with a job I have done I very well may have to sacrifice some of my other interests. But I am getting ahead of myself.

I experience often in myself a sense of restlessness, of being unable to sit still for very long, of being bored by repetitive tasks or even by repeating the same creative project. I enjoy new ideas but feel I do not always see them through without becoming distracted. On the positive side, I feel I have an emotionally richer life; I currently enjoy having both a private practice and teaching at a college (I have returned part time this year and will return full time this fall after a hiatus of 6 years from college teaching). I feel personally as though the experience of mothering a child has taught me so much about my own childhood and about being a therapist and unconditional love that I am very pleased I decided to have a child. For a long time, I was not sure whether it would be possible for me to have an academic career and also be a mother in the way that I would like and I hope I am achieving that.

Professionally, my decision to enter and stay in psychology was a difficult one. While I now feel that psychology is an absolutely perfect choice for me in so many ways, I had a tough time coming to that conclusion. I was always equally skilled in language and math and considered (at least briefly) careers in math, medicine or architecture and dreamed of artistic vocations such as drama or the visual arts. Somehow, with some interest and some luck, I ended up in graduate school in psychology. Graduate school was a very stimulating time in my life but upon entering academia after my Ph.D., I felt narrowly tracked and not sure how I might have a private practice, an academic career and a family too. I wanted what I called "some life experience" outside academia. So I got some: I got out of academia for six years, I got married to a doctor, I had a child and I worked at deepening my skills as as a psychotherapist. However, even during that time, I couldn't resist the lure of research and got hired as a consultant to a clinic to do a follow-up study of Down's syndrome children. Now I feel I have got "some life experience" and feel pleased and grateful to return to academia with a richer base of experience, both personally and professionally.

In addition to my work as a psychotherapist and psychology professor, I have a number of social interests that confirm my sense of self. I am physically active playing tennis on a team and running several times weekly. My wonderful and intense experiences as a mother have led me to a Mothers' Lodge support group with women from varied lifestyles (married, single, lesbian), which is an incredibly rich and nourishing activity for me. I enjoy solitude as well as quiet moments with my daughter or my cat. I attend a unique church called The First Existentialist Church which also challenges my spiritual side. So it seems I still have a full and varied life, yet the difference now seems to be that I have sought out activities that will be particularly satisfying just for me, unique yes, but also personally relevant.

RORSCHACH RESPONSES, PSYCHOGRAM, AND SELF–EVALUATION OF STUDENT 21

Student 21, taking the test in his fifties, was already established in a responsible position in the educational field.

In his self-evaluation, he spoke of a "self" who has met and handled a variety of situations and played an authoritative role within various groups.

He is of interest to us not only because he comes from a different age group among student psychologists, but because he, like Student 22, demonstrated ambi-equalness where color scores are dominant.

There is still too little known about how Rorschach himself envisaged an extrovert, as opposed to those with ambi-equal scores showing good color. Studies with large populations (Harrower, 1955b) may allow more precise definitions of both types to emerge.

TABLE 8–3
Rorschach Responses of Student 21

Card I			
1. 2 elephants or donkeys attached to a top or bell	W	FM, F	A
2. Dress dummy with see-through skirt	D	Fc	obj
3. 2 small dog heads (on top)	de	F	Ad
Card II			
1. 2 hats—red	D	FC	obj
2. 2 masks—red	D	FC	obj
3. 2 elephants kissing	W	FM	A
4. Female sex organs suggested by redness and shape of what looks like vaginal opening	D	CF	sex

TABLE 8-3
(Continued)

Card III

1. 2 musicians playing drum	W	M	H
2. Bow tie of red tuffets	D	FC, c	obj
3. Falling birds shot down	D	F, m	A
4. Falling flame	D	CF, m	fire

Card IV

1. Ape from the back	W	FM	A
2. Animal or bear rug	W	Fc	obj, A
3. Tree stump	D	F	obj, pla

Card V

1. Bat flying	W	FM	A
2. 2 jaws—animal	D	F	Ad
3. Nut cracker	D	F	obj
4. 2 male sex organs	D	F	sex

Card VI

1. Rug (animal)	W	Fc	A, obj	P
2. Hoof	D	F	Ad	
3. 2 Siamese old men (upside down)	W	M	H	
4. 2 profile masks	W	F	obj	
5. Faces of gargoyles	W	F	Hd	
6. Penis penetrating a vagina (sex act)	W	F	sex	

Card VII

1. Faces of two women conversing	D	F, m	Hd
2. 2 masques	D	F	obj
3. 2 Siamese animals whose exact shape is hard to define	D	FM	A
4. Inverted—two dogs kissing 2 horses' heads	W	FM	A

Card VIII

1. Coat of arms	W	F	obj
2. 2 animals climbing (red)	D	F/C	A
3. A blue corset	D	F/C	obj
4. 2 flags—blue	D	FC	obj
5. Helping hands	D	F	Hd
			sym

Card IX

1. Violin	D	F	obj
2. Key	D	F	obj

TABLE 8-3
(Continued)

Card IX			
3. 2 grotesque green faces (facing outward)	*D*	*F/C*	*Hd*
4. 2 pigs' snouts and faces, green—facing inward	*D*	*F/C*	*Ad*
5. 2 monks in pale orange garments seated and playing on some kind of instrument	*W*	*M*	*H*
6. A pale purple base or rocks	*D*	*FC*	obj

Card X			
1. Underwater photography in color (National Geographic)	*W*	*CF*	pla
2. 2 divers in reddish tank suits and grey helmets working underwater amidst an underwater scene of beautiful flowers and colored fish	*W*	*M, CF*	*H,* pla

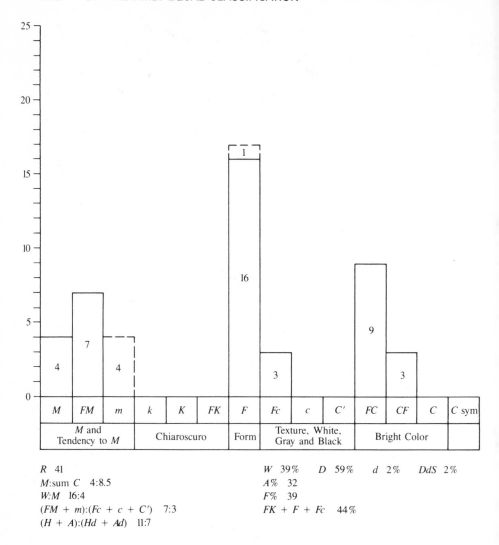

FIG. 8-4. A psychogram of Student 21

Self-Evaluation of Student 21

This record consists of a total of 41 responses, a bit above average. A study of the responses themselves indicates also a fairly good form level. These two factors would indicate a person of generally good perception and awareness of reality. In addition, a better than average number of *W*s (39%) with good form indicates a person with organizational ability and capacity for abstract and creative thinking.

The *D*s also occur in high proportion, a bit above average. This person would appear to be practical and possessing a degree of common sense, but with a tendency toward recognition of the obvious. The infinitesimal number of small *d*s (2%) seems to indicate an avoidance of small details. This individual probably does not like to handle minutiae but prefers that his secretaries do so. This person seems to be the executive type, more interested in over-all decision-making than in carrying out the little details.

The moderate number of *F* scores (39%) would indicate here a degree of stability and control and a clear awareness of reality. When to this are added a fair number of *Fc* scores and a good proportion of color scores (9 *FC*, 3 *CF*), we have indication of a fairly rich personality. The *Fc* scores indicate a fair sensitivity to people, a mature approach to life, tactfulness in social relations, and a general awareness of the finer distinctions in his world. The high *FC* scores and the moderate *CF* scores indicate a rich emotional life under fairly good control, although the *CF* score might indicate some occasional tendency toward impulsive behavior. Spontaneity and creativity might well be among his characteristics.

The four *M* scores are indicative of a feeling for people, ego strength, self-sufficiency, and a capacity for a rich and imaginative inner life. With the strong *M* and *Fc* scores, we can feel fairly certain that here is a person with empathy. Chances are he likes himself and others too.

The *FM* scores (7) indicate that this individual has a lusty animal instinct with lots of energy and drive. The content analysis reveals a fair variety of interests for the release of this drive and energy; but, with sex indicated three times in content, one suspects a strong sex drive or some problems in this area. The lack of other evidence of problems in the forms of anxiety or repression (excess of *K, k,* or *m*) would minimize the possibility of a sex problem. One might therefore suspect that this person had had psychotherapy, an experience which encourages openness in expressing sexual interests.

The ratio of *M* to sum *C* is 7 to 8.5. This would indicate that he seeks his satisfactions more readily from environmental factors than from his inner life, as rich as it may seem from the record.

The ratio of *W:M* is 16:4 or 4:1. This would indicate that this individual has an ambition or drive that goes considerably beyond his creative potential. He probably has some frustration resulting from the inability to achieve the goals he has set for himself. The three additional *m* scores indicate that such frustration may exist, but since it is secondary (additional), it is apparently being adequately controlled.

An examination of the content reveals a personality that is generally warm and accepting rather than hostile and fighting. Elephants are seen kissing; dog and horse head are seen kissing; the divers on Card X frequently seen fighting, are here seen as working amidst a peaceful under-water scene of beauty; the hands on Card VIII are seen as helping hands.

An original response like the blue corset must represent some meaning probably related to the examinee's childhood, perhaps a sexual response related to his mother.

Masques are seen three times in the record. These are sometimes considered as a camouflage to avoid exposure or detection. What is he hiding? Here again we get a suggestion of some repression of emotions or of unresolved problems.

In general, we see here an above-average, stable individual, the executive type, with a practical view of the world and with good human relations. He would probably make a good administrator in a school situation or a social work agency. His rich inner life and ego strength would produce a degree of creative leadership which he would tactfully yet firmly pursue and develop. Any underlying problems or frustrations he may have he is apparently handling well.

I believe that this record coincides very well with what I know about myself. I find the following to be some of my most significant qualities, which the Rorschach record has illustrated:

1. Common sense, practicality
2. Delegation of details to subordinates and enjoyment of decision-making, with considerable involvement of subordinates in this decision-making through executive conferences.
3. Moderately rich inner life. I am capable of spending much time alone, working, thinking, planning in areas of interests, although rarely stopping to enjoy some of the nuances of experience because of the drive to work.
4. Ambitions with principles. On two recent occasions I refused advancement "with strings attached." I felt great conflict about this at the time of decision.
5. Excellent human relations. I have especially good relations with staff below my authority and with my peers. I have moderately good relations with superiors. While I am tactful, respectful, and generally conforming, I refuse to kow-tow or be obsequious, a prerequisite for advancement for special consideration. I find some subtle conflict between my own creative leadership and the effort of some superiors to resist creative change. I frequently feel mild frustration in this area.
6. Executive ability. As an educator, I have always run a well-organized school with excellent pupil and teacher morale. This fact has led my

superiors to assign me, on two occasions, to problem schools requiring good human relations and strong organization.

7. Response to the obvious. I sometimes find myself impressed by the obvious and then surprised when others see the relationship too.

8. Strong emotions. My feelings are strong but I keep them under control. I have great patience and tolerance for failure, inefficiency, inadequacy, hostility. I am slow to anger but can become violent when anger is finally aroused.

9. Sensitivity. I am sensitive to tears in the movies. I respond only to vigorous music; I cannot carry a tune myself. I respond to visual artistic expression and nuances of color. I like both strong and soft colors.

10. Strong sex drive. I have strong sex drives but control them within acceptable limits. I enjoy immensely my associations with females, professional and social. I like stately older women and petite younger ones, but I do not respond to obese women, except to feel sorry for them.

11. Great energy. I feel best when I am in motion and expending physical energy, usually through rapid walking. Most associates have a hard time keeping up with me either on the street or about the school building I administer.

12. Distaste for minor detail. I have one major failing, according to my wife. Because of my many interests, my library is extensive and I spend much money on books in a variety of fields. While she does not object to this, she does object to the fact that I save clippings and correspondence of interest. My files are bulging; my cartons fill every corner in attic and basement; for long periods my desk is cluttered because I am busy. My wife feels all this messes the house. She is unquestionably right; it does. But I find it difficult to part with a book, a pamphlet, a letter, a clipping which interests me or which I feel I may refer to again. This may be a reflection of my distaste for handling minutiae.

13. Self-confidence; good self-image.

14. Unresolved problems. I suspect that I have some unresolved problems relating to my animal urges or repressed hostility. Evidence is in the occasional nightmares I have, always dealing with violence. I am usually being pursued by criminals with guns. On the night after I worked on this exam and this answer, my wife claims that I shouted out three times in my sleep. Upon waking I had no recollection of what had troubled me.

15. In general, I feel I have a satisfying life but time is running too fast. I have a very strong life urge and am troubled by the thought of nonexistence.

There seems to be at least a 90%, or better, correlation between my Rorschach record and my own personal description.

RORSCHACH RESPONSES, PSYCHOGRAM, AND SELF-EVALUATION OF STUDENT 22

Our next self-evaluator, Student 22, had an $M:C$ ratio of 8:4.5, the exact reverse of student 21; both being variants of Rorschach's ambi-equal record.

While her scores and initial experiences favor the introversive side, color is still more than adequately represented, so that the ambi-equal classification is now justified. One of the interesting aspects of her self-evaluation, as she reviewed her own development, is that she recognized and actually experienced herself as becoming ambi-equal, after a markedly introverted childhood.

Twenty-Two decides to provide for herself a frame of reference within the more general context of writing a self-evaluation. She chose to assess herself in terms of her potential effectiveness as a clinical psychologist. Her concept of clinical psychology showed insight and awareness of some of the personal qualities necessary for the role. In this connection, her knowledge of her own sensitivity and vulnerability in clinical situations was dealt with, for, sooner or later, all clinicians have to face the problem of involvement in the suffering of others and the need to develop the capacity of distancing themselves.

Twenty-Two took the course and responded to the Rorschach cards at a moment of feeling great well-being: "Right now I am enormously happy. . . . " Her Rorschach record (Table 8–4), psychogram (Figure 8–5), and self-evaluation follow.

TABLE 8–4
Rorschach Responses of Student 22

Card I				
1. Two winged gryphons, or lions: joined as though flanking either side a shield or coat of arms	*W*	*F*	obj	*P*

Card II				
1. Butterfly	*D*	*FM, FC*	*A*	
2. Stingray fish	*S*	*FM*	*A*	
3. Hookah-smoking caterpillar in Alice in Wonderland	*W*	*FM*	*(A)*	
4. Grey colored areas give a feeling of softness, shadow	*W*	*c, C'*		

Card III				
1. Head and thorax of a bug	*W*	*F*	*Ad*	
2. Owl's head with red eyes	*D*	*FC*	*Ad*	

TABLE 8-4
(Continued)

Card III				
3. Two humans—females, holding something in common	W	M	H	P

Card IV				
1. Frog with large hind legs	W	FM	A	
2. Winged creature	W	FM	A	

Card V				
1. Butterfly or bat	W	FM	A	P
2. Open mouth of a bird	de	F	Ad	
3. Top view, front of a bird (not a long perspective)	de, S	F	Ad	
4. Feeling of a bat flying	W	FM	A	

Card VI				
1. Indian totem—perhaps a thunderbird	D	Fc	obj	
2. Pope or bishop standing in robes with a mitered hat and outspread arms	D	M	H	
3. Two people talking	d	M	H	
4. Slug with feelers	di	FM	A	

Card VII				
1. Two elephants, back to back with trunks raised, as though in the circus	W	FM	A	
2. Two Indians—feathers sticking up	W	M, Fc	H	
3. Two women dancing	W	M	H	

Card VIII				
1. Two bears	D	FM	A	P
2. Animal climbing on rocks with a mirror image in a lake	W	FM, FK	ntr, A	
3. Wizard or being, hat, full robes	W	M, FC	(H)	
4. Piece of petrified wood	D	CF	obj	

Card IX				
1. Two humans with electrical energy passing between their fingertips	D	M	H	
2. Pelvic bones	D	F	anat	
3. Slice of ham	D	CF	Food	

TABLE 8-4
(Continued)

Card IX			
4. Two humans, crouching with arms outstretched with open hands	*D*	*M*	*H*

Card X			
1. Undersea world	*W*	*FC*	ntr
2. Esophagus, two lungs	*D*	*F*	anat.
3. Chick embryos	*D*	*FC*	*A*
4. Rosebuds	*D*	*F*	pla
5. Blue spider mums with leaves	*D*	*FC*	pla
6. Nuclear medicine scan of kidneys	*D*	*Fk*	anat

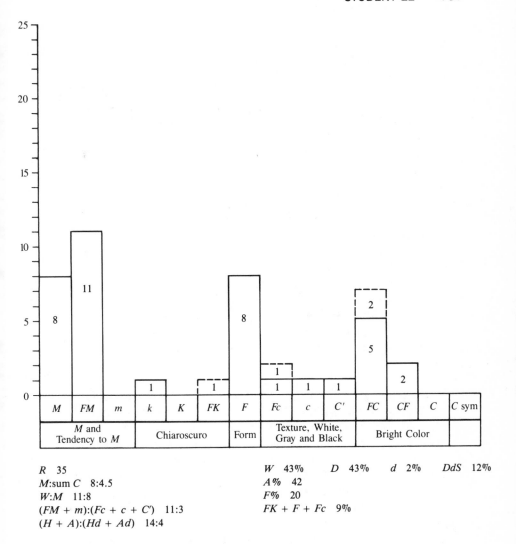

M	FM	m	k	K	FK	F	Fc	c	C'	FC	CF	C	C sym
8	11					8				5	2		
			1		1		1	1	1				

M and Tendency to M		Chiaroscuro			Form	Texture, White, Gray and Black			Bright Color			

R   35

M:sum C   8:4.5

W:M   11:8

(FM + m):(Fc + c + C')   11:3

(H + A):(Hd + Ad)   14:4

W   43%   D   43%   d   2%   DdS   12%

A%   42

F%   20

FK + F + Fc   9%

FIG. 8-5. A psychogram of Student 22

Self-Evaluation of Student 22

The analysis of one's own Rorschach is an exciting and unique experience. It is a rare opportunity to have such a tool of self-evaluation to provide a frame of reference. In the Rorschach we find an instrument to interact with personally, which can provide the insights of countless other records, while allowing individuality of response in form, content, and sequence. I jotted down my feelings after taking the Rorschach. Overall I was exhausted, and surprised that a task I had approached with skeptisism and "distance" had taken so much out of me. For evaluation purposes, I have chosen the potential effectiveness as a clinical psychologist for my frame of reference.

Overall manner of approach stresses whole responses rather than Ds, yielding a theoretical perspective. The emphasis on the whole is important for evaluating the whole client, and the Ds are not so poorly evidenced to inhibit analytical thinking. Moderately elevated Dd + S exposes a personal approach to things. All of these, given their proportions, I think are important to the clinician in his role as therapist. I think it is important to note the Dd + S, personal input or interpretation, and keep it in mind with respect to the rest of the record. The W:M ratio is not the optimum 2:1 ratio; here the M is slightly elevated. This has the potential to balance the elevated overall theoretical response style with strong inner resources. Hypothetically the clinician needs to be able to see the person as a whole, to break things down for analysis and synthesize them once again into a whole. Also therapy is an interpersonal interaction, so the ability to personalize the analysis and synthesis is important. It is especially important to balance the theoretical or the abstract with internal human aspects.

The total number of responses is in a comfortable range, not forced into the upper ranges nor reduced into the lower ranges. Average time per response is rather lengthy, here a function to some extent, of resisting the instrument initially and also a matter of taking utmost care with the task. Again in the light of a clinician, care and commitment is important. For the clinical student some resistance and skepticism is important for evaluation and development of one's own role. My earlier comment that I was impressed at how involved I became in the task emphasizes the potential for involvement. Here skepticism was utilized to gain perspective not to limit involvement.

High FM and M shows a person with high energy and strong drive with a lot of inner life to support it. Drive is important in any profession; it is crucial as a graduate student to keep "plugging away." What is important with this drive, however, is a strong M column to provide direction and depth for the drive. Without inner resources, the drive might yield very little as it would have little direction (it would be a less mature energy).

Color is a large aspect of this record. High FC indicates skill in handling emotions in a socially acceptable manner (getting along with people). Yet the CFs provide depth and meaningfulness to the FC expression which can be superficial. Emotions here are strong and open, perhaps too strong for the objective clinician? Since they are primarily *FC,* sufficient control is apparent.

The *F%* is slightly less than optimum (20%), nothing necessarily to be concerned about, yet a hint of vulnerability. The *Fc, c, C'* responses expose a sensitive, tactful side. Perhaps this sensitivity coupled with possible vulnerability yields a therapist who is "too sensitive," to himself or the pain of others. The additional *FK* points out the potential to remove oneself when the occasion demands it. Definitely a point to be developed for the clinician.

M:sum *C* is left to wind things up, not because it is less important, but *because* of its importance. Within Rorschach's framework this is an introvert.[1] This, in my estimation is a good place for a therapist. Working with people, constantly dealing with their conflicts and problems, it seems important to have a strong inner life to bear the weight. The introversion here is not so extreme as to remove one from people. Rather the strong *C* element indicates enjoying people and emotions. The stronger *M,* however, provides strength and depth for the clinician's role.

The general picture, then, is rather favorable for the potential clinician: The ability to synthesize, analyze his world, strong personal input and unique perspective, drive and inner strength to support it, sensitivity that has the potentiality of perspective when necessary, strong, open emotions and an introspective basis for reflection and recuperation.

The record appears to be of someone with considerable strength for a clinician's role. Where exactly do I fit in to all of this? In general, I was not surprised by the record. The abstract, synthetic approach is readily apparent from my "success" in academia. I am an "intellectual" type, always enjoyed school, manipulating theories and constructs. The *D%* seems appropriate as well. With everyday matters, I am sufficiently practical to take care of things that have to be done. As a matter of fact I am perpetually amazing my roomates with taking care of household matters. There is no question, however, that I prefer not to spend an enormous amount of time breaking up my world into these practical parts. The *Dd + S%* is very representative of my style. I think I have a rather unique response style to my world and cognitively I think that this type of style is important. Quite frankly I am bored by those who are too "matter of fact" about their world and do not have a strong personal response to their environment. Again my perception of myself is reinforced by those around me who comment that I am quite unique in my perception and response to

---

[1]Actually, within Rorschach's framework this individual shows an ambi-equal orientation.

the world. There is more to indicate this than just $Dd + S$. The $W:M$ ratio points to this as well. Strong inner life has enormous impact on the way I synthesize my world. I do not feel, however, that it is so large as to swamp my ability to deal with things as they really are. I rarely if ever feel that I am overwhelmed by my personal input. I rather enjoy it!

Drive and energy are two very strong characteristics I have attributed to myself. I am happiest when involved in numerous activities and accomplishing a wide variety of projects. School is important to me and achieving well demands a good deal of time. I need to balance this with weaving and artistic creation, growing plants, etc. The high FM is perhaps some indicant of impulsive energy. At times I make rapid decisions, and I tend to plunge into new projects. Impulsiveness or maybe spontaneity well characterize my approach.

Moderately low $F\%$ highlights a vulnerability that others relate to me, that often I am not aware of myself. The level of my sensitivity is somewhat reflected in the psychogram; however, I expected it to be more elevated. I am sensitive to others' feelings, to others' pain and am moderately concerned by my lack of objectivity at times. Observing clients at the Psychology Clinic, I find myself upset and depressed over their problems, or life situations. I often house strangers in trouble without regard to my own safety, and am considered by some to be foolish and too involved for my own good. The additional FK shows the potential to remove or distance myself when necessary. This is one potential strength that needs development. I know that I have utilized it in the past. I worked as a candystriper in a hospital during high school. Initially I ached my whole shift, with others' pain. I had to learn to distance myself in order to do my job effectively, and truly care for them. During college I worked with emotionally disturbed children. Again I felt so much for them initially that my job was quite difficult. It required less time, however, for me to balance my caring for them and my objectivity in order to work effectively. I am also sensitive to my own feelings. I commit myself entirely to my environment: people and activities. This personal commitment exposes me to distress which others, who are more removed, avoid. This distress is not so severe as to make life miserable, rather it gives depth. This depth is further reflected by my emotions.

The psychogram shows strong affect. I guess I consider myself someone who enjoys, explores and expands her feelings. The $M:$sum C ratio is interesting, especially in relation to $FM + M:Fc + c + C'$.

The introversion is more marked in the latter, in fact dramatically so. If this is interpreted as a developmental phenomenon, it is apparent that at this point I am tending more toward ambi-equal. I think this is the case. As a child I was very introspective, almost to extreme, preferring to be by myself. Now I am excited and stimulated by people, as well as satisfied to be by myself. In fact I often seek time just for myself.

The psychogram presents a very positive picture. What is more interesting to me is the content. Obviously the popular responses are there, not in enormous abundance, aging pointing my personal perceptual style. The *A%* is high, yielding a childlike quality. In examining these *A*s there is high fantasy and playful content: II, 3—*hookah-smoking caterpillar* from Alice in Wonderland; V, 1—*2 elephants back to back with raised trunks as though in the circus.* Also response I, 1—*gryphons,* shows mythical beings. I think this childlike or playful quality reflects an open, almost naive (childlike) response style which may bring difficulty with my vulnerability. On the other hand, it yields a unique experience level often lost in adulthood. *M* responses are also interesting in that a few have symbolic or powerful roles: VI, 2—*bishop in regalia with arms outstretched;* VIII, 1—*wizard;* IX, 1—*two people with electrical energy (power or communication) passing between their fingertips.* People are important to me and powerful influences on my life, as well represented by the content. Another interesting aspect of content are the three anatomical responses. I was a premedical student as an undergraduate and come from a family of doctors (father, mother, brother). In fact, I am a bit of a surprise for them pursuing psychology. A rather unique response, whose meaning I am not sure exactly how to interpret, is II, 4—*grey colored areas give a feeling of softness.* In this I saw no form, I just had a "feeling" of softness texture and shadow. Perhaps symbolically this is an aspect of sensuality.

In addition, the first and last responses are of interest. I, 1 is form ruled, an object, a rather distant "How do you do" to the instrument. The content is rather personal, though, gryphons or lions, mythically very powerful beasts. The last response—*nuclear machine scan of kidneys*—is the only indication of anxiety, especially important since it is the last response. It was obviously the last moment possible to expose this element within myself.

The record reveals a positively developed and developing individual. To a certain extent I am embarrassed. I feel this paper has been a thesis on "how wonderful I am" or have the capacity to be. Partially this is a function of where I am in space and time. Right now I am enormously happy. I am in graduate school, pursuing a goal I have held for years. I am intellectually stimulated and challenged. There is some anxiety reflected in the record. There is no readily apparent conflict. Having been generously blessed as a human with many capabilities and at the same time living in a healthful environment, the Rorschach is not perhaps such a surprise.

RORSCHACH RESPONSES, PSYCHOGRAM, AND SELF–EVALUATION OF STUDENT 23

Our fifth example in the ambi-equal group showed a more marked introversive trend but nonetheless offsets this with strong and excellent color, her $M:C$ ratio being 13:7.5.

Student 23 offered us one of the most lively and colorful reactions to the Rorschach inkblots. Apart from her clearly ambi-equal development, with excellent movement and color responses, there is a very wide range of interests and obviously well assimilated cultural references.

The field of art is handled with genuine familiarity, as for example, "a lamp which produces light à la Van Gogh" and "ceiling paintings of biblical figures in a few cathedrals in Rome." There is a spontaneity about her observations with no attempt to impress. Human beings are expressing a variety of moods, both active and passive: skiing, dancing, exercising "bending back touching their legs"; as well as "having a conversation," "holding hands," "warming their hands over a stove," "sleeping or daydreaming."

Throughout the record there is a liveliness and *joie de vivre* which is conveyed to the reader. Very sharp perceptions impart the feeling of an ongoing visual experience rather than passive reaction. The taking of this record is, to quote Rorschach, "a task experienced as play." Student 23's Rorschach record appears in Table 8-5, her psychogram in Figure 8-5.

TABLE 8-5
Rorschach Responses of Student 23

Card I

1. Two Cossacks dancing, holding hands together. They are wearing kind of furry coats and hats and boots. They seem friendly, and dancing the familiar Russian dance.	W	M, Fc	H, cloth
2. They could also be angels or Santa Clauses, because they seem to have beards and wings. They look glad and joyous.	W	M	H
3. A crown (just the form)	W	F	obj
4. A torn apron (shading & texture)	W	Fc	cloth
5. Two people, could be skiers, wearing heavy fur coats and hats, a scarf on			

TABLE 8–5
(Continued)

Card I

their neck. They are talking to each other. It's windy, the scarves are flying.	W	M, Fc, Fm	H, cloth
6. A woman in the center, her hands lifted. Praying or dancing.	D	M	H
7. Two birds, their wings in a dynamic position, as if that very moment they stopped flying and rested on some rocks	D	FM	A, nat

Card II

1. Two bears dancing around a fire, with their paws touching each other	W	FM, CF	A, fire
2. Rabbits resting on rocks (without the red parts on top)	W	FM	A
3. Two people sitting on small stools warming their hands over a stove, having a conversation	W	M, FC	H, obj
4. A white Chinese lamp with light à la Van Gogh	DS	FC', CF	obj
5. A red butterfly	D	FC	A

Card III

1. Two women making food or washing clothes or carrying a basket. They seem to be talking to each other	W	M, F	H, obj
2. In the background wall decorations or lamps	D	FC	art
3. A red butterfly	D	FC	A
4. Or a bow tie	D	FC	cloth
5. Acrobats on trapeze	D	M	H
6. A view of a road, trees at the horizon, and two squirrels sitting on the side looking at their tails (perspective, card upside-down)	W	FK, FM	nat, A
7. Head of giraffe	D	F	Ad

Card IV

1. A big bear	W	F	A
2. A person wearing heavy boots (unproportional, upper side too small)	W	M, Fc	H, cloth
3. An animal rug	W	Fc	A, obj
4. Upper part of a vase with handles	D	F	obj
5. Head of a crocodile swimming out of the mud	D	FM, Fc	Ad nat

TABLE 8–5
(Continued)

Card IV			
6. Head of a Lassie dog from the back	D	F	Ad
7. Two dancers in an exercise bending back touching their legs	d	M	H
8. A flower	d	F	plant
9. A man's profile with a big nose	de	F	Hd

Card V			
1. A butterfly or a bat flying	W	FM	A
2. Two people leaning on a tree, their arms folded, their legs stretched, sleeping or daydreaming	W	M, F	H, plant
3. A dancer in the middle of a dance, holding two dancers on both sides	W	M	H
4. A rabbit between rocks	D	FM	A, nat

Card VI			
1. A guitar, or a caricature of an old broken guitar	W	F	obj
2. A night butterfly	D	F	A
3. Two heads with arms lifted. Could be two people praying (looks like ceiling paintings of biblical figures in a few cathedrals in Rome)	D	M	Hd, art
4. A head of a man with a beard	D	F	Hd

Card VII			
1. Two women with pony tails in profile, sculpture-like	D	F	art, Hd
2. Heads of bears with horns, funny, like fairy tales	D	F	Ad
3. Two squirrels with long ears sitting on rocks watching the landscape	D	FM	A, nat
4. Two poodles looking at each other	D	FM	A
5. Rocks in the desert, or canyon (reminds me of the landscape in the Negev in Israel)	W	Fc	nat
6. A horseshoe eaten by rust	W	Fc	obj

Card VIII			
1. Two cats or rats climbing on rocks	W	FM, F	A, nat
2. A hanging lamp or decoration, mobile	W	FC	art
3. A starfish or crab	D	F	A
4. Heads of frogs sticking their heads from the water colored by the sunset	D	FM, CF	A, nat

TABLE 8-5
(Continued)

Card VIII			
5. Two blue flags	D	FC	obj
6. A sunset on a lake	W	CF	nat
7. A modern painting, harmony. The cold colors send "messengers" to the warm colors	W	C symb	art

Card IX			
1. A glass of ice cream	D	FC	food, obj
2. A head of a baby	D	F	Hd
3. Two persons playing a flute, wearing long orange gowns	D	M, FC	H, cloth, obj
4. A head of a horse looking from behind a colorful curtain (mainly the colors of the curtain)	W	CF, FM	obj, Ad

Card X			
1. Two starfish or crabs	D	F	A
2. A view in the sea, sea creatures and plants	W	FC	nat
3. Two jumping rabbits	D	FM	A
4. Profiles of young girls (just form)	Dr	F	Hd
5. Lions sitting looking at each other	D	FM	A
6. A galloping horse	D	FM	A
7. A painting board of a painter	W	CF	obj, art
8. Two dolphins with a ball, holding it together like in the circus	D	FM, F	A, obj
9. Spring	W	C symb	abst
10. Eiffel tower in Paris	D	F	obj
11. Boots	D	F	obj
12. A mobile, colorful	W	FC	art
13. Saxophones	D	F	obj

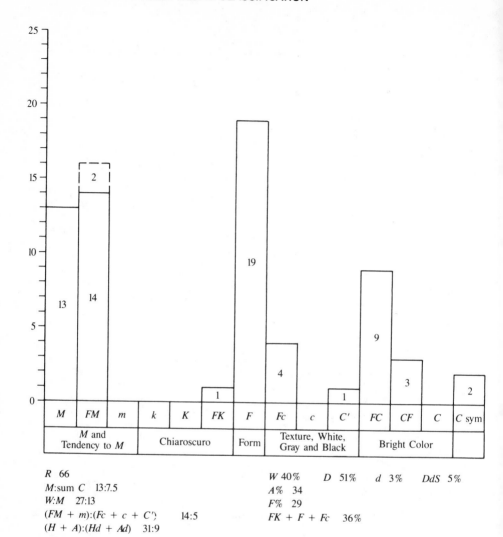

M	FM	m	k	K	FK	F	Fc	c	C'	FC	CF	C	C sym
13	14 (2)					19	4		1	9	3		2
									1				
M and Tendency to M			Chiaroscuro			Form	Texture, White, Gray and Black			Bright Color			

R 66

M:sum C   13:7.5

W:M   27:13

$(FM + m):(Fc + c + C')$ 14:5

$(H + A):(Hd + Ad)$ 31:9

W 40%   D 51%   d 3%   DdS 5%

A% 34

F% 29

FK + F + Fc   36%

FIG. 8-6.   A psychogram of Student 23

Self-Evaluation of Student 23

At present I am studying for the M.A. and working as a research assistant for the second year. I plan to continue my studies toward the doctorate. I find academic work interesting and satisfying. I also have interest in clinical work and actually started a clinical program in Israel. (My "coming back" to the experimental field was not planned. My husband had to come to New York for a few years and it was too late to apply to most schools.)

I was working for 2 years in a vocational guidance institute and served in the Israeli army as an interviewer and psychotechnician (testing of Air Force candidates, etc.).

My social life in Israel was very active and at points interfered with my studies. As we get to know more people here, I face the same situation. When there is such an interference I find it difficult to decide what is more important, and try to be active in both areas. Since I got married 3 years ago, my career became less important and it was my husband rather than me that at some points pushed me to continue my studies.

I was curious to see on my Rorschach indication of these, namely the conflict between my social activities and studies and between my interest in academic work vs. clinical work.

An initial look at my psychogram reveals a distribution over the 3 main determinants with a tendency to higher responsiveness on the *M* and *FM* side. It seems that energy is directed in both inner and outside direction, a first indication of my interest in both the areas I've just indicated.

An examination of the basic ratios reveals the following picture:

M:*FM* ratio of 13:14 suggests inner resources, imagination and ability for constructive utilization of fantasy and inner experience which are satisfying. There is an awareness of impulse life that does not interfere with the value system. There is no indication of conflict between the two, yet impulse life is not subordinated to the value system. The content of the *M* responses reveals perception of people mainly engaged in social interaction (like talking, friendly) and many times dancing (according to Freudian theory sexual sublimation. To me it makes more sense in light of the fact that I love to dance and actually, around the age of 14, I wanted to become a dancer). The content of the *FM* responses suggests tendency to *M* (like dancing animals). This might indicate some effort in the direction of making impulse life subordinate to the value system. As far as I know myself, I tend to agree with the first hypothesis; I feel "independently" satisfaction in inner experience in the form of intellectual as well as impulse life, and I am not aware of any conflict and enjoy both. Ability for empathy with other people is suggested by the content of the *M* responses, and the *Fc*, *FK*:*F* suggests a need for affection in the "normal optimal range."

Examination of the color responses (9 *FC,* 3 *CF,* and 2 *C* symb) shows emotional responsiveness to outside stimulation with ability to control it. Yet the *CF* and *C* symb suggest some uncontrolled reaction or spontaneous reaction to emotional stimuli. It indicates also some control of emotional response through intellectual approach. I am quite aware of this, and enjoy it under some situations.

The M:sum C 13:7.5 shows a stronger tendency to rely upon inner life for comfort and stimulation (the introversive tendency). The $FM + m$:$FC + c + C'$ and the 36% responses to Cards VIII, IX, and X, according to Klopfer indicate that this tendency is "natural." Yet the representation of the color response (sum $C = 7.5$) is quite high, and indicate perhaps some conflict between the inner experience and the reaction to outside stimulation. (If my interpretation of the Szondi is correct, I find on the m factor 3 positive and 2 negative reactions, which might indicate or suggest some conflict about the ability to enjoy contact with other people, as suggested in "Appraising Personality"). I am not aware of this conflict as resulting from negative experience with people. It makes more sense to me as a result of the simultaneous stimulation from both outside and inside sources.

F% of 29% is in the normal range, but on the low side. In the presence of the fairly good control by M, FC, and Fc, according to Klopfer it might suggest ability for intellectual control, but a stronger emphasis on the more personal ways of reaction, and a more spontaneous and sensitive reaction to others. And if I know myself this is so. I am able to behave in an impersonal way and control myself logically and formally when the situation demands it, but I prefer a more personal behavior and tend to introduce it when possible. One thing I did not like about my service in the Army was the strong pressure for the F type of control. I did not enjoy it but I maintained it without getting into any discipline troubles at all. When I started my studies in the university I felt a relaxation, as it called for much more flexibility and personal relations.

Intellectual ambitions and interest is suggested by the productive capacity ($R = 66$). The W:M ratio of 27:13 is in Klopfer's words optimal and suggest "enough creative potential to fortify a real drive to intellectual achievement." This surprised me a little, since I feel that I am not always using my potential in an "active practical" way. I am more involved with the process of inner experience than with doing something "practical" with it; it sometimes takes me a long time until I actually write a paper, even if I already know for a long time what I want to write in it.

A further examination of the W responses, and a few W perhaps indicate something in this direction. Many of the W responses are organized and elaborated, but a few are very general like "spring" "a crown" "a bat flying." The M responses seem more dynamic and elaborated (whether they are W or D). This perhaps indicates the incomplete or more exactly the feeling I have about not finding active outlet to the inner resources as suggested by the *W:M* ratio.

There is no indication of tension and inadequate feelings toward the self (no *K* or *m*), no marked anxiety (no *k, c, C'*), and the one *FK* might suggest some effort to tolerate and understand anxiety when it occurs. *FK* may also suggest a tendency for self exploration, looking, or observing the self from a perspective. I am seldom aware of this tendency.

Some criticalness, but not overcriticalness is suggested by both *W* and *H + A:Hd + Ad* of 31:9. This is another indication of the ability to perceive the human as a complete figure, perhaps accepting both body and mental aspects of the human.

The succession is orderly, flexible enough as not to interfere with efficiency. Relation to reality is firm as indicated by the form level and content of the responses. The responses indicate no aggression or direct sexual response, which might suggest no conflict in this area, or satisfaction, sublimation or control. (The Szondi gives the same impression, in the form of two open responses on the sexual vector.)

The record further reveals interest in art which is true. The *P-O* relation is not clear since I don't know how to score Originals. (I will not be surprised to find some trend in this direction.) The six populars indicate ability to perceive the world as others do. The *A*% is in the "optimal range" (34%). It does, however, suggest some stereotypy or at least conformity to some degree, perhaps moreso than I am aware of.

The sequence of the determinants shows a tendency to use first the inner resources, but when emotional stimulus appears (Card II) there is adequate reaction.

The *W* indicates again ability and concern with the abstract and theoretical, but enough *D* to secure "staying on the ground," with no interest in the minutiae of experience (*d*). And taken together with the *M* and *Fc* responses, which indicate a need or ability to interact with other people and to empathise with them, it points to what I described as my simultaneous interest in both academic and clinical work. (The Szondi might indicate this through the 2 negative and 1 positive reactions to the *p* and 2 negative reactions on the *k*. Some conflict between expanding to other people and keeping to myself. In this connection I would mention the "animal that I would choose to be" is dog. And the reason for this is "because it is Wise and Friendly." I remember that when I wrote it I really just wanted to write something. I was not serious about it because I did not feel any desire to really become a dog. But it turned to be quite significant. A closer examination of my sentence completion reveals similar things.)

The contrast between inner and outside experience is indicated as I mentioned, by both the Rorschach and Szondi. A certain intellectual tendency is indicated in dealing with emotional stimulation (C symb). It reminds me of a line of poetry written by Wordsworth: " . . . in that sweet mood when pleasant thoughts bring sad thoughts into the mind." It is suggesting a "translation" of mood which is caused by the beauty of Nature into thoughts. This might be my solution (of which I am not aware) to the conflict; approaching the outside stimulation not directly but rather restructure it through my inner experience. And if I interpret it correctly it might be represented by the "pleasant thoughts" that I many times experience in front of an impressive art work, a concert or a beautiful landscape.

A second "solution" of which I am aware is my interest in the area of personality and clinical research; it might give outlet to both my intellectual and abstract interest and the interest in other people.

As a last indication of these tendencies I want to mention the general themes of my T.A.T. stories: there are 2 scientists, an interaction between a mother and a daughter that has to do with giving support and advice, and 2 family situations, that might represent the other facet of my life which is very central.

I just want to mention that my previous knowledge of some of the more popular responses might have interfered with my individual production. I don't know in what direction and I actually can't tell which responses are not "purely" my own responses."

9

The Rare Extrovert

That Student 24 is the only Rorschach extrovert in our series raises two questions: First, is our sample too small? Out of the 300 or so students who participated in the Instruction–Insight method over the years, 50 at most, for one reason or another, returned their material. Of these 50, the 27 cases we have used were chosen because they provided all the items necessary for the particular study of their Inside Stories.

The second question is: Are students less likely to be taking courses in psychology and becoming psychologists if their personality, in general, is of the more active and outgoing variety—students whose main interest may be in doing rather than contemplating, introspecting, and theorizing. This indeed might be a plausible explanation, except for the fact that early studies (Harrower, 1955b) on several classes of medical students provided essentially the same *lack* of clear-cut dominance of color responses over those of human movement. As we have seen, Figure 8.1 shows this distribution in a class of 166 members.[1]

Thus the smallness of the sample does not appear to be the problem, nor are psychologists the only professional entity illustrating the lack of the extroversial type.

How did Rorschach himself envisage the extrovert? He gave an interesting warning:

Introverted individuals are colloquially contrasted to extroverted. There is a disadvantage in this terminology, however, in that it might be concluded that

[1]Subsequent to these published studies, large populations of ministers, nurses, adolescents, and patients in therapy gave essentially the same results, although the Unitarian ministers did show considerably more extroverts relative to all other populations.

introversion and extroversion are really opposites; let me repeat again that this is not true. The psychological processes producing introversion and extroversion are not opposite, but different. They are as different as thinking and feeling, as motion and color. (Rorschach, 1942, p. 82)

He further epitomized the outstanding qualities of the extrovert, as contrasted to the introvert, in the following way:

Stereotyped (rather than creative) intelligence
More reproductive ability
More "outward" life
Labile affective reactions
More adaptable to reality
More extensive than intensive rapport
Restless, labile motility
Skill and adroitness
    (Rorschach, 1942, p. 78)

Specific examples of scoring in Rorschach extroverted cases are few. But he did state, "A subject with $2\,M$ and $4\,C$ would have to be designated as more extratensive than introversive" (Rorschach, 1942, p. 83). Perhaps more interesting are his observations, such as, he found a dislike of interpretation among extroverts when taking the test. Self-evaluation or assessment was accompanied by displeasure. He found the extrovert subjects, however, were better related to reality. Elsewhere he stated that while for the introversive individual the taking of the test is play, for the extrovert it is work.

At this point, we should introduce Student 24, our sole extrovert (his Rorschach responses appear in Table 9-1). In the first place, it is obvious that the sum of his color responses clearly outweighs that of his human movement responses, his score being M:sum C = 2:10—a large and convincing difference.

With reference to Rorschach's comments on reproductive ability, we have an unusually good example in Student 24's self-evaluation. His approach to his task was more academic than introspective or clinical. Where most students have taken the self-evaluation assignment as an opportunity to "dig into" their own psyches and correlate their Rorschach findings with experiential ones, Student 24 retained the more conventional, academic approach of relating his work to the available text—in this instance, that of Bruno Klopfer. Rather than experimenting with putting the new learned material into his own words, he used many direct quotes. He felt safer in reproducing the accepted authority. To call attention to this difference in presentation, we have italicized these quotes, so that even at face value, a different text appears.

Although for our present purposes the high color scores are the outstanding feature, looking at his psychogram (Figure 9-1), another important characteristic is the height of the Animal Movement (*FM*) column. This not only dwarfs the *M,* but competes with the Form column in terms of dominating the psychogram. His text shows concern with the masculine gender and strong and aggressive varieties of animals in action. The "armed artillery piece" again emphasizes masculine interests, and the need for action is clearly marked: "Animals coiled to strike," "Animals waiting to attack" and "ready to jump." The gentler side of life, that of kissing, is achieved by fish rather than by humans.

Student 24 is of further interest to us since we know something of his interests and activities. He was teaching languages in high school prior to entering the psychological program and during his academic work. Subsequently he graduated to research rather than to a clinical program. Later he switched to administration, becoming first dean and then president of a community college—at this point, clearly a man of action living in and coping with the stress of the outside world.

TABLE 9-1
Rorschach Responses of Student 24

Card I

1. Bat	W	F	A
2. Hide	W	Fc	A obj
3. Winged animal standing in water	W	FM	A
4. Crest with eagle at the top	W	F	emb

Card II

1. Two roosters in a fight	W	FM	A
2. Male animal bending down to drink	W	FM	A
3. Two ibex face to face	D	F	A
4. Two-horned animal looking out at me	D	FM, Fc	A

Card III

1. Two African women bending over pot: hermaphrodite women? Looks like penis at knee bend	W	M	H
2. Huge butterfly in center	D	F	A
3. Baby hanging from umbilical cord	D	M	H

Card IV

1. Skin hanging up to dry	W	Fc, m	A obj
2. Animal face	d	Fc	Ad
3. Vaginal tract	D	F	sex
4. Serpent coiled to strike	d	FM	A
5. Shrubbery	D	Fc	nat

TABLE 9-1
(Continued)

Card IV

6. Crest for shield	W	F	emb
7. Human head with touseled hair	d	Fc	Hd

Card V

1. Bat	W	F	A
2. Two animals who have locked horns	W	FM	A
3. Animal, buffalo type, which has dived into water: male animal	D	FM	A + sex
4. Bat	W	F	A

Card VI

1. Totem top	D	F	obj
2. Skin drying	D	Fc, m	A obj
3. Armored artillery piece in water bank	D	F, c	obj
4. Shrubbery	d	Fc	nat
5. Dog head yelping	d	FM	Ad

Card VII

1. Skin removed from oddly shaped animal	W	Fc	A obj
2. Two rabbits perched, ready to jump	D	FM	A
3. Harlequin faces	D	F	Hd
4. Open clam shell	D	F	A
5. Dog head	D	F	Ad
6. Finger pointing	d	m	Hd
7. Skin drying	W	Fc	A obj
8. Shield with pennants hanging	W	Fm	emb

Card VIII

1. Two rodent-type animals climbing up to top of hill	D	FM	A, nat
2. Water	D	C	nat
3. Butterfly	D	FC	A
4. Animal perched, waiting to attack prey	D	FM	A
5. Shield with pennants	D	FC	emb

Card IX

1. Water in an unusual vessel resting on sponge	W	CF, m	nat obj
2. Weirdly shaped animals moving to left	D	FM	A
3. Mushroom cloud from atomic bomb	D	K, m, CF	exp
4. Mask with two eyespaces	W, S	FC	mask

TABLE 9-1
(Continued)

Card X

1. Anatomical chart from dictionary	W	CF	chart
2. Could also be an insect chart	W	CF	chart
3. Trachea, lungs	D	F	anat
4. Animals ready to jump	D	FM	A
5. Wishbone	D	FC	A obj
6. Sides of beef	D	CF	Food
7. Crabs	D	F	A
8. Sea horses	D	F	A
9. Caterpillars	D	F	A
10. Dirt, soil	D	C	nat
11. Irish lute or harp	D	FC	instr
12. Fish kissing	D	FM	A
13. Amoebae	D	FC	cell

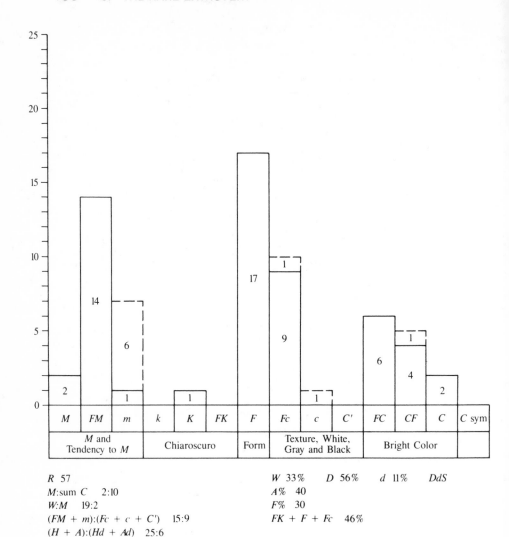

FIG. 9-1. A psychogram of Student 24

Self-Evaluation of Student 24

My approach to the interpretation has been to (1) Itemize the indications separately with respect to the immediate sources in the test responses, (2) Add supplementary material provided by other tests, (3) Integrate the information into a substantiated whole. Quotations are from the first volume of Klopfer's *Developments in the Rorschach Technique*.

L is a married man, thirty years old, who has been teaching languages in high school for the past two years while pursuing graduate studies in psychology. His manner of approach to the Rorschach (*W*%) suggests that he is *"interested in and capable of viewing the relatively separate facets of his experience as an interrelated whole. This is not found except with persons of superior intellectual ability who have been able to mobilize their capacities to serve their interest in seeing relationships between the various aspects of their experience and making sense of their world."* At the same time there are indications (*D*%) of his ability to apply his intelligence to practical, everyday, common-sense matters and a lack of interest in organizing matters. His abstract (*W*%) and concrete (*D*%) approach are both at the same degree above average. This could be due to a balanced approach in which case there would be no contradiction, or to an insecure approach to his life which causes him to hold on to obvious facts. More information will be needed to arrive at a justifiable assumption from these indices.

There are indications that L has an *"overly high level of aspiration, with ambition outstripping the creative resources of his personality,"* (*W*:*M* = 19:4) Or, it could also be that he has *"a very strong drive for accomplishment, with perhaps much accomplished, but at the expense of other important satisfactions."* In any case, the number of his responses (57) does not suggest that he is completely underproductive since the *"average number of responses falls within a range of 20 to 45."* His number of responses also suggests that he is *"perceptually responsive and receptive to the world about him,"* i.e., he maintains contact with the world and reacts readily to changes in it.

His response time falls within the average limits which suggests that he is not below average in his intellectual capacities as suggested earlier or that he is not greatly depressed at this time. His detail responses (*H* + *A*:*Hd* + *Ad* = 25:6) indicate that he is not highly over-critical. The number of popular responses (6 + 2 per 57 responses) is close to the average (5 per 20 to 45 responses), though the additional responses suggest the possibility of *"an overemphasis upon conventionality, perhaps through training or because of fear of error."* This latter view would support one of the evaluations made earlier in considering L's (*D*%) manner of approach. His percentage of animal responses (44%) is above the optimum level of 20%–35%, but does not exceed the upper average limit of 50%. From this we can conclude that he is able to see the world as others see it.

L appears to be an *"individual ruled by immediate needs for gratification rather than by long-range goals. . . . An immature behavioral impulsivity cannot be inferred, however, unless CF also exceeds FC, implying that the individual tends to act out his impulses without socialized restraint.''* L's *CF* does not exceed his *FC* which prevents a total endorsement of immature impulsivity, but it points to a possible problem area which we will have to relate to his other tendencies. This much can be admitted: An abundance of drives which may be indicative of an aggressive attitude kept in check by his realistic (*F*) approach. There are other indications that his tensions are too strong to permit him to *"utilize his inner resources for the constructive solution of his everyday problems of living.''*

There are counterindications (F% = 30%), however, in that his *"ability to view his world in an impersonal matter-of-fact way serves as an aid to controlled adjustment. He is able to be impersonal on many occasions but has not stripped himself of his responsiveness to his own needs and/or his reactivity to strong emotional impact from the outside.''* The lack or absence of constriction is also apparent in other responses, viz., (*FK + F + Fc*)% = 46%, where 75% suggests neurotic constriction.

Comparing his responses with the four signs of inadequate outer control:

1. (*CF + C*) > *FC*
2. Achromatic < ½ Chromatic
3. Minus form level in color responses
4. Sum C > *2M* and *F%* < 30%,

and the three signs of inadequate inner control:

1. *F%* > 50
2. Minus form level responses
3. *F%* < 20

we find that he does not fulfill any of these requirements. The dynamic quality in his personality has probably been utilized or controlled in a way which is not self-destructive, though possibly less productive than it could be.

The absence of anxiety (*FK, K,* or *k*) also contradicts the expected frustration from all these drives (*FM*). This may be due to a *"lack of awareness of affectional anxiety, either because such anxiety is in fact minimal or because the individual has built up mechanisms to defend himself from awareness of anxiety.''* This lack of awareness is contradicted in a way by other responses (*Fc*) which *"indicate an awareness of and acceptance of affectional needs experienced in terms of desire for approval, belongingness, and response from others retaining a passive recipient flavor but refined beyond a craving for actual physical contact. It is believed that this is a development essential for the establishment of deep and meaningful object relations and that it occurs only where the basic security needs have been reasonably well satisfied."* These responses also suggest sensitivity which may mean easily hurt feelings, awareness of any cloud in the emotional atmosphere or a tactful awareness of the needs and feelings of others. *"The better the control system reflected by the rest of the psychogram, the more likely it is that Fc is associated with a tactful sensitivity."*

L's responses suggest a rich, balanced, emotional life (FC = 6, CF = 4, C = 2), but there is further evidence of a conflict or tension with respect to his introversive-extratensive balance, namely his contemplative vs. outgoing drives. The three indices for this balance indicate that he may be (1) outgoing (M:sum C = 2:10); (2) contemplative ($FM + m$:$Fc + c + C'$ = 15:9) in a mathematically exact inverse proportion; or (3) within the average limits of this balance (number of responses to Cards VIII, IX, and X = 39%; average level = 30%–40%). It is likely that these apparent differences in estimating his balance of activity reflect shifts in L's orientation which have been suggested since the ability to shift equally from the abstract to the concrete was first noted above.

SUMMARY

The test results suggest that L is a man possessing good intellectual capacities and a capacity for a balanced emotional life. He gives evidence of being able to enjoy and utilize his inner resources on certain occasions while responding to external demands just as freely on others. His major conflict or tension stems from the abundance of his drives. He has apparently found a way to cope with his reservoir of energies which is satisfactory in maintaining control, if not entirely productive. He gives evidence of being sensitive to the needs of others, but indicates a tendency to demand unrealistic perfection from others which probably limits his capacity to enjoy others as much as he could. His level of aspiration is too high, which probably reduces his overall effectiveness. His ability to see life in the conventional ways most likely provides a meeting ground with others who would otherwise be upset by his aggressiveness.

This diagnosis from the Rorschach profile coincides precisely with what I know about myself, so much so that I might question the subjective bias in my interpretation of the results.

10

An Established Psychologist Looks Back after 20 Years

RORSCHACH RESPONSES, PSYCHOGRAM, AND SELF-EVALUATION OF STUDENT 25

Student 25's record is chosen to reflect an inside story for several reasons. In the first place she was one of the older students taking the course at the age of 44. Secondly, the passage of time has enabled us to trace her progress in the psychological field. She is now an established therapist, has held academic positions, and published in the field of her special concern.

Most important, she has been interested enough to look back at her original self-evaluation and at her early experiences, intellectual and emotional. This reevaluation is particularly pertinent for our study.

Her content in the Rorschach record (Table 10–1) shows what she described as the "Preoccupation with life-death." Her later history shows how this theme has been successfully woven into her career.

From her psychogram (Figure 10–1) we see her dominant pattern was one which we subsequently found in many psychological students: namely the "Twin Towers" of M and FM as the chief feature of the graphic expression of a Rorschach record.

TABLE 10–1
Rorschach Record of Student 25

Card I			
1. A larva (middle), anticipating its future as a moth	*W*	*FM*	*A*

TABLE 10-1
(Continued)

Card I			
2. A bat	W	F	A
3. A deformed human-like figure, without a head or feet, throwing its clawlike hands up in despair, besieged on each side by a winged animal	W	M	Hd

Card II			
1. Two clowns or devils (profile) with warts on their noses and sticking out tongues, wearing dunce hats, clap each others hands and knees, as in playing patty-cake. They are in sitting position, with legs stretched out to their left (can't be seen). The red patch below them symbolizes hellfire.	W	M, CF	H
2. Two animals rubbing their turned up snouts against each other; A crab or lobster creeping out from behind them	W	FM, FC	A
3. A butterfly	D	FC	A
4. An airplane nosing its way through clouds	S	F, m	obj
5. Two small puppets or midgets sitting back to back over a mountain cliff. They are holding each other up by their position.	DrS	M, FK	H

Card III			
1. Two French poodles facing each other, with their front paws on top of a miniature bomb. It will not explode as long as they keep in this rigid position. The bow tie between them is the prize the poodle with the greatest perseverance will win. Above them are two homunculi, acting as judges.	W	FM, FC	A
2. A crab	D	F	A
3. Tree branches or trunks	D	F	Pl

Card IV			
1. A dragon-like animal with side-way eyes, two long front teeth and two tusks, trying to push its big body	W	FM, Fc	A

TABLE 10-1
(Continued)

Card IV

forward. It has a short, bushy tail.			
2. Two dancers resting with their heads on a cloud or a rock, their bodies hanging in the air	*dr*	*M*	*H*

Card V

1. A bull charging with two daggers (only the hilts are showing) pierced into a hump on its back	*W*	*FM*	*A*
2. A nut-cracker	*d*	*F*	obj
3. Two men lying down on inclines	*W*	*M*	*H*

Card VI

1. Two reptiles or worms lying sideways, touching each other ventrally, within the intestines of another animal	*W*	*FM*	*A*
2. Artery, going through heart or liver	*D*	*k*	*At*
3. A bird	*D*	*F*	*A*
4. Two Pinocchio-like faces	*D*	*Fc*	*Hd*
5. Vagina with lower abdomen	*Dr*	*Fc*	sex

Card VII

1. Sponge-like formation, growing upward	*W*	*Fc, m*	*Pl*
2. Two black Africans in a native dance, raising their arms, as a mock-symbol of the Statue of Liberty	*D*	*M, FC'*	*H*
3. Two two-faced people (Dr. Jekyll and Mr. Hyde), each face looking into different direction, with animal bodies, sitting back to back	*W*	*M*	*Hd*

Card VIII

1. A pyramid of butterflies	*W*	*FC*	*A*
2. Two miniature bears, added for support or balance, climbing up pyramid	*D*	*FM*	*A*
3. Stained slides of leaves or organs	*W*	*FC*	*Pl, at*
4. Two women-faces	*di*	*F*	*Hd*

Card IX

1. An owl behind icebergs	*W*	*FM, c, CF*	*A*
2. Two witches riding above clouds,	*W*	*M, K*	*H*

TABLE 10-1
(Continued)

Card IX			
pointing at each other threatingly			
3. Two heads turned upward and two heads turned downward with big overhanging face on each side	*D*	*M*	*Hd*

Card X			
1. Mitosis in paradise	*W*	*CF, m*	abstr
2. A carnival mask	*DS*	*FC*	mask
3. Two rats climbing on a totem pole, on	*D*	*FM*	*A*
4. Top of two embryos of impending noble birth, as they have	*D*	*CF*	*H*
5. Coat of arms attached to their protuding cortex; while	*D*	*F*	obj
6. A victorious Indian, standing on his head, is waving two gigantic feathers, heralding their birth.	*D*	*M, FC*	*H*
7. Two faces on top of each other, lower with moustache, upper with side-beard.	*WS*	*FC*	*Hd*

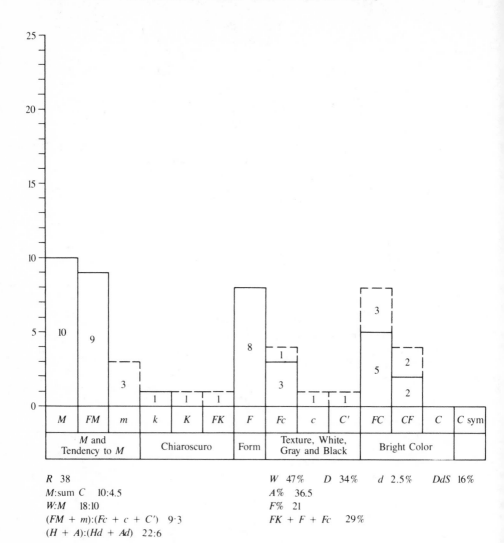

R 38
M:sum C   10:4.5
W:M   18:10
(FM + m):(Fc + c + C')   9·3
(H + A):(Hd + Ad)   22:6

W   47%   D   34%   d 2.5%   DdS 16%
A%   36.5
F%   21
FK + F + Fc   29%

FIG. 10-1. A psychogram of Student 25

Self-Evaluation of Student 25

Reading through my Rorschach production, I picked up two themes
going through it, which seem to reveal the core aspects of the
personality. One I shall call the "life-death" dimension, the other the
"contact" dimension. The latter is reflected in people and animals
doing things to each other, being in active, physical contact with each

other. (See Cards II, 1, 2, 5; III, 1; VI, 1; IX, 2, for the more obvious examples).

The preoccupation with the "life–death" dimension is most strikingly brought out in the very first answer to card I: the nonliving anticipating life; in a more symbolic and less optimistic way, also in the third percept. It bursts out again in the first percepts of the third plate (perhaps also in the fifth plate), culminating in the first percept of plate X, and here the whole theme of birth is carried through percepts 3, 4, 5, and 6. It is not the frequency in which this concept appears that is so startling, but rather the charged emotional tone of it, and the fact, that it is always the very first percept, and that it is always followed immediately by very controlled, stereotyped percepts. This sequence alone suggests a problem in the area of emotional control; after every "outburst" an effort seems to be made at control.

At this point I would interpret the contact-dimension as reflecting a great need for close interpersonal relationships, indicating the outward-directedness of my personality make-up. On the other hand, the life–death dimension points to the most inward aspects, revealing a struggle of the inner life, to come to terms with an irreconcilable dichotomy.

With these intense needs for inner- and outer-directedness, I would predict to find the hypertensive personality type, who lives rather exhaustively, spending too much energy in all directions. Yet in spite of these conflicts, the prevailing mood is one of optimism, pointing to good adjustment and a strong ego. I shall now consider the scores and see how well the above assumptions are reflected in it.

Looking at the psychogram we find indeed a rather balanced personality type, though with the greater emphasis on the introtensive side.

The proportion of M to FM indicates a ready acceptance of impulses, which however can be subordinated to other values. This lack of impulse repression as well as the relatively low F score are aspects of myself I am well acquainted with. There is very little rigid, conformist-type control, however, control is brought in, in a more flexible way, indicated by the $Fc, FK,$ and FC scores.

Looking now specifically at the contact-dimension, we find indeed an awareness and acceptance of affectional needs for other people, as well as of other people. This is reflected by the substantial Fc score, as well as by the $FK, K,$ and k score. It is interesting to note that these latter determinants, as well as the m score, all indicative of anxiety, are only present as additional determinants. I would interpret this as an indication that good adjustment ability, a strong ego, a feeling of security (Fc) and the generally optimistic mood (very positive responses to colors), by far outweigh the anxiety determinants. The *W:M* ratio reflects the ability to organize and to realize intellectual achievements.

Though I could not have predicted in any way, what my Rorschach would look like (as a matter of fact, I have been entirely unaware of some of the major aspects in my personality make-up), once confronted with it, I recognize and can confirm every aspect of it as a reflection of my subjective experiences of myself.

Reevaluation After 20 Years

It is now 20 years ago since I took your course in projective techniques with my self-administered Rorschach test. After evaluating it and writing my report, at the end of the semester, I don't think that I have ever looked at it again, or have given it much thought. All the greater was my surprise now, when reading my records to find that the main theme running through it has been the leitmotif in my life. But I shall return to that aspect a little later.

I am trying to sort out the kind of impact the self-knowledge I had gained from my Rorschach analysis has had on my life. In retrospect I can see that it could have served as an excellent predictive tool. But though I discovered aspects of my personality, assets as well as weaknesses, I had not previously been aware of, I do not remember that at any point I *consciously* made a decision or embarked on a different path as a consequence of this newly acquired self-knowledge. Not consciously—not in these terms. But some things did happen, in indirect ways, that may have affected my entire career as well as my personal life quite drastically. To gain a better understanding of these changes I need to give a brief account of my pre–self-evaluation life style.

I was 44 years old when I took the Rorschach. I had never had a job, I had never worked, that is, with the exception of two adventure filled years during the war, in Morocco, where I was a member of the OSS. But that occupation hardly qualifies as a "job." I was not a "homemaker" either, though I had two children. I had accompanied my husband, a career officer, on his overseas assignments, and there was always a staff around, freeing me from all obligations. When we finally stayed long enough in one place, making it possible for me to attend college, I was 38 years old, well read, well traveled, fluent in a number of languages, but otherwise rather uneducated—I had only finished 5 years of "gymnasium" that's roughly equivalent to 10th grade—undisciplined and beset with feelings of insecurity as to possible academic achievements. Thus, very reluctantly, under some pressure of one of my professors, I took the Comprehensive Examination. It was my second year in graduate school, the same semester that I took the projective techniques course. I remember looking at my classmates at the beginning of the test and thinking that I would gladly change places with each one of them, since I was absolutely convinced that they were far more knowledgeable than I was. I have always been keenly aware of my intellectual limitations, though I was also aware of my potentials.

Several months after taking the Comprehensives I learned that of those 24 students who had taken it for the first time, I had been the only one to pass it. I felt happy, relieved, and very surprised. I was convinced that it was due to some freak occurrence, since I had no doubt that most of the students who had failed were far more qualified than I was.

That same evening we had our weekly Rorschach class. When I walked in a student was just telling you that I was the only one who had passed the test. You responded with something like: "I am not astonished. It can be expected of someone who responds 'Mitosis in Paradise' to the 10th Card." Your comment had a far greater effect on my gaining self-confidence than the fact of having passed the test. It made me believe that I really may have some special qualifications. Toward the end of the semester, when I finally evaluated my own Rorschach and wrote the report, I discovered certain encouraging patterns of my personality, which helped to make me dare to think seriously about becoming a professional.

I am emphasizing the *pattern* which emerged on the basis of ratios with their hypotheses, the prevailing themes and the flavor of the entire production, rather than discrete qualities, many of which I had been aware of, while missing the relationship between these often contradictory appearing characteristics. I had functioned well. I had generally "felt good" about myself, but there always was a feeling of something missing. Though I have been a rather introspective person, I did not know that my dissatisfaction revolved primarily around vaguely discerned, unfulfilled potentials.

I had thought of myself as resourceful, creative, original, nonconforming, impractical, tense, impatient—all of which was confirmed by my Rorschach. The surprising revelations derived from relations such as $W{:}M$ ratios. My overemphasis on Ws and Dds and my underemphasis on D and d responses did not come as a surprise. I knew that I saw forests at the expense of trees, that I saw things differently than others, that I lacked patience to appreciate details;

but all of this had smacked of the somewhat talented dilettante. The 18:10 $W:M$ ratio was an indication that I could do something with my resources. Organize them, bring order into something that had always felt like chaotic, disorganized, undisciplined potentials.

My low $F\%$ seemed to convey a lack of control and discipline. This also is a correct but one-sided view of myself. And as indicated in the Rorschach protocol, this lack is balanced by Fc, FK, and FC scores (29%), which are indications of more flexible controls. The almost equal proportion of M to FM percepts reflects a ready acceptance of impulses—indeed repression is one of my lesser used defense mechanisms—yet I experience total control over my impulses.

According to Rorschach interpretation, my personality type is introversive (M:sum $C = 10:4.5$) though phenomenologically I would describe myself as hypertensive, living rather exhaustively with intense inner- as well as outer-directed needs. My one regret is to have only one life (not to give it to my country) but not to be able to lead the most diverse life-styles simultaneously and to the fullest. I find myself in constant conflict situations of having to choose between equally attractive alternatives. In spite of it, I experience life as deeply satisfying. Is that reflected in my "balanced" Rorschach protocol?

All determinants, with the exception of C, are represented, and in proportions that would indicate good adjustment ability, a strong ego, an overall sense of security, and an optimistic mood (very positive color responses). Anxiety determinants are present, though only as additionals. I somehow have the feeling, that every one of my characteristics as well as their opposites are allowed to develop and find expression, because of my weak repressive defenses. Now to the main theme which I found running through my Rorschach protocol. I shall first quote parts of the report I wrote 20 years ago:

> I picked up two themes going through it, which seem to reveal the core aspects of the personality. One I shall call the "life–death" dimension ... [it] is most strikingly brought out in the first answer to card I: the nonliving anticipating life; in a more symbolic, less optimistic way, also in the third percept. It bursts out again ... culminating in the first percept of plate X, and here the whole theme of birth is carried through percepts 3, 4, 5, and 6. It is not the frequency in which this concept appears ... but the charged emotional tone ... that it is always the first percept ... followed immediately by very controlled stereotyped percepts. ...
>
> I would interpret the contact-dimension (discussed in report at length) as reflecting a great need for interpersonal relationships, indicating the outward-directedness ... on the other hand, the life–death dimension

points to the most inward aspects, revealing the struggle of the inner life to come to terms with an irreconcilable dichotomy.

As a supplement to my Rorschach analysis I wrote a TAT report, which utterly validated the Rorschach interpretations. The following is a paragraph taken from the TAT report.

> ... to get the flavor of the main themes, we find that indeed three of the four stories carry the life–death motif.... (the first story deals with birth and the last one ends with immortality) ... the nature of the theme is revealed: It is life that maters, not death. Death is transcendental, in the way that it is never an end but a means to achieve something (ideals, integrity, immortality). The same optimism (as in Rorschach) is also found here. Though death runs through the stories, the emphasis is on life. This seems to reveal that the conflict is not based on an anxiety or fear of death, but rather on living life too intensely.... The first TAT story, just like the first Rorschach percept, reflects a victory of life.

Up to that time, 1966, I had not been aware of my preoccupation with death. I did know that I was "insanely" in love with life, and that I had considered the human condition, with its Juggernaut approach of death, as tragic. But I also loved tragedy—the ephemeral, which makes life so immensely valuable. I had not been aware of the main goal or the theme of my life, which was "coming to terms with death." My Rorschach and my TAT report are the first written acknowledgments of that preoccupation.

Some years later, when, as an assistant professor, I had the first opportunity to devise an entirely new course, I chose The Psychology of Death. It was one of the first courses in that field to be taught at a college in the United States. I became a thanatologist. Not in the sense of working with dying patients, but by pursuing the study concerning the impact our knowledge of death has on our life. I have done a great deal of research on the subject, interviewing literally hundreds of individuals in depth, participated in symposia, written articles and a book entitled *Death and the Creative Life.* Yes, I did become a "professional"—doing research, teaching, and psychotherapy. True to my makeup, I would like to pursue each of these endeavors "full-time" incapable of giving up any one of them. Would I have become a psychologist had I not taken the projective techniques course? Most probably "Yes!" But the self-knowledge I gained certainly helped in many respects. It gave me confidence that I could actualize my potentials.

The need to accomplish something, to make a contribution, to leave a mark had always been there. But I needed the positive confirmation that was reflected in my Rorschach protocol to strengthen my self-confidence. I must admit that I "liked" my Rorschach profile, as is clearly indicated by the report I wrote at that time.

11

Career Change on the Basis of Self-Evaluation

Student 26 made the most far reaching change in her lifestyle and choice of career as a result of studying her Rorschach findings. She changed from clinical psychology to medicine.

It is clear in reading her self-evaluation that she was becoming more and more aware of a basic lack of interest in the generalized concepts she was grappling with in her psychological training. From having felt herself to be dumber than her peers at this apparent failure, she was able to detect that her way of envisaging the world had assets which are more appropriate to factual knowledge and practical procedures. In a letter explaining her decision she wrote:

Having to analyse my own Rorschach was perhaps the most valuable assignment that I was ever given in graduate school. While I knew only too well how very much I wanted to study and practice medicine, I never realized how much better suited I was to work in the basic sciences than in psychology.

Since my basic motivation seems to be a deep abiding concern for the well-being of others, when it appeared that I would be unable to go on in medicine, I thought that clinical psychology would be a viable alternative. After two years of struggling with the abstractions coming to this area, I was almost ready to conclude that I was just much dumber than my colleagues, but after evaluating my Rorschach I began to realize that I just saw things much differently and had a very different orientation.

It was only after completing the course and two weeks of careful consideration that I realized that I could only be happy and capable of making a significant contribution in medicine. While I still face the major hurdle of being accepted into medical school, I have no regrets about my decision and find that I am now much happier and healthier than I have been in a long, long time.

Sharing her note with the head of the department elicited this reply: "I was so glad to see the note from S and get some understanding of her decision. I did not get to talk to her at all, either before or after her decision so her note was most helpful."

Student 26 was accepted in medical school and has completed her training. Her Rorschach record (Table 11-1), psychogram (Figure 11-1), and self-evaluation follow.

TABLE 11-1
Rorschach Responses of Student 26

Card I

1. Angry dog's head, wolf's head	W	F	Ad
2. Four ghosts	S	(M), C'	(H)
3. Hands reaching out	d	F	Hd
4. Jagged rocks jutting upward	D	Fc	N
5. Two trees	d	F	Pl
6. Dissected brain	W`	F	At

Card II

1. Butterfly	D	FC	A
2. Top	S	F	obj
3. Christmas tree ornament	S	F	obj
4. Two small animals fighting	D	FM	A
5. Arrowhead	d	Fc	obj
6. Pelvic bone structure and coccyx	W`	F	At
7. Two large bears with injured hind legs placing their front paws together	W`	FM	A
8. Wolf's head	d	F	Ad

Card III

1. Two women facing each other	W`	M	H
2. Butterfly	D	FC	A
3. Low table	D	F	obj
4. Large crab	D	Fc	A
5. Two lions with long tales	D	F	A
6. Head of a poodle	d	Fc	Ad
7. Exaggerated profile	D	F	Hd
8. Hands being warmed over a fire	dd	F	Hd
9. Two furry bear cubs	D	Fc	A
10. Boots	d	F	obj

Card IV

1. Old man in robes bending down in	D	M	H

TABLE 11-1
(Continued)

Card IV			
prayer			
2. Elephant or large curly-haired dog	D	Fc	A
3. Dangerous precipice	d	F	N
4. Vertebral column (portion)	D	Fc	At

Card V			
1. Butterfly	W	Fc	A
2. Wishbone	d	F	obj
3. Two worms coming up out of the ground	d	FM	A
4. Butterfly sitting on a branch	D	Fc, FM	A
5. Two drumsticks	d	F	Fd
6. Fingers raised in a victory ("V") sign	d	F	Hd
7. Sharp claw	dd	F	Ad
8. Two men facing in opposite directions	d	M	H
9. Front profile of a man holding a microphone	d	F	Hd
10. Priest in robes with his hand placed above the head of another man	dd	M	H

Card VI			
1. Butterfly with ragged wings	D	Fc	A
2. Totem pole	D	Fc	obj
3. Two men, back to back, standing on top of a mountain giving signals with their arms	D	M	H
4. Neural cell—myelin sheath, nodes of Ranvier	D	F	At
5. Bird's nest—parents and baby birds	d	FM	A
6. Portion of a heart, valves	d	F	At

Card VII			
1. Smooth-winged butterfly	D	Fc	A
2. Front end of an elephant dancing	D	FM	A
3. Dog's face	d	Fc	Ad
4. Door hinge	d	F	obj
5. Cork of a bottle with a corkscrew	d	F	obj
6. Glass bowl	S	F	obj
7. Woodpecker's head	d	F	Ad
8. Large white dogs—front end	S	FC'	Ad

Card VIII			
1. Two pink bears climbing	D	F/C, FM	A
2. Pansy	D	CF	Pl

TABLE 11-1
(Continued)

Card VIII

3. Arms and hands reaching out	*d*	*F*	*Hd*
4. Two lakes with a bridge over them	*D*	*CF*	*N*
5. Uterus, Fallopian tubes	*D*	*F*	*At*
6. Snoopy on top of his dog house (playing "Red Baron")	*d*	*(FM)*	*(A)*
7. Body of a seagull soaring	*S*	*FM*	*A*
8. Centipede on a twig	*d*	*F*	*A*

Card IX

1. Large green butterfly	*D*	*FC*	*A*
2. Fingers stretched out	*d*	*F*	*Hd*
3. Fetus	*D*	*M*	*H*
4. Pair of sorcerers	*D*	*M*	*H*
5. Water fountain	*D, S*	*K*	diff.
6. Head of a teddy bear	*di*	*F*	*(Ad)*

Card X

1. Two blue crabs	*D*	*FC*	*A*
2. Rabbit's face	*D*	*F*	*Ad*
3. Two yellow lions roaring	*D*	*FC, FM*	*A*
4. Planaria	*D*	*F*	*A*
5. Two green seahorses	*D*	*F/C*	*A*
6. Two pink appendices	*D*	*F/C*	*At*
7. Wishbone	*D*	*F*	obj
8. Gray insects with long antennae on a branch	*D*	*FC, Fc*	*A*
9. Blue spiders	*D*	*F/C, Fc*	*A*
10. Yellow sparrows	*D*	*F/C*	*A*
11. Green grasshoppers on green leaves	*D*	*FC*	*A*

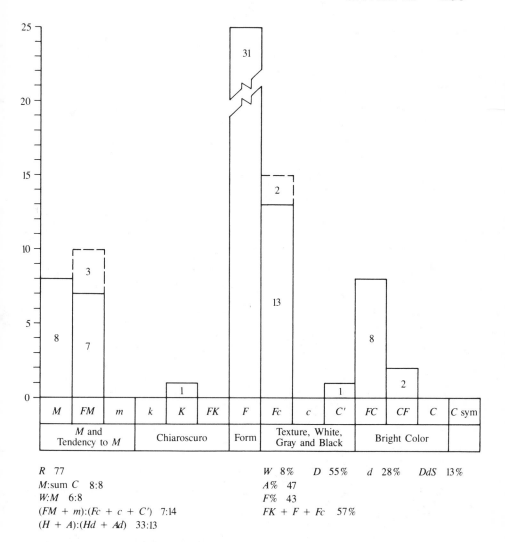

FIG. 11-1. A psychogram of Student 26

Student 26 first discussed her findings using the third person, following it with a section entitled *Supporting Evidence* where she spoke personally:

Self-Evaluation of Student 26

On the basis of the Rorschach and the Wechsler-Bellevue, S appears to be of high-average to superior intelligence, with the Wechsler-Bellevue suggesting a somewhat higher IQ than the Rorschach. A previous administration of the WAIS confirms the superior status, with an IQ score of above 130.

There appears to be some degree of imbalance in her manner of approach, with W significantly deemphasized (W = 8%), d moderately emphasized (d = 30%), and DdS slightly emphasized (DdS = 13%). The very low W% suggests that she lacks theoretical mindedness and interest in generalities, and has very little need to see the world as a meaningful total kind of response. She may be expected to experience significant difficulty when required to participate in abstraction, posing a rather serious handicap for her future in clinical psychology. The D% reflects her practical bias. There is a definite emphasis on d, reflecting her close attention to details and moderate degree of compulsivity. Also, DdS is emphasized, indicating a rather individualistic way of looking at the world, with possible tendencies toward obstinacy and stubbornness. In S's case, the oppositional tendencies may well be directed against herself in the form of self-destructive or self-critical tendencies, especially as feelings of inadequacy. Additionally, her balance on introversion–extroversion appears to indicate ambivalence and doubt. A $W:M$ ratio of 6:8 suggests that she may have problems in organizing ideas.

While S's productivity is better-than-average (R = 77), it should be noted that this score may be somewhat artificially inflated by the number of F responses, elevating the total quantity rather than the quality.

Her relation to reality appears to be essentially firm, with a relative absence of minus responses. Several responses, however, may show a slight trend toward a minus quality. The F% of 43, while not out of normal range, is somewhat higher than that which might be expected in her profession. Her focus on logic, fact, rationality, practicality, and accuracy suggest that she might be much more at home in basic science rather than social science. The combination of F and D suggest a tendency toward being rigid and demanding. While some inner experiences and resources are definitely available to assist in the interpretation of things (M = 8), the F% suggests that such interpretations are determined more by outer experience than by inner experience.

Thought content is fairly restricted in range, as is reflected by a rather high A% (47%), and there is a relative lack of original trends. S's perceptions are fairly simple, but the use of descriptive phrases and texture prevents the percepts from being designated as sparse. In general, her interests are rather limited and reflect little exposure to the world.

However, constructive fantasy appears to be readily accessible (M

= 8). S has a fairly rich inner life, with the capacity to live within herself and enjoy inner experiences. She definitely appears to have the inner resources necessary to provide stability. However, since the *M:*sum *C* ratio is 8:8, with sufficient *F* to hold things in balance, she may be described as "vulnerable," being innervated from both inside and outside.

It definitely appears that S may be experiencing some difficulties with her emotions. While *FC* and *CF* reflect good strong emotions, and the predominance of *FC* responses over *CF* and *C* suggest that the emotion is fairly well incorporated within a meaningful framework, the number of *FC* responses (12) appears to be somewhat excessive. This may indicate that her emotions are somewhat overtrained to be appropriate, leading to a tendency toward superficial, facile interpersonal relationships. The high proportion of *F/C* responses also suggest "conventional good manners." Further problems may be reflected by the elevated *Fc* score (13 + 2). She is no longer simply extremely aware of other individuals and sensitive to their needs, but has very possibly reached a level of ultrasensitivity and self-consciousness. In her case, sensitivity appears to be a burden, rendering her highly vulnerable. In line with this, S may have a slight tendency toward inability to experience full emotions, as is reflected by the *Ć* responses.

The presence of energy and clearly sufficient drive is reflected by a good *FM* column (*FM* = 7 + 3). If S were in a basic science area or medicine, her drive would undoubtedly be well-directed.

On the basis of the Rorschach, anxiety does not appear to be marked (*K* = 1). In this particular case, the anatomical responses may be better interpreted as a reflection of this person's deep and abiding interest in medicine.

S definitely appears to have adequate control and self-discipline, and may well have a tendency toward overcontrol and rigidity.

Supporting Evidence

While it is difficult to interpret intelligence on the basis of the Rorschach, the suggestion in this case that intelligence is within a range from high average to superior is supported by a WAIS score of 130+. This intelligence, however, might well be expected to be (and definitely is) expressed in certain fact-oriented areas rather than in highly abstract areas.

The Rorschach certainly confirms my detail-oriented approach to life. I tend to focus on small bits of information and remain thoroughly fascinated by them, having tremendous difficulty if I am required to integrate them into a complex, meaningful whole. Needless to say, I have a great deal of difficulty with such abstractions as are common to personality theory. Usually, the best that I can do is to memorize discrete amounts of information and answer any exam question with a conglomeration of rather disorganized facts. Trying to manipulate such facts into a meaningful totality requires a great deal of time and effort. However, when it comes to my fact-oriented biochemistry or neuroscience courses, even though the material seems "difficult" to my brilliant but theoretical-minded friends, I can perform quite adequately. I am, without doubt, an analyzer rather than a synthesizer. I definitely am practical and very compulsive, and may be somewhat stubborn, with a tendency toward having an individualistic way of looking at things. The manner of approach suggested by the Rorschach receives further support from the Myers-Briggs Type Indicator (MBTI). As an introverted-sensing type (ISTJ), I am characterized as having a "complete, realistic, and practical respect for the facts," with a strong preference for having "everything put on a factual basis, clearly stated, and not too unfamiliar or complex." This type, however, tends to look at things from an "intensely individual angle," which certainly supports the suggestion that this Rorschach-person looks at the world from an individualistic point of view. In addition, ISTJ's are "patient with detail and routine," which would definitely be expected from my manner of approach.

The high productivity (especially the high percent of F responses) fits with my compulsion to totally analyze things. I can become completely fascinated by such tasks in which I can break things down and discover how many tiny pieces can be distinguished.

Assessing relation to reality is particularly difficult when scoring one's own profile. "Objective" scoring was a definite problem, and I suspect that I was quite generous in not scoring minus responses in several instances. This tends to fit in with a need to see what I want or need to see, although I generally tend to be realistic. The $F\%$ certainly substantiates my focus on logic, rationality, fact, and practicality, in agreement with my Myers-Briggs type. I undoubtedly would make an excellent scientist/physician with this orientation and accompanying accuracy. While the Rorschach suggests that I may rely more on outer experience than inner experience to interpret things, I find that I do rely very heavily on my inner life for interpretations, particularly in personal areas (which has a tendency to really get me in trouble at times). My $F+$ and d combination is highly accurate when it suggests that I might be rigid and demanding—I definitely am! Some of the other projectives make me less certain about my relation to reality.

The restricted range of content is probably quite accurate. I tend to be fairly content concentrating on the same fairly limited interests, having no overwhelming desires to try something new. Again, this is highly characteristic of introverted sensing types who "dislike new problems unless there are standard ways to solve them," "like an established routine," and "enjoy using skills already learned more than learning new ones." The lack of original trends is definitely characteristic of myself and of ISTJ's in general.

An M score of 8 (granted, some of the Ms aren't too great!) suggests that my "constructive fantasy" should be readily available. While I generally regard myself as totally lacking in creativity, I do seem to have quite an imagination in certain areas. A friend once informed me that anyone who could invent the fantasies that I came up with had to have quite an imagination—I just wish I could channel it in a more useful direction. I very definitely do have the capacity to live within myself and enjoy inner experiences and generally prefer to do so when I have the option, being markedly self-sufficient. The vulnerability associated with the approximately equal $M:$sum C ratio would certainly be applicable to me. I very often do feel pounded from both inside and out, which leads to considerable discomfort. If M reflected introversion in the conventional sense, I would expect that my M column would far outshadow all others. On the MBTI, I had a score of zero on extroversion, which is quite accurate—I am an extreme introvert, but have learned to go through the motions of functioning as extroverted-oriented.

The energy and drive suggested by the good FM $(7 + 3)$ column is extremely accurate. If my drive were not well directed, I sincerely doubt that I currently would be in graduate school. I frequently am accused by friends of operating primarily on "sheer guts." Considering that the last 12 years of my life have been spent in and out of hospitals, I really would have to conclude that I must have quite a bit of energy and drive to keep going.

The aspects of the record dealing with emotional tone appear to be the greatest source for concern, and probably correctly so, since I do have a history of problems in dealing with my emotions. If I were to be optimistic, I would interpret my FC column $(FC = 12)$ as reflecting available, but possibly somewhat overcontrolled, warmth. Being a realist and knowing my history (and knowing myself fairly well), I would have to conclude that at least to a slight degree these emotions may be better described as being "overtrained to be appropriate," leading to "superficial, facile interpersonal relationships." While I tend to have excellent intellectual insight, I am almost totally lacking in emotional insight. My usual pattern is one of "keeping though the number of *FC* responses might be interpreted as improvement in ability to express emotion, I suspect that my *F*% still manages to keep a tight rein on things. In certain situations where I know intellectually that I should be feeling certain emotions, I frequently feel nothing, but do manage to express the "appropriate" emotion, very much in accord with the interpretation from the Rorschach. The two *CF*s may be accurate reflections of strong emotions—with certain friends with whom I am very close, I do manage to feel very strong, genuine emotions. In such cases, I know that it is "safe" to feel. The ultra-sensitivity and self-consciousness reflected by the high *Fc* (13 + 2) column couldn't be more accurate. While I can be highly sensitive to others and their needs, in general, my own sensitivity is so exquisite that I am highly vulnerable. As much as I hate to, I probably would have to conclude that I am somewhat paranoid. Certainly, anyone who is as sensitive as I am may well be expected to have problems in experiencing full emotions—such experience would simply be too painful. With such great vulnerability, one's goal soon becomes self-protection at all costs.

While the Rorschach did not suggest high anxiety, I definitely do tend to be highly anxious, particularly in situations involving evaluation and/or the possibility of rejection. My anxiety does seem to be basically situationally induced rather than an extremely deep-seated personality trait leading to diffuse, free-floating anxiety.

This Rorschach-person very definitely accurately described as having adequate control, with perhaps a slight tendency toward overcontrol and rigidity. Prior to therapy, I was extremely rigid, anxious, and "uptight," but I seem to have shown substantial improvement in that respect. Because of the nature of my life for the past few years extreme control and self-discipline have been absolutely essential to my continued functioning. Without it, I would have given up long ago.

After completing medical school, Student 26 began residency training in diagnostic radiology and has now been in private practice for several years.

12

Self-Understanding within the Family Unit

The contribution of Student 27 is one of the most original. She envisaged the task of self-evaluation as an opportunity to relate her Rorschach-self to the Rorschach profiles of her parents and sibling. She was keenly aware of the fact that Rorschach patterns must be seen as ways of relating to the environment, and she found one important aspect of her own environment to be the psychological makeup of her parents.

The actual Rorschach responses of the family have not been included, but ample evidence for the reader with Rorschach knowledge is provided by the four psychograms (Figures 12-1, 12-2, 12-3, 12-4) and the accompanying basic ratios. We also have here evidence from three other tests, namely the Wechsler–Bellevue, the Szondi, and the Sentence Completion.

The Szondi test may not be familiar to some of our readers, but comments concerning its use have been included, particularly where they reinforce findings of the Rorschach. In our bibliography will be found two references relating to this test: chapter V of *Appraising Personality* (Harrower, 1952); and *Introduction to the Szondi Test* (Deri, 1949)

STUDENT 27'S PROJECTIVE STUDY OF A FAMILY AND THEIR PSYCHOLOGICAL INTERRELATIONSHIPS

Evaluation of the Father of Student 27

In viewing the results of a projective assessment it is interesting to see the patterns that emerge in the individual's way of relating to his environment. Particularly important in this relationship is the interaction of his patterns and those of the people around him. When viewing the figure drawings of a man for example, it is informative to see that his male figure is much larger than his female figure, but it reveals a great deal more about his life situation to see that his wife's are that way also. When only one person's projective record is studied, the picture obtained is only that of his way of experiencing his psychological world, but when those of two or more people who live in close proximity emotionally are viewed, the scope is broadened to include the similarities and contrasts in their perceptions and modes of experiencing as well as the effects that these might have in interaction.

A family is the ideal group to which this view of projective relationships would apply. Not only are a husband and wife close emotionally, which would lead to the expectation of some type of interaction in their patterns, but their children are doubly bound by emotional ties and dependency which suggests an even stronger interrelationship between their patterns and those of their parents. This paper will attempt to view one family projectively to see if their similarities, contrasts, and interactions can indeed be observed.

J, the husband, is a 51-year-old accountant who is employed by a small firm in the southeast. He is intelligent as shown by his scores on the Wechsler-Bellevue which place him in the superior range for adults. He has a capacity for theorizing and organizing as well as the ability to see the world uniquely and originally as shown by his W and $Dd + S$ percentages on the Rorschach. His tendency to be introspective and to stand back and look at himself is revealed by the presence of three FKs in his Rorschach. This also supports his high intelligence level. Introspection coupled with a critical attitude, indicated by his $H + A:Hd + Ad$ ratio, suggests that his criticism may be self-directed. This is supported by his plus m on the Szondi which indicated a strong need for support from the environment. The large number of FMs on his Rorschach profile suggests drive and liveliness. The fact that he is minus s on the Szondi suggests that this drive may be sublimated instead of directly expressed. Closely associated with his liveliness is his spontaneity, revealed by his response on the Sentence Completion test, "When an animal is wild it has a freedom not enjoyed by domestic animals." His minus k response to the Szondi suggests that he would be very adaptable and easy to get along with.

In the area of emotional responding, the fact that 33% of his responses were made to Cards VIII, IX, and X indicates that he is sensitive and responsive to emotions, but the low sum C suggests that these emotions do not have much overt expression. This control of his emotions is also shown by his plus *e* response on the Szondi. His sensitivity is supported by the *Fc*s on his Rorschach profile. In viewing his emotional responsiveness in relation to other aspects of his personality it would appear that he finds the warm, positive emotions more comfortable and easier to express than the more violent, aggressive ones. This is suggested by the fact that he has a high need for support from other people and tends to be adaptable. This plus the fact that his aggressive drives are somewhat sublimated indicates that he would feel most comfortable behaving in a warm, positive manner. This is also supported by the fact that his *FC*s, indications of his most developed emotions, are a flower and a coral reef, both beautiful things, while his *CF,* a less developed experience, is the powerful, violent explosion of an atomic bomb.

In summary, J is an intelligent, introspective individual who may be somewhat self-critical. Though responsive to emotions, he is emotionally controlled and feels more comfortable with his warm, positive feelings. He is lively and spontaneous with a high level of drive that tends to be sublimated. His approach to the world is somewhat original though he does have the ability to organize and integrate facts.

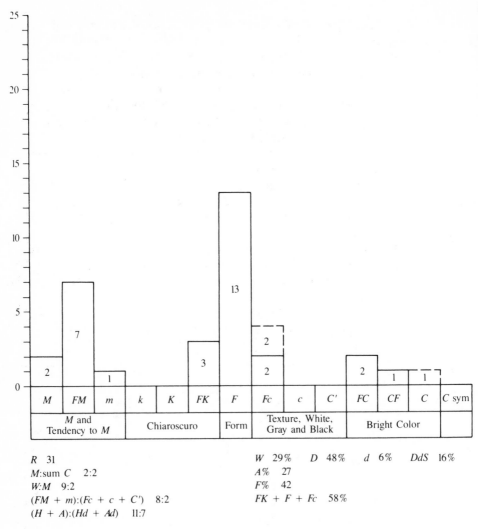

R   31

M:sum C   2:2

W:M   9:2

(FM + m):(Fc + c + C')   8:2

(H + A):(Hd + Ad)   11:7

W   29%   D   48%   d   6%   DdS   16%

A%   27

F%   42

FK + F + Fc   58%

FIG. 12-1.   A psychogram of father of Student 27

Evaluation of Mother of Student 27

R is a 48-year-old housewife who has had employment experience as a bookkeeper. She also is intelligent with her scores on the Wechsler–Bellevue placing her in the superior range of functioning. Her approach to the world is unique and original as shown by her elevated *Dd + S* percentage. The large number of *FM*s in her

Rorschach responses suggests that she has a great deal of drive and a certain liveliness. The fact that her Szondi revealed an ambivalent *s* suggests that this drive may be sublimated as well as directly expressed. Her large number of *M*s on the Rorschach indicates a rich inner life with a large number of inner resources. This number of *M*s also supports the fact that she is highly intelligent. She is also introverted and somewhat anxious, as shown by her *M*:sum *C* ratio and the presence of three *K*s in her Rorschach. Her responses to the Szondi revealed the fact that she is adaptable (minus *k*) and needs support from the environment (plus *m*). The responses to her Sentence Completion test, which suggest that depression is a problem and indicate her concern with family ties, combined with her anxiety and need for support suggest that she may be experiencing some of the typical symptoms of the menopause.

In the area of emotional responsiveness, her responses to Cards VIII, IX, and X suggest that she is responsive to emotional stimuli, but there is a lack of direct expression of this as indicated by her low sum *C*. The fact that her *FC* is greater than her *CF + C* indicates that she is capable of controlled emotional responsiveness, but the fact that the *CF + C* is so low (*CF + C* = 1) may suggest that this control is excessive. This is supported by her minus *hy* on the Szondi which shows that she needs to hide her emotions. The fact that her *FK + Fc* is less than 1/4 *F* suggests that there may be some denial or repression of her need for affection. This is supported by her minus *h* on the Szondi. It is somewhat countered, however, by her selection of a cat as the animal she would most like to be because a cat is loved, protected, and secure. It appears that R also may find the positive emotions easier to express. This is supported by her responsiveness to emotional stimuli coupled with her reduced emotional expression and the fact that all of the color responses given were of the warm, beautiful type, i.e., two butterfly responses and ice cream.

In summary, R is an introverted, intelligent woman with a rich inner life and an abundant supply of drive. Her mode of handling her drive is sophisticated with both direct expression and sublimation being present. Though sensitive to emotional stimuli in her environment, she is controlled in her emotional expression. She is an adaptable individual who finds her environment pleasant and supportive.

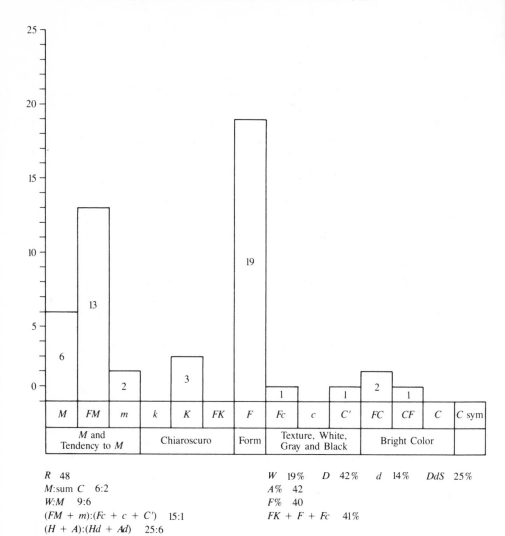

R 48

M:sum C 6:2

W:M   9:6

(FM + m):(Fc + c + C')   15:1

(H + A):(Hd + Ad)   25:6

W 19%   D 42%   d 14%   DdS 25%

A%   42

F%   40

FK + F + Fc   41%

FIG. 12-2.   A psychogram of mother of Student 27

Self-Evaluation of Student 27

There are some definite similarities in the psychological patterns of these individuals who have been married for 27 years. First, they are both intelligent people who are somewhat inner-directed. They have a high level of drive which is channelled by sublimation. Their methods of emotional expression are strikingly similar. Both, though sensitive to emotional stimuli, are emotionally controlled and tend to find expression of their warm, positive emotions easier than of their more active, aggressive impulses. Both are adaptable individuals who seek support from their environment. Also both tend to have a unique, original perception of their environment. In regard to contrasts between them, he tends to be more spontaneous while she has a richer inner fantasy life. An interesting interaction between them was revealed by their figure drawings. Her figure of a male was definitely much larger and more detailed than that of her female. His male was also larger and his female had her hand behind her back. This would indicate that both perceive the male to be more dominant and capable, and the woman as weaker and dependent. This could be seen as a concrete instance of their joint acceptance of a cultural norm perhaps due to their tendency to conform. In general this marriage would be a quiet comfortable one in which both individuals would be unlikely to express hostile, aggressive emotions and would tend to be easy-going and adaptable. It would be kept from becoming too dull and placid by their liveliness and original ways of viewing the world.

Having viewed the psychological environment of this marriage, it is interesting to see what kind of children it produced. Their daughter JL is a 23-year-old graduate student at a large southern university. Like her parents she is intelligent as shown by her college board scores of 1450 and introverted as shown by her M:sum C ratio. The most striking aspect of her Rorschach profile is her large number of Ms, 19. She has a great many inner resources, but there is a danger that she may become too absorbed in and happy with her inner life to the exclusion of some other important experiences. Her W:M ratio is 10:10, almost exactly the opposite of the optimal 2:1 ratio. This indicates that she has more ideas than she has the capacity to organize and use. Like her parents she has a great deal of drive, shown by a large number of FMs, which tends to be sublimated. She is adaptable (minus k) and needs support from her environment (plus m). She is spontaneous, as shown by her Sentence Completion response "When an animal is wild, it's free," and sensitive as shown by the presence of Fcs on her Rorschach.

In the area of emotional expression she is very similar to her parents. While she is sensitive to emotional stimuli, having 33% of her responses to cards VIII, IX, and X, her sum C, or indication of emotional expression, is low for her large number of responses. Her Szondi indicates that she feels the need to control her emotions. Her emotions are pretty well-developed as indicated by the fact that the number of FCs is greater than the number of CFs on her Rorschach. The FCs are generally of a soft positive quality such as the red and yellow butterfly on III while the *CF*s are the most explosive tongues of fire on III or the explosion on II. Since *FC*s express emotion that is more developed and intellectually controlled, it may be easier for her to control and express her positive emotions while those such as anger or aggression are more difficult. This is also supported by her sublimation of aggressive impulses as shown by her Szondi (minus *s*).

In summary she is an introverted intelligent young woman with a rich inner fantasy life. She is emotionally controlled, though responsive to emotional stimuli. She is spontaneous with a high drive level which tends to be sublimated. She is also adaptable. It is easy to see how her psychological pattern developed in this family situation. Her mode of emotional responding exactly parallels that of her parents. It would be expected that a child, raised in an environment where everyone was emotionally controlled and freely expressed only their positive emotions, would follow that pattern also, particularly when the child was an adaptable, conforming one. Her method of handling drive by sublimation is also modeled after those of her parents. Her rich inner fantasy life is also understandable in the family context. In a situation where both parents were inner-directed, either introspective or introverted, and where there was an emphasis on emotional control at the expense of emotional expression, naturally a child would develop the inner fantasy aspect of his psychological life most highly. This would be particularly true of an intelligent sensitive child.

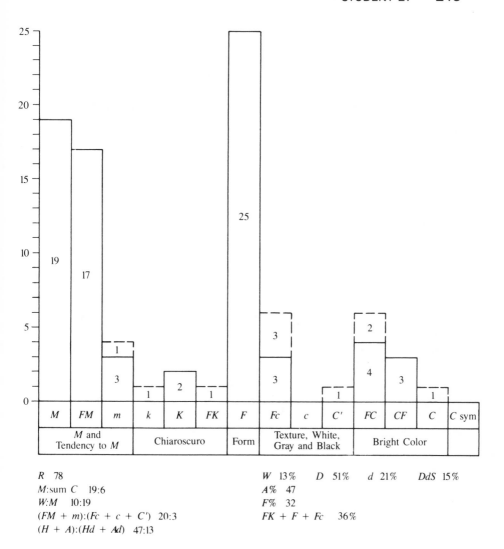

FIG. 12-3. A psychogram of Student 27

R 78	W 13% D 51% d 21% DdS 15%
M:sum C 19:6	A% 47
W:M 10:19	F% 32
(FM + m):(Fc + c + C') 20:3	FK + F + Fc 36%
(H + A):(Hd + Ad) 47:13	

Evaluation of Brother of Student 27

Their son J. O. is a 20-year-old college junior, majoring in mathematics. He also is an intelligent person as shown by his scores on the Wechsler-Bellevue. He is introverted as shown by his *M:* sum *C* ratio and has a high drive level which is sublimated. His approach to the world is one that is intent on organizing experience into meaningful wholes.

Like the rest of his family he experiences the world as positive and needs support from people, having a plus m on the Szondi, but unlike them he is not adaptable, but rather feels the need to assert his individuality, as shown by his plus k.

His manner of emotional expression is very similar to that of the rest of his family. He is sensitive to emotional stimuli, but his level of emotional expression is low. He feels the need to both control and hide his emotions, having a plus e and minus hy on the Szondi. Like his mother's, his FCs and CFs contain only beautiful soft images such as two babies on card IX. This suggests that he too is most comfortable with his positive emotions.

It is easy to see how his similarities to the rest of the family, such as his intelligence, introversion, drive, and emotional expression came about. Perhaps more interesting is his obvious difference, the plus k on the Szondi, or his need to assert his individuality. This is understandable in view of a family constellation that is so compatible and psychologically similar. A definite assertion of individuality would be a possible way that he could feel that he was a separate person with his own identity in this family of similar people. Perhaps his sister's method of establishing this separate identity is found in her distortion of the family pattern by piling up an enormous number of Ms. There is another possible explanation of his plus k. This lies in the fact that it is normal for a person in his age group to feel the need to assert their individuality and to find their own identity.

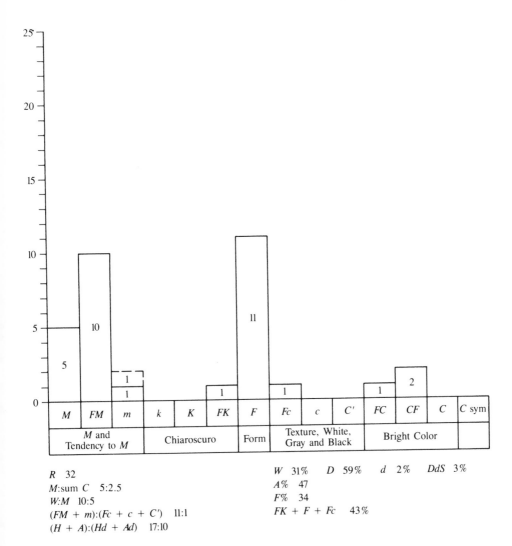

FIG. 12-4. A psychogram of brother of Student 27

R 32

M:sum C   5:2.5

W:M   10:5

(FM + m):(Fc + c + C')   11:1

(H + A):(Hd + Ad)   17:10

W 31%   D 59%   d 2%   DdS 3%

A% 47

F% 34

FK + F + Fc   43%

Summary Evaluation of Family of Student 27

In summary this is a family with many marked similarities: their intelligence, introversion, and methods of handling drive and emotions. The patterns on which they coincide would tend to make theirs a peaceful household without any overt strife. Perhaps more important, however, are the ways in which each differs from a dominant family pattern and how the family constellation of traits can be seen to cause these diversions. Such evidence of individuality is what keeps them from becoming dull and uninteresting and suggests that each one's psychological composition is affected by and affects those of each of the others.

13

Epilogue

In these concluding remarks, I revert to the quote from Koffka (1935) given in the Introduction: "Writing a book is a social act. What good can society, or a small fraction of it, at best, derive from it? How have I attempted to meet this challenge in the small fraction of society for which projective techniques are relevant?"

First, I wanted to call attention to a way of teaching the projective tests, which involves the student both intellectually and emotionally. Whether we like it or not, all of us experience a peculiar quickening of interest when material is directly relevant to our own lives. While scientific reporting exemplifies *par excellence* the *lack* of personal involvement, some aspects of the human condition, particularly clinical work, require an *awareness* of our emotional and intellectual selves in order—ironically—that we can become *less* personally involved in dealing with others. The various forms of therapeutic training have become witness to this.

In the late thirties and forties, clinical psychologists were struggling to attain a professional status equal to that of psychiatrists. Diagnostic reports were aimed at finding pathology and subtle deviations from the "normal" which could vie with the pronouncements and diagnostic labeling already established by psychiatrists.

There existed no categories, no labeling, which described the strengths and the balance of well-functioning persons. A much more positive frame of reference was needed, not to substitute for, but to add to, the psychiatric dictates.[1]

---

[1]Isabel Briggs Myers' book *Gifts Differing* reflects the need to envisage the person in terms of various positive factors as well as problem areas. Published in 1980, this point of view was not available at that time.

In developing the Instruction–Insight method of teaching the Rorschach, my main interest was to provide potential psychological clinicians with an awareness of their own creativeness and strengths and, equally important, what used to be called "the defects of one's qualities"—their inevitable blind spots.

Secondly, I was interested in paying more attention to Rorschach's basic categories, to modernize the wording, and to demonstrate graphically dominant trends, which are emphasized in a psychogram. Of course this is what psychograms have always done, but the challenge was to see by way of the students' self-evaluations whether they experienced these dominant trends and envisaged them as a major component in their thinking, feeling, and acting.

Of the five basic Rorschach types, the introverted, the extroverted, and the ambi-equal have acquired a current use or meaning; but the other two descriptive groups—coarted and coartive—have a somewhat archaic flavor and have little resonance with our terminology. In large-scale studies, I have spoken of the "impoverished" record and the "meager" or "mediocre" record, respectively, to reflect some aspects of Rorschach's original terms (Harrower, 1965a).

The importance of the psychogram is that it allows us to both utilize Rorschach's ideas and demonstrate the dominance of certain components and the lack or nonexistence of others.

The various sections of this book deal with different dominant trends. The individual with the high R—many responses—is coping with the pressure of a bombardment from his evoked responses, at times engulfed by his own productivity (Students 1 and 2). The low R maintains order easily, but may well lack excitement which can be educed from a rich and evolving perceptual world (Students 3, 4, and 5).

The high F, with his strong logical control, may be to some extent defrauded of a variety of potential emotional contacts (Students 6 and 7), or may require such a high $F\%$ to offset strong FM and color scores (Student 8); while the low F is concerned with the spectre of lack of control (Students 9, 10, and 11).

The high M runs the risk of retreating into a too-personal world, and may lack the means to evoke direct, warm relationships, despite his capacity for empathy and understanding of the psychic world of himself and others (Students 12, 13, 14, and 15). The high FM is challenged as to how to handle strong drives constructively, and must avoid being at the mercy of impulse (Students 16, 17, and 18).

The ambi-equal types, whom Rorschach considered to be "unusually gifted and talented," can be *embarras de richesse,* overburdened with the possession of too many possibilities, an inner and an outer world of great richness (Students 16, 17, and 18).

In studying our ambi-equal students, it would seem as if within the ambi-equal group there are trends toward either the introversive or the extroversive way of life. We have yet to find ambi-equal ratios which are exactly equal in terms of M: sum C scores (see Figure 8-1).

Our sole extrovert displayed a different frame of reference, a need for action and concreteness, a need to use the published material of others for amplification rather than exploring the self through internal scrutiny (Student 24).

We have an example (Student 25) of a student showing that the self-assessment of 20 years earlier has proved relevant in understanding subsequent life experiences.

A fundamental change in career was successfully made on the basis of understanding certain qualities displayed in the Rorschach record (Student 26). And finally, a self-evaluator (Student 27) saw the interrelationship of projective findings in a close family group.

How can our material be used? It may open up a new approach for those who plan to teach the projectives, and for those who supervise the work of younger clinicians in practice.

It may allow students studying the Rorschach for the first time to become explicitly aware of these Rorschach-based categories and to find their own niche within the Rorschach framework. Hopefully, the constructive potential of their individual types will be utilized to the full and potential dangers bypassed, or better still, through understanding, converted into assets.

For example, Student 26 called attention to the fact that when she was able to understand her own lack of interest in various kinds of conceptualization, she then realized that her low $W\%$ was not so much absence of something indispensable, but the counterpart of her highly utilizable ability to handle details, large and small.

Student 6's interest in research, rather than in therapeutic endeavors, is a proper avenue for his F-dominated way of perceiving, while Student 27's concern over the social implications of a small group allowed her special insights into her own family.

To what extent do Rorschach records and psychograms change? Long-term follow-ups are rare, for obvious reasons. But the four records which follow show testing of one subject at ages 30, 50, 60, and 80. The circumstances under which these records were taken are, to some extent, pertinent material in understanding them.

The first testing, done by Zygmunt Piotrowski, occurred at a moment of a dramatic career change in the subject's life, namely a shift from the security of the academic fold of established psychology to a new venture into the field of medicine. The subject, working in the neurological laboratory of Dr. Kurt Goldstein, was utilized for Piotrowski's collection of subjects from various walks of life in the early days of the use of the Rorschach test. (See Table 13-1 and Figure 13-1.)

Twenty years later, settled into a rapidly emerging new career, this subject had the opportunity of taking part in many interesting experimental endeavors. When great interest centered in consciousness-altering drugs, the second test responses given in Table 13-2 preceded a series of experiments using LSD, under the auspices of the clinician-scientist Dr. Harold Abramson. (The psychogram appears in Figure 13-2.)

Ten years after that, following many months of anxiety and concern over the painful terminal illness of the subject's spouse, a third record was taken (See Table 13-3 and Figure 13-4). The underlying reason for taking the test at this time was to participate at a moment of extreme emotional and personal stress.

TABLE 13-1
Subject, Aged 30, Tested, Scored, and Interpreted
by Zygmunt Piotrowski

Card I

---

1. Somebody impersonating a bat, in a sort of theatrical performance. Rising up from the back of the stage.	*W*	*M*	*H*
2. Not a bat so much as a sort of a spectre.	*W*	*M, K*	*H*
Gives the impression of conveying atmosphere rather than an interpretation of anything. The more analytically one looks at it, the more one sees that it isn't just that. For instance, *the figure of the man,* in the middle holding the wings, one can see that he has no head—that would be against it—although that would be my first impression.			

Card II

---

1. They all bear sort of a resemblance to spinal cord sections. The general distribution of it. I suppose they all do, by their symmetry.	*W*	*CF*	*At*
I find this less atmospheric, much less able to give a spontaneous interpretation.			
2. Two absolutely distinct *red-faced gnomes playing this game* (clap hands) with each other. I would say they were counting, sort of squatting			

TABLE 13-1
(Continued)

Card II

(knee bent as we used to do in gym).	W	M, FC	H
3. I can also dissociate this red and see it as two Aberdeen *puppies with their noses next to each other.* That's now amazingly clear . . . with their eyes and the markings.	D	FM	A

Card III

1. These are two funny *little page boys in tights,* with very pointed shoes, their behinds sticking out a mile. There's some central thing here, *like a cauldron they've been carrying between them, which they're setting down.* The red is completely dissociated, has no meaning whatever.	W	M	H
2. It's also possible for me to see it as a drawing of a Japanese vase, rather a bowl, the shading, and in that case the central red thing is taken in.	D	FC	obj

Card IV

1. Here's a ram's face up at the top.	d	F	Ad
2. *A ram in enormous boots, sitting* on a tree stump. Or a sheep with its paws out like this (to sides) and legs in enormous wading boots (sprawled out).	W	FM	A

Card V

1. Oh, this is the back view of some creature with enormous wings. I always have the *impression of someone masquerading . . .* at a fancy dress ball. Somebody dressed up like the devil . . . with a huge cloak . . . falling off at the sides here . . . with Satyr's horns.	W	M	H

Card VI

1. That's like a *rug on the floor* . . . like one of these skins that somebody's shot. All except the top.	D	c	A-obj

TABLE 13–1
(Continued)

Card VI			
2. That's just like an appendage. I can see it perfectly clearly as an animal's head and whiskers, but it's sort of out of keeping with the rug part.	D	F	Ad
Card VII			
1. The predominant thing . . . *the impressionistic Parisian ladies gesticulating over a cup of tea . . .* although I don't see the cup of tea. A Matisse drawing. They both have these enormous plumes in their hats. The narrow waistline and the bustly dress. Of course . . . the most atmosphere of all of them. The texture is quite similar to nicely done water color.	W	M	H
2. I can also get something different, like a vase, the Rubin figure, in the space here.	S	F	obj
Card VIII			
1. These are *two pink sloths* coming up from the sides, just *sort of wandering around, stepping up from one rock to another.*	D	FM	A
2. The other pink things look like the heads of *little fetal pigs.*	D	FC	Ad
3. The whole thing might be symbolic of the rise of the animal kingdom like the "trees of life," "fish emerging," etc.	W	F	Abs
Card IX			
1. The orange things at the top are sort of *witches with lobster claws.* They are being sort of belched up by this green smoke from some kind of fire at the bottom.	W	MC^2	H

---

[2]A symbol devised and utilized by Piotrowski, which he explains in his book *Perceptanalysis* (Piotrowski, 1957).

TABLE 13-1
(Continued)

Card X			
1. My first impression was like a plate of specimens, absolutely disconnected, like in a bacteriology class, more like a group of little sea animals ready for someone's inspection.	W	CF	A
2. I can see it in a more unified way. The two red masses as *two ladies with two tall gray hats on, holding blue-gloved hands* and the general impression that they're *trying to cross a crowded thoroughfare,* with a lot of stuff around, and they're sort of headed in that direction (through the card).	W	M, FC	H

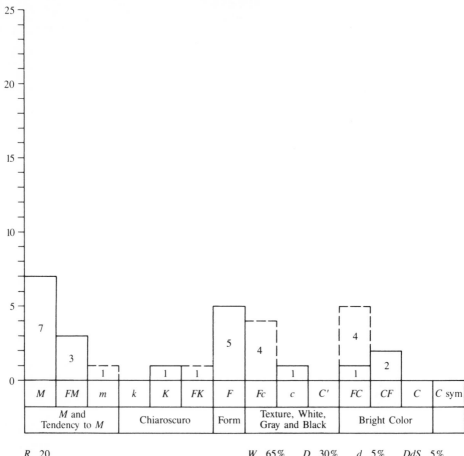

R 20

M:sum C 7:2.5

W:M 13:7

$(FM + m)$:$(Fc + c + C')$ 3:1

$(H + A)$:$(Hd + Ad)$ 8:2

W 65% D 30% d 5% DdS 5%

$A\%$ 30

$F\%$ 25

$FK + F + Fc$ 25%

FIG. 13-1.   A psychogram of MH, 1937

TABLE 13-2
Subject, Aged 50, Tested for Stability
and Creativity in LSD Experiments
Conducted by Harold A. Abramson, M.D.

Card I

1. Two Santa Clauses flying off with	D	M	H
2. *Gesticulating figure*, sack of toys slipping off their backs, carrying them off to the pole—snowy background	D	M	H

TABLE 13–2
(Continued)

Card I

3. Toys stuffed in sack, teddy bears, dolls	*D*	*Fc*	obj
4. Kidney-shaped shadow, as in X-ray	*di*	*Fk*	

Card II

1. *Two red-faced clowns playing patty-cake. Red underwear* shows	*W*	*M, FC*	*H*
2. Two bears with rough fur *touching noses*	*W*	*FM, Fc*	*A*
3. *A red butterfly*	*D*	*FC*	*A*
4. A top	*S*	*F*	obj
5. Vagina	*dd*	*FC*	*Hd*
6. Rock profiles, a face on a crag	*de*	*F*	*Hd*

Card III

1. *Two men setting down a basket*	*W*	*M*	*H*
2. *A dental plate with two small teeth in front*	*D*	*FC*	obj
3. A gay, tumbling animal somer-saulting, monkey-like	*D*	*FM*	*A*
4. A genie with turban doing a snake act	*d*	*M*	*H*
5. A dog lying down	*d*	*FM*	*A*
6. *A butterfly*	*S*	*F*	*A*

Card IV

1. *A goat-like animal with heavy fur sitting on an alligator, gesticulating wildly with its arms*	*W*	*FM, c*	*A*
2. Two faces, noses in the air	*d*	*F*	*Hd*
3. An old man bent in prayer in a graveyard	*dr*	*M*	*H*
4. A poodle with its tail up	*d*	*FM*	*A*

Card V

1. *A policeman with a cellophane cap over his bowler*	*D*	*M, k*	*H*
2. Two men lying down, arms akimbo, with furry wraps	*D*	*M, c*	*H*
3. The face of an animal	*dr*	*F*	*Ad*
4. *Man dressed in bat wings*	*W*	*M*	*H*

Card VI

1. That's like a *rug on the floor . . .* like

TABLE 13-2

(Continued)

Card VI

one of these skins that somebody's shot. All except the top.	*D*	*c*	*A*-obj
3. Fish-like with filmy fins	*D*	*Fk*	*A*
4. Two possums or polar bears talking	*di*	*FM, C'*	*A*
5. Two people close together in furry jackets	*d*	*M, c*	*H*

Card VII

1. *Two women gesticulating in a lively discussion*	*W*	*M*	*H*
2. Two Russian dancers with big headgear	*W*	*M*	*H*
3. Two puppets, cartoon people, funny men	*D*	*F, m*	*H*

Card VIII

1. *Pink salamanders climbing up*	*D*	*FC, FM*	*A*
2. Two calf heads	*D*	*F*	*Ad*
3. A blue bed jacket with fur collar	*D*	*CF, Fc*	obj
4. Two people on top embracing, having climbed a mountain	*dd*	*M*	*H*
5. Other people sitting at their feet	*dd*	*M*	*H*
6. Someone in bed under a white counterpane	*drs*	*M*	*H*

Card IX

1. *Two magicians in tall hats, working a miracle,* being borne aloft in their fire and smoke	*W*	*M, CF, k*	*H*
2. Deer's heads with beards	*di*	*F*	*Ad*
3. A big green face with a little	*D*	*M*	*Hd*
4. dentist looking in the mouth of the patient	*D*	*M*	*H*
5. *A washerwoman type, or a nanny, catching small child by the hair*	*D*	*M*	*H*
6. Child trying to catch something	*D*	*M*	*H*

Card X

1. Hectic crabs catching a green bull by the tail	*D*	*FM*	*A*
2. *Two ladies in 1800 dresses, holding blue-gloved hands* and also holding crabs. They are *picking their way through a busy animal-cluttered*			

TABLE 13-2
(Continued)

Card X

| garden | D | M, FC | H |
| 3. Discussion by two animals at the top | D | FM | A |

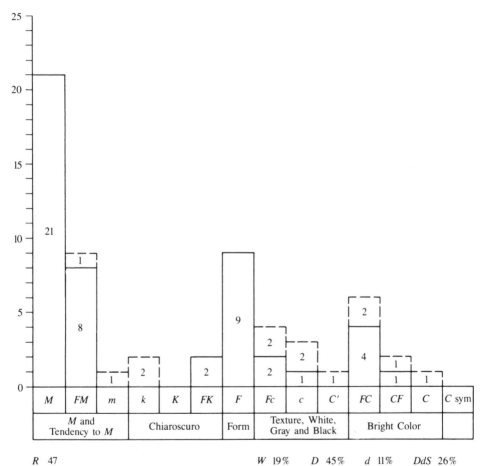

FIG. 13-2.   A psychogram of MH, 1956

TABLE 13-3
Subject, Aged 60, Tested During Terminal Illness of Spouse

Card I

1. *Woman being borne aloft* by two flying Santa Clauses	*W*	*M*	*H*
2. *Dogs' heads*	*D*	*F*	*Ad*

Card II

1. *Two red-faced Cossacks playing patty-cake*	*W*	*M, FC, Fc*	*H*
2. *A red butterfly*	*D*	*F*	*A*

Card III

1. *Two people setting down a burden*	*W*	*M*	*H*
2. *Red butterfly*	*D*	*FC*	*A*
3. *Dental plate*	*D*	*FC*	obj
4. Tumbling animals	*D*	*FM*	*A*

Card IV

1. *Huge animal, heavy fur, riding on another animal, a crocodile*	*W*	*FM, Fc*	*A*

Card V

1. *London Bobby, in his hat and cellophane cap*	*D*	*M, Fc*	*H*

Card VI

1. *Animal skin*	*W*	*Fc*	*A*-obj
2. Small man inside worm-like animal	*d*	*M*	*H*

Card VII

1. *Two ladies talking*	*W*	*M*	*H*
2. *Two ladies dancing*	*W*	*M*	*H*

Card VIII

1. *Animals climbing*	*D*	*FM*	*A*
2. *Blue flags*	*D*	*FC*	obj
3. *Pink fetal pigs*	*D*	*FC*	*A*
4. Flower	*D*	*FC*	nat

Card IX

1. *Witches fencing*	*D*	*M*	*H*
2. *Woman running after child*	*D*	*M*	*H*
3. Moose head	*di*	*F*	*Ad*
4. Pink bed jacket	*D*	*FC, Fc*	obj

TABLE 13-3
(Continued)

Card X

1. *Two ladies in pink holding blue-gloved hands*	D	M, FC	H
2. *Green worms*	D	FC	A
3. Yellow lions	D	FC	A
4. Yellow flower	D	FC	nat
5. Spiders	D	FC	A
6. *Wishbone*	D	F	obj
7. Dog	D	FM	A

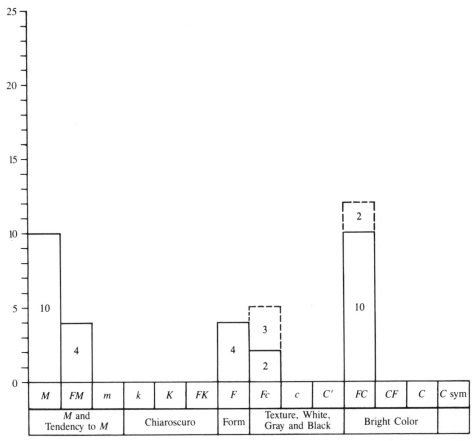

R 29
M:sum C 10:5
W:M 7:10
(FM + m):(Fc + c + C') 4:2
(H + A):(Hd + Ad) 20:2

W 24%   D 69%   d 3%   DdS 3%
A% 34
F% 14
FK + F + Fc 6%

FIG. 13-3. A psychogram of MH, 1967

TABLE 13-4
Subject, Aged 80, Tested after Completing *The Inside Story*

Card I

1. I see 3 figures, the 2 outside are males, *the inside one is female. The men are lifting her up* and flying away with her. She has her hands up, not in protest, sort of going with the upward movement. She is dressed in a somewhat transparent garment, around her waist a belt with a light buckle. Her lack of head does not seem to bother me. The men are doing the flying, strong upward movement, she is going along.	W	M, mFK	H
2. On the sides are *dachshund heads;* the dachshunds are looking outward.	D	FM	Ad
3. The two upper white spaces could be small cloaked figures.	S	M	H

Card II

1. *Two Russian dancers,* because they are doing the down on the knee type of dancing. They have met in the middle and *are doing a patty-cake kind of dance.*	W	M	H
2. *They have red faces, clown-like, and dunce caps* on their heads.	D	FC	Hd
3. Two Scottie dogs *approaching each other*	W	FM	A
4. At the bottom a well-formed *beautiful red butterfly*	D	FC	A

Card III

1. *Two men bowing to each other carrying something together setting something down*	W	M	H
2. *The center a red butterfly*	D	FC	A
3. *A very good denture piece,* red, the piece that goes against the gum, with little teeth inside it	D	FC	obj
	dd	F	Hd
4. Far side, gesticulating little animals with an unnecessary protuberance out of the top of the head	D	FM	A

TABLE 13-4
(Continued)

Card IV

1.	The *good old furry bear sitting on the trunk of a tree,* pathetic little arms	W	Fc, FM	A
2.	Huge boots	D	F	obj
3.	Head of an animal, dark eyes	Dd	F	Ad
4.	On either side in the white space 2 little ladies sitting down hands up toward their faces	S	M	H
5.	Two men's faces with pointed noses	de	F	Hd
6.	The boots turned sideways show an old lady, hunched, ahead of her are two other small figures like children	D	M	H

Card V

1.	Bat-like	W	F	A
2.	Two men on either side, pre-historic men in the sense that they are clothed in deep rich fur. They are like twins arms akimbo lying exactly the same way.	D	M, c	H
3.	In the *center a London Bobby's hat*	D	F	obj
4.	Somebody, maybe a dancer, im-personating a body but the legs are going to dance	D	M	H

Card VI

1.	*Essentially the bearskin*	W	Fc	A-obj
2.	Lying on this a beautiful polished bedpost	D	Fc	obj
3.	Feathers on the side	d	Fc	A-obj

Card VI

1.	*Two ladies gesticulating describing a party, tight-waisted dresses.*	W	M	H
2.	Feathered plumes in their hair	d	Fc	A-obj
3.	Central detail also faces, a clown or animal.	D	F	Ad
4.	Two fluffy animals facing outward crouched	D	Fc, FM	A

Card VIII

1.	*The pink animal climbing up*	D	FM	A

TABLE 13–4
(Continued)

Card VIII

the side.			
2. *Brilliantly beautiful blue flag*	D	FC	obj
3. *Two fetal pigs* just born.	D	FC	A
4. Georgia O'Keefe skull on the desert	S	F	anat
5. A coat of arms	W	F	emb

Card IX

1. Two figures at the top, men fencing with long fingers. They have *witch-like hats,* they are *sparring* and trying to reach each other.	D	M	H
2. In the green large faces, a moron-ish character	D	F	Hd
3. *A woman chasing a child just about to catch it*	D	M	H
4. A red bed jacket, good to wear in bed for entertaining in bed with fluffy sleeves	D	Fc, FC	Clo

Card X

1. The *central red figures, grey hats,* each holding an animated crab-like creature.	D	M, FM, FC	H, A
2. Creatures waving a green furled flag.	D	FC	A, obj
3. A blue bra in the center, texture of satin.	D	FC, Fc	Clo
4. Two lion dogs.	D	FC	A
5. *Green caterpillars* nosing up to the rabbit's head.	D	FC, FM	A
6. Yellow jonquils	D	FC	Flo
7. *Wishbone*	D	F	obj

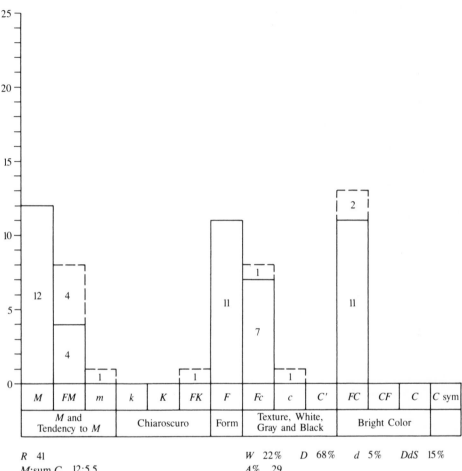

FIG. 13-4. A psychogram of MH, 1986

The fourth record (see Table 13-4 and Figure 13-4) was taken as a celebration of having reached the age of 80, combined with the completion of the book, *The Inside Story*.

Without going into self-evaluations, a few comments may be made relating to similarities and changes in these records. I have spoken elsewhere at some length (Harrower, 1958) about "core" responses, namely, those which appear in repeat records, as opposed to answers which occur in only one. In this instance it will be seen that the italicized responses show the continuity in this particular series. In addition to the repetition per se, perhaps even more interesting are the slight variations in description which may reflect mood changes relevant to the time of each test.

See, for example, a core response to Card III. In the earliest record, we have "two funny little page boys in tights," etc. In the second test the response is "Two men setting down a basket." In the third, "depressed" record, the response has become "Two people setting down a burden."

Another core response occurs to Card VIII. In the first record, this response is "two pink sloths . . . stepping up from one rock to another." In the second test, this is "Pink salamanders climbing up"; in the third, merely "Animals climbing"; and in the fourth, the salamanders climb with direction again.

In Card I, the headless figure is at first a man; then becomes a (sexless) "gesticulating figure"; and later becomes female when aided by the men Santa Clauses who "bear her upward."

It may also be seen that in the "depressed" record taken at age 60 there is, in general, less amplification of responses, a reduced verbal output, producing a shift toward sparseness on the sparse/rich scale discussed in chapter 1.

In terms of the similarities between the four records, the major finding is unquestionably the consistently low $F\%$: 20%, 19%, 14%, 25%. In addition, despite changes in absolute values of the M and sum C, M is always greater than C throughout the series.

Readers may be interested in looking for other differences and similarities among the four reports. While such longitudinal studies are difficult to achieve, it would be valuable if more were attempted.

References

Alcock, T. (1963). *The Rorschach in Practice*. Philadelphia: J. B. Lippincott Co.

Deri, Susan. (1949). *Introduction to the Szondi test*. New York: Grune & Stratton.

Harrower, M. (1950). The most unpleasant concept test. *Journal of Clinical Psychology, 3,* 213–233.

Harrower, M. (1952). *Appraising personality: The use of psychological tests in the practice of medicine*. New York: W. W. Norton & Co.

Harrower, M. (1955a). Who comes to court? *Journal of Orthopsychiatry, 25,* 15–25.

Harrower, M. (1955b). A Psychological testing program for entering students at the University of Texas School of Medicine, Galveston. *Texas Reports on Biology and Medicine, 13*(3), 406–419.

Harrower, M. (1958). *Personality change and development as measured by the projective techniques*. New York: Grune & Stratton.

Harrower, M. (1958b). The most unpleasant concept test: A graphic projective technique for diagnostic and therapeutic use. In *The Clinical Application of Projective Drawings*. Springfield, IL: Charles C Thomas.

Harrower, M. (1965a). *Psychodiagnostic testing: An empirical approach*. Springfield, IL: Charles C Thomas.

Harrower, M. (1965b). "Clinical psychologists at work." In B. Wolman (Ed.), *Handbook of Clinical Psychology*. New York: McGraw-Hill.

Harrower, M. (1971). Letter to a valued colleague. *International Mental Health Research Newsletter, 13*(1), New York.

Harrower, M. (1977). The Rorschach and self-understanding: the instruction-insight method. *Journal of Personality Assessment, 41*(5), 451–460.

Harrower, M., & M. E. Steiner (1951). *Large scale Rorschach techniques*. Springfield, Il: Charles C Thomas.

Harrower, M. (1960). (with Vorhous, P., Roman, M., & Bauman, G.). *Creative variations in the projective techniques*. Springfield, Il: Charles C Thomas.

Klopfer, B. (1954). *Developments in the Rorschach technique*. Yonkers-on-Hudson, NY: World Book Company.

Koffka, K. (1935). *Principles of Gestalt psychology*. New York: Harcourt, Brace.

Myers, I. B. (1980). *Gifts differing*. Palo Alto, CA: Consulting Psychologists Press.

Piotrowski, Z. A. (1957). *Perceptanalysis.* New York: Macmillan.

Rorschach, H. (1942). *Psychodiagnostics: A diagnostic test based on perception.* English Edition translated by Paul Lemkau, M.D. New York: Grune & Stratton.

Index